AF323686

The Image of Manhood in Early Modern Literature

Recent Titles in
Contributions to the Study of World Literature

Virginia Woolf: Feminism, Creativity, and the Unconscious
John R. Maze

The French Revolution Debate in English Literature and Culture
Lisa Plummer Crafton, editor

Jane Austen and Eighteenth-Century Courtesy Books
Penelope Joan Fritzer

James Joyce and Trieste
Peter Hartshorn

True Relations: Essays on Autobiography and the Postmodern
G. Thomas Couser and Joseph Fichtelberg, editors

The Adventure of the Detected Detective: Sherlock Holmes in James Joyce's *Finnegans Wake*
William D. Jenkins

Afro-Cuban Literature: Critical Junctures
Edward J. Mullen

The Tales We Tell: Perspectives on the Short Story
Barbara Lounsberry, Susan Lohafer, Mary Rohrberger, Stephen Pett, and R.C. Feddersen, editors

Robin Hood: The Shaping of the Legend
Jeffrey L. Singman

The Myth of Medea and the Murder of Children
Lillian Corti

African-British Writings in the Eighteenth Century: The Politics of Race and Reason
Helena Woodard

Styles of Ruin: Joseph Brodsky and the Postmodernist Elegy
David Rigsbee

The Image of Manhood in Early Modern Literature

Viewing the Male

Edited by
Andrew P. Williams

Contributions to the Study of World Literature, Number 95

GREENWOOD PRESS
Westport, Connecticut • London

Library of Congress Cataloging-in-Publication Data

The image of manhood in early modern literature : viewing the male / edited by Andrew P. Williams.
p. cm.—(Contributions to the study of world literature, ISSN 0738-9345 ; no. 95)
Includes bibliographical references and index.
ISBN 0-313-30766-0 (alk. paper)
1. English literature—Early modern, 1500-1700—History and criticism. 2. Masculinity in literature. 3. English literature—18th century—History and criticism. 4. English literature—Male authors—History and criticism. 5. Male authors, English—Psychology. 6. Gender identity in literature. 7. Men in literature. I. Williams, Andrew P. II. Series.
PR428.M37I43 1999
820.9'353—dc21 98-41688

British Library Cataloguing in Publication Data is available.

Library of Congress Catalog Card Number: 98-41688
ISBN: 0-313-30766-0
ISSN: 0738-9345

First published in 1999

Greenwood Press, 88 Post Road West, Westport, CT 06881
An imprint of Greenwood Publishing Group, Inc.
www.greenwood.com

Printed in the United States of America

The paper used in this book complies with the Permanent Paper Standard issued by the National Information Standards Organization (Z39.48-1984).

10 9 8 7 6 5 4 3 2 1

This book is dedicated
to the memory of Dr. John McManmon

Contents

Acknowledgments

I would like to thank the following for their generous assistance: Dr. Ode Ogede for reviewing drafts of my own chapter and the introduction. His comments and insightful suggestions proved extremely valuable. Mrs. Frances Nelson and Dr. Tom Evans whose computer expertise made a difficult task a bit easier. And my wife Cathi, without whom I would still be looking for the margin key.

Introduction

Andrew P. Williams

This volume, *The Image of Manhood in Early Modern Literature: Viewing the Male,* grew as an extension of a panel I chaired at the 1997 American Society for Eighteenth-Century Studies Conference in Nashville, Tennessee. The panel, "Images of Manhood and the Masculine Ideal," discussed the ways literary representations of masculinity both validated and challenged cultural assumptions concerning the composition of the "ideal male" in early modern English literature. While the panel presenters mainly explored various social barometers for measuring the worth of the "ideal male" in the early modern period, one critical commonality seemed to emerge when the discussion moved from representations of early modern manhood to issues of manhood in general: Any discussion of what it means to be a man is a significantly difficult undertaking because masculinity is not a neutral site of critical discourse. The history of masculinity is inherently bound to the history of gender inequity, patriarchy, and the exploitation of both men and women. As a critical subject, masculinity cannot, and should not, be excused from the misogyny and violence that have historically accompanied individual and cultural expressions of manhood and what it meant to be a man. However, the problematics of "masculine" discourse run deeper than the broad social effects that accompany displays of manliness; the term "masculinity" itself presupposes a single, fixed standard of referential criteria for the identification of the masculine-self. Invariably, as the panel seemed to suggest, this standard represents a narrow categorization of "appropriate" gender behaviors that ultimately promote and reinscribe the patriarchal privileges of a certain class: Primarily, white, heterosexual men of wealth. It is obvious that any discussion of masculinity cannot be divorced from its connection to the power inequities that have generally defined Western gender relationships; however, it must also be noted that not all forms of masculine selfhood are defined by the limited, heterocentric parameters of Western gender politics. Though convenient, the term "masculinity" is inapplicable as a blanket descriptor of the many, and often contesting, versions of the masculine-self where, simply put, there is no one way to be a man.

Instead, it is necessary to recognize that the dynamic facets of masculine self-identification and their historical interaction with issues of race, gender, and class make inappropriate any essentialist definition of masculinity as some particular quality or essence. Masculinity is not an ahistorical phenomenon; it cannot be separated from the social and historical contexts that shape and reshape the ever-changing cultural definitions of what it means to be a man. Nor can masculinity be identified solely through a lone set of cultural signifiers unique to any one historical moment. Arbitrarily constructed images of the "ideal man" have historically served as templates for measuring social expectations of appropriate masculine behavior. However, ideal forms of manhood and manliness are nothing more than fictions of gender ideology and wishful thinking that perpetuate and valorize existing systems of domination and inequality. To accept the fiction of the "ideal male" is to accept that there is only one true form of the masculine-self. However, while "ideal masculinity" may exist only as a construct of the social imagination, many conceptions of masculine selfhood and identity do coexist within society to produce a complex web of "masculinities."

The numerous and multifaceted ways by which masculinities emerge and are expressed within culture facilitate the necessity of a broad ranging and sweeping (re)examination of what it means to be a man. Clearly, the emergence of queer studies, feminist theory, and postmodern cultural criticism have radically challenged the political and social dynamics and privileges that have traditionally been associated with certain socially encoded "norms" of manhood. These critical approaches have sufficiently—and rightfully so—deconstructed the power basis of the notion of the "ideal male," revealing it to be less of an idealized state of masculine perfection, and more of a method for defining the parameters of hegemonic dominance. The fiction that is the "ideal man," the possessor of the key to true natural manhood, is a fiction of social and economic disenfranchisement, designed to reinscribe the dominant political structures that make certain men "ideal" and others, well, not so ideal.

But it is not enough to simply pluralize the word "masculinity" and expect that the acknowledgment of alternative "masculinities" will provide a sufficient impetus for deconstructing social and economic privileges that attend hegemonic forms of masculine identity. Criticism needs to be directed toward the social processes that define and inscribe hegemonic masculinities and their relationship to both men and women. Historically, definitions of masculinity have been grounded in their difference and opposition to femininity. In the most simplified of terms, to be a man has traditionally meant not to be a woman. This distinction, of course, is fraught with gender-based ideological constructs that demand the "natural" subjugation of women as conditional for the maintenance of patriarchal social structures. However, as the proceeding volume will show, the construction and maintenance of a masculine identity routinely included the necessary cultural and political subjugation of other men as well. As such, the literary representation and identification of manhood in early modern English literature is routinely grounded in the subtle promotion of misogynistic biases and the maintenance of a patriarchal hierarchy, which relies upon the disenfranchisement of both sexes. Taking this as a starting point, the essays in *The Image of Manhood in Early Modern Literature: Viewing the Male* thus begin the discussion of masculine representation during this time by foregrounding two critical perspectives: The representation of any particular type of masculinity requires the identification and repression of some type of socially or culturally defined "inferior"; and the dynamic social and political milieu of the early modern period in England was significant in the development of various and often contesting masculine identities.

Within the study of masculinity, the early modern period stands conjunctive between the Renaissance, where conceptions of manhood can be seen to have been primarily dominated by the chivalric and humanistic tradition, and the latter half of the eighteenth century, which marked the beginnings of modern conceptions of gendered character and masculine identity. However, rather than merely functioning as a transitional period between these two historical moments, the early modern period emerges, in what can be seen, as a key moment in the evolutionary dynamics of masculine representation. Significantly, several social and historical developments had marked effects on the cultural criteria that constituted masculine identity, as well as the means by which those identities were represented. Briefly, the early modern period experienced an evolutionary shift in the understanding of gender characterized by a more defined separation of biological processes between the sexes; the Puritan revolution, the Restoration, and the shift in political power from the courtier class to the ever-growing middle class forced open the parameters of masculine representation to include the trappings of bourgeois society; and as the difference between the public and private spheres became more pronounced, the public demonstration of masculinity became increasingly necessary as the "social field" replaced the battlefield as the appropriate arena for masculine display.

Perhaps the most important development affecting the representation of masculinity in the early modern period can be attributed to the growth of print as a primary mode of cultural discourse. This development indelibly linked the literary text to the mass production and dissemination of ideologically laden depictions of masculine ideals and antiideals. At this time, the literary text, the poem, and the play became the dominant medium by which models of masculinity were presented to society and negotiated. As a result of their wide circulation and popularity, they provided society with models or types of masculine self-fashioning which became a foundation of the cultural dialogue, especially during the latter half of the seventeenth century, concerning what it meant to be a man. This, of course, is not to say that the literary text was the sole medium for masculine representation; on the contrary, the virtual explosion of the "pamphlet war" between the sexes during the latter portion of the seventeenth century textualized and commodified what has been routinely referred to as a "crisis in masculinity." Crisis was certainly the state Jeremy Collier saw at the end of the seventeenth century when, in his *A*

Short View of the Immorality, and Profaneness of the English Stage (1698), he called to task the English stage for promoting a version of masculinity that was prone "to stain the Imagination, to awaken Folly, and to weaken the Defences of Virtue."

Despite the dramatic fervency of Collier's plea for moral reformation, the phrase "crisis in masculinity" seems to suggest a potential displacement of masculinity as a stable subject position in the early modern period. Indeed, what constituted "proper" and "ideal" masculine behavior was being renegotiated within early modern culture with an enthusiasm England had never before experienced. However, whether this constitutes a state of crisis or not seems to be a matter of perspective. Obviously for the female population who believed that English masculinity was becoming increasingly effeminate and less "manly," this was most certainly a period of crisis. But for the nonhegemonic modes of masculine self-identity at this time, masculinity as a subject position was certainly not in a state of crisis; instead, the cultural discussion and renegotiation of what it meant to be a man was now forced to address and acknowledge such "unmanly" components of self-identity and expression as effeminacy and homosexuality as viable and essential elements of certain masculine identities, an acknowledgment that proved problematic to hegemonic ideal forms of masculinity such as the libertine and the heroic-ideal. What some may label as a gender "crisis" of the early modern period actually proved to be an opportunity for contesting modes of masculine self-identity to become engaged within the cultural discussion of what it meant to be a man, and to have a significant impact on the ways manhood would continue to be defined.

Rather than reveal any particular "crisis in masculinity," the original essays collected in *The Image of Manhood in Early Modern Literature: Viewing the Male* explore what can be described as various sites of masculine anxiety. Through the term site, I mean to suggest that forms of masculine self-identity, "masculinities," produce regions of gendered behavior and social dynamics particular to the "masculinity" involved. As such, all forms of masculine self-identity relate to, and interact with, the society of both men and women in various ways, producing what can be seen as moments of male anxiety concerning the successful display and maintenance of the particular "masculinity" that, with the rapid growth of the print-culture in England during the early modern period, became increasingly represented within the literary text as focal points for gender tension and conflict. As the essays in this volume illustrate, at these particular moments in early modern English literature, where masculine self-identity necessitates some form of social intercourse or performance, the act of "being a man" often makes brutally apparent the troubling and tenuous nature of manhood itself.

Though differing in subject and critical approaches, each essay in this volume identifies specific literary texts (or collections of texts) as indicative of potential sites for various formations of masculine anxiousness in early modern England, as well as illustrates the literary and cultural dynamics involved in the representation of "masculinities" during this period. Written with the student of the early modern period in mind, the essays in *The Image of Manhood in Early Modern Literature: Viewing the Male* provide an overview of the evolving and often contesting images of manhood that came to populate the verse, drama, and prose of the early modern period; images, which when viewed together, ultimately reveal the fragile complexities and deep-rooted anxieties of both masculinity and masculine representation at this time.

Masculine Disaffection and Misogynistic Displacement in Carew's Love Lyrics

Ian McAdam

In 1979 Lynn Sadler remarked that Carew "is mainly known as a facile versifier of erotic love poems who happened to write an extraordinary elegy on Donne."[1] He was notorious in his own day for the highly erotic "A Rapture," which, perhaps not surprisingly, continues to attract critical attention. While much of Carew's love poetry consists of fairly conventional Petrarchan lyrics, he cannot be dismissed as simply a "facile versifier," and, like other poets of the early seventeenth century, he conducts what Gordon Braden refers to as "an incisive critique of Petrarchism."[2] Yet the peculiar nature of Carew's anti-Petrarchan critique deserves further examination. Although Carew seeks to replace the psychologically repressive idealism of Petrarchan love, his imagined modes of masculine sexual freedom and fulfilment remain, in their assertion of a new idealism, qualified by a misogynistic displacement of the very restraint and repression he opposes.

As Heather Dubrow points out, distinguishing Petrarchan from anti-Petrarchan lyrics "is by no means easy" since "Petrarchism regularly incorporates attacks on its own vision"; at the same time, she warns that the assumption that "so-called anti-Petrarchism is merely a convention of Petrarchism which never seriously challenges it" is a "common interpretation that neglects the intensity and even choler with which certain poets attack Petrarchism."[3] In fact, Dubrow believes that the "misogynistic hostility and anger that often impel both Petrarchism and the reactions against it can be even more pervasive and virulent than we sometimes acknowledge."[4] For Dubrow the source of this hostility is an "unending slippage" rather than "clear-cut separations" between such categories as male and female, powerful and powerless, and successful and unsuccessful. However, these "slippages" are arguably less acute in Carew than in historically earlier poets; indeed, Anthony Low has offered a reading of Carew that removes him from the Petrarchan context altogether:

> In different, less forgiving circumstances, Raleigh and Sidney learned the politics of desire for an unobtainable object, desire that was an inextricable mixture of frustrated religious,

political, and amatory ambitions. The political experience of these earlier courtier-poets reverberated with and reinforced a Petrarchan stance in their love poetry. Carew's psychosocial circumstances, to the contrary, taught him a politics and an amatory strategy based on cynicism, libertinism, and scorn for authority.[5]

I suggest that, while Carew's particular brand of self-possession does not seem haunted by uncertainty about masculinity *per se*, his poetry nevertheless offers an interesting case of male hostility in response to identifiably Petrarchan social and literary conventions. Carew's challenge to Petrarchan conventions surpasses an ironical or cynical deflation of Platonic and masculine, courtly ideals, and constitutes a bold reexamination of traditional gender roles. More honestly and directly than many earlier satirists of Petrarchan love poetry, Carew focuses on, and resents, the real male suffering—including emotional pain, sexual frustration, and, most significantly in "A Rapture," social expectations of "manliness"— behind the conventionalized posturing of the Petrarchan lover, so that his lyrics represent not so much an attempt to manipulate women under the guise of subservience, as they expose the cost of exercising power dishonestly and indirectly under a system that codifies and suppresses human sexuality. However, in the process, the poet underestimates or misidentifies the ways the system also intensifies the sufferings of women, who are often regarded as capitalizing on their construction within traditional roles. Thus Carew's love lyrics contain an interesting critique of gender inequity from a male perspective but remain notably misogynistic since resentment of the social construction of sexual experience is displaced onto the opposite sex itself. This misogyny arises primarily, not through a subtle extension of Petrarchan ideals of manhood, but through an assertion of a new ideal of manliness, one that carries its own profound misogynistic streak. There exists, nevertheless, some evidence in the poems to suggest that Carew, through this process, is struggling toward a more equitable and mutually satisfying understanding of the relation between the sexes.

Among Carew's critics, then, I am in accord with those who identify a recognizable masculine personality behind the poems' various personae. It may be helpful, however, to briefly consider a less "essentialist" approach. Renée Hannaford, for example, has argued:

> the modes of personation characteristic of Carew's dramatic love lyrics . . . display Carew's profound awareness of the conflict between private personality and public role in a society which placed a high value on sociability (or good courtiership). Techniques of self-presentation . . . [reveal] an understanding of personality (akin to Montaigne's) as fluid, changeable, volitional, subject to occasion—in short a self-fashioned artifact, rather than something fixed and constant.[6]

There is no denying that Carew adopts a variety of roles and attitudes in his lyrics, allowing him to explore various emotional responses to the conventions in question. Yet even Hannaford's reading identifies a tension between "private personality" and "public role," a distinction that in itself raises the issue of the nature of the poet's interiority, and makes problematic the portrait of the poet as simply an untroubled socialite engaged in the game of superficial self-fashioning and artful self-presentation.

The tension or conflict identified by Hannaford has been noted by other critics. Kevin Sharpe, for example, observes that "Carew's poems undoubtedly mirrored his age. . . . Carew's poems presented a variety of images, not all of them reassuring, images which not only reflected men's self-perception, but the divorce between the self and self-perception. . . . Carew . . . turned his glass this way and that to show the different aspects and faces of his subjects." Sharpe thus shows at the outset of his discussion an admirable sensitivity to the complexities of Carew's poetic practice, but unfortunately he goes on to assume a kind of moral and didactic program that results, I believe, in an overly sanguine reading of the psychological tensions in the poetry: "In the private and public worlds, Carew's mirrors educated and informed as they reflected values in different lights and from various perspectives. They became, that is, not the accoutrements of vanity but the mirrors of morality."[7] Sharpe has some difficulty establishing Carew's moral program in light of Carew's own reputation for libertinism—"a man who, we recall, was brought close to death, if not finally killed, by a life of licence and by syphilis"—not to mention the unrestrained eroticism of his most famous poem: "'A Rapture' is, we might say, a laboratory in which Carew creates an ideal condition so that we may better explore an actual problem." The "ideal condition" is an Elyzium where "men live virtuously by acting according to their instincts"; the "actual problem" of reconciling "love and passion, appetite and order" was, Sharpe suggests, for Carew found in marriage, an odd resolution for a man who never married. Even odder is the poem that Sharpe cites as an example for this "resolution of tensions," "On the Mariage of T. K. [Thomas Killigrew] and C. C. [Cecilia Crofts] the morning stormie." For Sharpe, the marriage celebrated in the poem "reconciles contradictions rendering chaste what was impure, honourable what was otherwise shameful, moral what was immoral."[8] The poem is in fact an extremely unpleasant and voyeuristic expression of masculine sexual aggression, which concludes:

> But ere thou feed, that thou may'st better taste
> Thy present joyes, thinke on thy torments past.
> Thinke on the mercy freed thee, thinke upon
> Her vertues, graces, beauties, one by one,
> So shalt thou relish all, enjoy the whole
> Delights of her faire body, and pure soule.
> Then boldly to the fight of Love proceed,
> 'Tis mercy not to pitty though she bleed,
> Wee'le strew no nuts, but change that ancient forme,
> For till to morrow wee'le prorogue this storme,
> Which shall confound with its loude whistling noyse
> Her pleasing shreekes, and fan thy panting joyes. (25–36)[9]

While the speaker clearly approves of such manly assertion in the bridal bed, modern readers must question the "morality" of this "resolution," since the bridegroom is apparently invited to satisfy past Petrarchan "torments" of restraint and deference with a masculine sexual potency barely distinguishable from a consuming violence and brutality.

In light of the doubtfulness of parts of Sharpe's argument, it may be easier to accept Anthony Low's reading of Carew as an anti-authoritarian libertine who broke with his family connections and, in spite of his role as a courtier, was skillful enough to earn for himself a kind of "freedom or space for independent movement," which Low sees as "an early adumbration of the growth of modern individual subjectivity, of the impulse to establish an identity within, yet independent of, the social matrix."[10] It is certainly true that Carew's secular worldview for the most part excludes the kind of destabilizing religious anxiety or doubt[11] that characterizes earlier poets— "My unwasht Muse, polutes not things Divine" (3)[12]—and I find far less religious tension in the poetry than Sharpe attempts to suggest. In Carew's opus there is little of that heightened inwardness of Reformation Protestantism (as in Wyatt's version of the penitential psalms, for example) that leads, through the apparent internalization of the divine, to a confusion of self with other. Moreover, the frequently retold episode of Carew's irreparably offending his patrons Sir Dudley and Lady Carleton (his father's niece)[13] does suggest an assertive and independently minded young man balking under the rigors of obsequious servitude. Yet, ironically for a critic who opposes the materialist conviction that "culture shapes people but people cannot shape culture,"[14] Low's discussion of Carew goes to the opposite extreme from Sharpe's, and the homology between Carew's pragmatic individualism and the market economy of seventeenth-century England results in readings that at times seem excessively cynical and impersonal. The "truth" about Carew's psychosocial attitudes would seem to lie somewhere between the approaches of Sharpe and Low. In fact, Sharpe's speculation that "a strong personal sense of the ungoverned anarchy of his own appetite and passion, some internal quest for order and regulation, might have dominated Carew's life as well as his poetry"[15] is ultimately borne out by a careful reconsideration of the poems themselves, which, taken as a whole, seek fitfully to replace outmoded Petrarchan conventions with new models of regulation.

Carew's resentment of the ideal of Petrarchan adoration is, in his love lyrics, frequently patent. "Ingratefull beauty threatned" is a good example of what Kerrigan and Braden in *The Idea of the Renaissance*[16] call the "I made you, I can break you" lyric:

Know Celia, (since thou art so proud,)
'Twas I that gave thee thy renowne:
Thou hadst, in the forgotten crowd
Of common beauties, liv'd unknowne,
Had not my verse exhal'd thy name,
And with it, ympt the wings of fame.

That killing power is none of thine,
I gave it to thy voyce, and eyes:
Thy sweets, thy graces, all are mine;
Thou art my starre, shin'st in my skies;
Then dart not from thy borrowed sphere
Lightning on him, that fixt thee there.
Tempt me with such affrights no more,
Lest what I made, I uncreate;
Let fooles thy mystique formes adore,
I'le know thee in thy mortall state:
Wise Poets that wrap't Truth in tales,
Knew her themselves, through all her vailes.

The frustration here is similar to that of the speaker in Donne's "Elegy 7" who, having taught his mistress everything he knows, is outraged to discover she is as intelligent and capable as he, and quite willing to seek out other lovers. However, in Carew's lyric the lover claims only to have heightened her beauty and sexual allure; he resents her pride and disdain, for his intention was to heighten his own sexual pleasure, as he insinuates in his choice of verbs: "I'le *know* thee in thy mortall state." The concluding couplet repeats the insinuation, but also, I think, raises an ambiguity: "Wise Poets that wrap't Truth in tales,/Knew her themselves, through all her vailes." This might suggest, even more unpleasantly, that the veiled body of sacred Truth is simply a mortal woman that the male poet can deceive, strip, and take sexual advantage of. Yet Carew's introduction of "Truth" raises other possibilities. Wise or clever poets may wrap Truth in the veils of Petrarchan conventions, but the *truth* is, in fact, that women do have enormous sexual power over (heterosexual) men, and that beauty and attraction are not simply conventions or constructions of the Petrarchan poet or of other kinds of social ideology (contrary to the claims of currently fashionable radical constructionism). The Truth hints at the very real presence of masculine anxiety over sexual relations. There is, here and elsewhere in Carew, a strong insistence on the *reality*, the naturalness, of sexual desire, a need to honestly face it and come to terms with it. To take another example, at the beginning of "To A. L. Perswasions to love" the poet states:

Thinke not cause men flatt'ring say,
Y'are as fresh as Aprill, sweet as May,
Bright as is the morning starre,
That you are so, or though you are
Be not therefore proud, and deeme
All men unworthy your esteeme. (1–6)

Hannaford argues that the "rudeness of [the speaker's] opening remark he quickly counterpoises with 'or though you are'; psychologically this operates as a witty ploy to attract and keep the attention of a woman accustomed to receiving artful compliments."[17] We might, however, wonder why the speaker's "witty ploys" should be so self-contradictory—insulting in order to compliment—and I am willing to attribute a greater honesty to the speaker; he deconstructs the hackneyed Petrarchan convention but, in a striking irony, the power of beauty remains, in fact seems even more real in the absence of the conventions, and in the honest admission of the speaker.

It is partly this recognition that the power of sexual attraction exceeds any discursive formulation used to express it that renders Carew's love poetry intriguingly anti-Petrarchan. Braden, upon examining some of Petrarch's own lyrics, suggests that what the Italian poet "is actually in love with may well be his own imaginative powers." This critic concludes:

> More than one poetic career in the Renaissance begins with an episode of Petrarchism not merely in response to empty fashionability but, we may guess, because such an episode provides entry to an expanded feel for the mind's autonomy in shaping and contemplating the inner landscape of its desire. With such a beast, however obliquely, in view, the lover might well be thought to connive in his own sexual frustration; the laurel and not Daphne might well have been the real goal all along.[18]

Such a goal is decidedly not Carew's, whose art seems therefore less narcissistically self-indulgent than the kind of poetry Braden describes. Carew, to judge from the insistent masculine desire expressed (sometimes rather brutally) in his poems, definitely seeks sexual consummation. Yet the boldness of the desire does not establish him simply as a licentious and irresponsible trifler or seducer. Rather, he projects a different type of masculine identity, one that accepts the union of lovers as elemental.

Carew expresses a recurring need in his poetry for real romantic and sexual reciprocity. For example, "Disdaine returned" conveys both his great dissatisfaction for the typical Petrarchan admiration from afar and his hopes for a different kind of relationship, a new kind of ideal, romantic union:

> Hee that loves a Rosie cheeke,
> Or a corall lip admires,
> Or from star-like eyes doth seeke
> Fuell to maintaine his fires;
> As old Time makes these decay,
> So his flames must waste away.
>
> But a smooth, and stedfast mind,
> Gentle thoughts, and calme desires,
> Hearts, with equall love combind,
> Kindle never dying fires.
> Where these are not, I despise
> Lovely cheekes, or lips, or eyes.
>
> No teares, Celia, now shall win,
> My resolv'd heart, to returne;
> I have searcht thy soule within,

And find nought, but pride, and scorne;
I have learn'd thy arts, and now
Can disdain as much as thou.
Some power, in my revenge convay
That love to her, I cast away.

He disdains her now because he has not found their "hearts with equal love combined." With his penchant for introducing ambiguity in the final lines, Carew suggests either that he will now solicit, with the help of some supernatural power, a former love (whom, ironically, he had "cast away") in order to be revenged upon Celia; or that he wishes some power to infect Celia's heart with the kind of sick and constrained love he has felt for her but now relinquishes, so she will feel and suffer for him as he has done for her. There would presumably be no better way of getting even.

What is missing in "Disdaine returned" is some recognition of the speaker's own responsibility in the construction of women as proud and scornful. That the male lover shares complicity in the Petrarchan game gone wrong is suggested by the intriguing ambiguities of "A divine Mistris," which seems on first reading a deceptively simple poem:

In natures peeces still I see
Some errour, that might mended bee;
Something my wish could still remove,
Alter or adde; but my faire love
Was fram'd by hands farre more divine;
For she hath every beauteous line:
Yet I had beene farre happier,
Had Nature that made me, made her;
Then likenes, might (that love creates)
Have made her love what now she hates:
Yet I confesse I cannot spare
From her iust shape the smallest haire:
Nor need I beg from all the store
Of heaven, for her one beautie more:
Shee hath too much divinity for mee,
You Gods teach her some more humanitie.

Nature, the poem suggests, is always in some way flawed, so the mistress, as the ideal object of Petrarchan admiration, must be framed by "hands farre more divine;/ For she hath every beauteous line." "Line" here may refer to her bodily form or figure, but also suggests lines of poetry, and we begin to suspect the divine creator is really the male poet. It is somewhat ironic, then, that the speaker laments: "Yet I had beene farre happier,/ Had Nature that made me, made her;/ Then likenes, might (that love creates)/ Have made her love what now she hates." He is at least partly responsible for this proud creature, and in fact admits his continuing dependence on her ideal image: "Yet I confesse I cannot spare/ From her iust shape the smallest haire." But he seems unaware of the double bind the mistress experiences under this Petrarchan construction: having to be perfect, blamed for being perfect. "She hath too much divinity for mee,/ You Gods teach her some more humanitie," he concludes, without realizing the "Gods" that have stripped her of humanity are really his own poetic powers, or at least his own dependence on the social and poetic conventions that define his role and his powers.

This kind of dependence takes on a slightly different form in a longer, more complex, and more tender lyric, "To A. D. unreasonable distrustfull of her owne beauty," where the poet attempts to move beyond the sense of Petrarchan paralysis present in "Disdaine returned." A. D. has been dismayed at her reflection in the mirror, but the "love-sick"(23) poet assures her, "If then Love flow from Beautie as th'effect/ How canst thou the resistless cause suspect?" (35–36). He concludes:

It not endeares your bountie that I doe
Esteeme your gift, unless you doe so too;
You undervalew me, when you bestow
On me, what you nor care for, nor yet know.
No (Lovely Doris) change thy thoughts, and be
In love first with thy selfe, and then with me. (69–74)

It is possible to argue here, as do Kerrigan and Braden with respect to Spenser's *Amoretti* 45, that the male poet encourages a "trust [which] can reconcile pride and dependence, supplying a basis for communion within which her self-absorption has nevertheless a privileged place."[19] I am tempted to replace the term "self-absorption" here with "self-esteem," and then argue that the speaker recognizes his mistress must have her own sense of self and integrity before they can proceed with a meaningful romantic communion. However, the problem with this argument is that the emphasis in the poem remains on the woman's physical beauty; she is not encouraged to establish her own moral, intellectual or spiritual integrity, and thus she exists disturbingly only as a kind of template for the male poet's process of self-fashioning.

Carew's critique of Petrarchism is not always so subtle and restrained as it is in "To A. D." As already mentioned, his attack on the conventions more often takes the form of an urgent insistence on sexual consummation. In "To a Lady that desired I would love her" the male resentment is again patent. "Now you have freely given me leave to love/ What will you doe?" (1–2), the poet asks. Don't be the typical disdainful Petrarchan mistress, he says, just to enjoy watching me die: "Dispence a nobler Fate,/ 'Tis easie to destroy, you may create"(9–10):

Then give me leave to love, and love me too,
        Not with designe
To rayse, as Loves curst Rebells doe,
        When puling Poets whine,
Fame to their beautie, from their blubbr'd eyne.

Griefe is a puddle, and reflects not cleare
Your beauties rayes . . . (11–17)

But if you keep me happy, the poet argues, "I'le make your eyes like morning Suns appeare" (26). He promises to spend "Rich Natures store"(31) to dress her beauties if she—and this is the price her "mine of Pleasure/ In equall thankfulnesse/ . . . but unlock"(33–35), so that poet and mistress "blesse"(35) each other in joyful reciprocity. Beautiful poetry will not arise from a Petrarchan sublimation of sexual energy, but from the pleasure of sexual fulfilment; Carew calls Nature "the Poets Treasure"(31), and suggests that Nature inspires those who enjoy her most freely.

Carew's most notable celebration of idealized sexual licence is, of course, the notorious "A Rapture." The poem begins with an energetic dismissal of the personified giant Honour who is identified as "but a Masquer," a social construction that more noble and valiant lovers need not fear:

We shall see how the stalking Pageant goes
With borrowed legs, a heavie load to those
That made, and beare him; not as we once thought
The seed of Gods, but a weake modell wrought
By greedy men, that seeke to enclose the common,
And within private armes empale free woman. (15–20)

Celia is invited to fly with the poet to "Loves Elizium"(2), where the "Queene of Love, and Innocence,/ Beautie and Nature, banish all offence"(25–26). But, as Paula Johnson argues, while Carew turns his back on the artificial moral and social constructions of the civilized court world, he does so only to enter into an equally artificial fantasy of the creative imagination:

. . . although honor is manmade and delusive, art, also manmade, is the revelation of invention and craft. This snow-gold-ivory figure, the virginity of whose treasure multiplies its price, is the product of the poet's ars amatoria, which thus obliquely confirms the high value of body and art and of the poet's experience of both. But unfortunately . . . this success of ingenium makes for a human failure, since in transforming the woman's body into precious artifice, Carew denies to it any possibility of response, any interior. It slips paradoxically into the same category as the "vast Idoll" [Honour], having no value and no life in itself, but only the value the poet imputes to it, which rests in turn only on his own enjoying and beholding.[20]

Nevertheless, one cannot help qualify this reading by asking why, if the fantasy that Carew creates is so "artificial," has it seemed so intensely pornographic, in a real physical sense, to generations of readers? There is in Johnson's phrase "the high value of body and art" an ontological conflation that requires more careful consideration. Carew's poem is in part a radical and satirical appropriation of Petrarchan conventions; he may give the reader another blazon of sorts, but he describes body parts and the female body in such a way that no poet before or perhaps since has dared. Johnson herself qualifies her claim of complete passivity on the part of Celia by recognizing that she is finally imagined as physically active in sexual intercourse:

My Rudder, with thy bold hand, like a tryde,
And skilfull Pilot, thou shalt steere, and guide
My Bark into Loves channell, where it shall
Dance, as the bounding waves doe rise or fall:
Then shall thy circling armes, embrace and clip
My willing bodie, and thy balmie lip
Bathe me in juyce of kisses, whose perfume
Like a religious incense shall consume,
And send up holy vapours, to those powres
That blesse our loves, and crowne our sportfull houres . . . (87–96)

Moreover, in the penultimate verse paragraph, Carew gives a list of mythological revisions with which he hopes to warm the heart of any reader tired by the tedious history of Petrarchan disdain and frustration; here Carew significantly implies that the women have been equally frustrated. In "Love's Elizium" he believes, Penelope displays "Her selfe before the Youth of Ithaca,/ And th'amorous sport of gamesome nights prefer,/ Before dull dreames of the lost Traveller"(128–30). Daphne breaks out of her laurel bark and runs:

To meet th'embraces of the youthfull Sun:
She hangs upon him, like his Delphique Lyre,
Her kisses blow the old, and breath new fire:
Full of her God, she sings inspired Layes,
Sweet Odes of love, such as deserve the Bayes,
Which she her selfe was. (134–39)

Daphne escapes her objectification; no longer a symbol of sublimation, she herself becomes a female poet celebrating sexual liberation. And last, but not least, Laura ends the discourse of Petrarchism by lying down in Petrarch's learned arms and wiping away his tears.

However, this fantasy of sexual liberation is disturbingly problematic, as critics have remarked, by the poem's conclusion, although there has been no easy agreement on just what Carew here implies. The poet once more, in his address to Celia, criticizes the giant Honour:

nor is it just that Hee
Should fetter your soft sex with Chastitie,
Which Nature made unapt for abstinence;
When yet this false Impostor can dispence
With humane Justice, and with sacred right,
And maugre both their lawes command me fight
With Rivals, or with emulous Loves, that dare

Equall with thine, their Mistresse eyes, or haire:
If thou complaine of wrong, and call my sword
To carve out thy revenge, upon that word
He bids me fight and kill, or else he brands
With markes of infamie my coward hands,
And yet religion bids from blood-shed flye,
And damns me for that Act. Then tell me why
This Goblin Honour which the world adores,
Should make men Atheists, and not women Whores. (151–66)

Here Carew refers to "religion," presumably Christianity, quite different from the religion of sexual freedom he has celebrated earlier. As Paula Johnson summarizes, the poet asks "how one can do what is right when one's culture insists with equal vehemence on two incompatible kinds of behavior."[21] It is the dilemma of the Renaissance male: Admonished by orthodox Christianity into submission and Augustinian passivity, and encouraged by traditional chivalric and manly codes of honour to be assertive and heroic, yet here, as so often, the assertiveness takes destructive rather than creative forms. But what about the final lines? Johnson argues:

Honor makes men "Atheists"—despisers of religion, bad people; so, asks the poet, why shouldn't it make women bad people too? The inversion [of values in the poem] has failed. For the analogy to work, one would have to find a term for unchaste women that would carry positive overtones. As the last line stands, the word "whores" suddenly re-inverts the whole moral world that the poet has been so carefully setting upside-down.[22]

Braden, on the other hand, believes that "the main weight of the poem effectively puts the word 'whores' in quotation marks, challenges the reader consciously to reject the established connotations, in response to just the semantic lack Johnson describes."[23] Yet what gets ignored in discussions of the last two lines is that men become atheists by *obeying* Honour's precepts, but women would only become whores by *breaking* Honour's rules. The poem then definitely does not qualify the term whore; it is said angrily, misogynistically by the speaker, who in effect argues that since he must suffer danger and violence and take great risks by obeying the codes of Honour, his mistress should, through sexual repayment, disobey the very code he is fighting to uphold. The system itself is corrupt, ridiculous, and self-contradictory, but Carew displaces his anger at the absurdity and hypocrisy of such social constructions onto the mistress herself, who, he suggests, should not hesitate to offer him sexual consolation for his troubles. But she then suffers a kind of contempt, the label of whore, for doing so, since the "Idoll"(6) valiantly fought for is false. She is thus punished for his inability to realize his ideal fantasy of sexual freedom, and his failure here to escape the traditional codes of "manliness"; in fact, she becomes, along with his male competitors, a target of his violent aggression.

Despite the unpleasantness, the disturbing quality of the poem, it is worthy of attention because of the psychological dilemma it illuminates. We stand to learn something from Carew's lyrics even today, since, I will venture to suggest, the kind of displacement I have identified—resentment toward various kinds of illogical or destructive social constructions of human sexual experience expressing itself as resentment of the opposite sex—is a not infrequent phenomenon on *both* sides of the battle line in past and present gender wars. Carew's experiences are, quite probably, representative of the evolution of masculinity through the crucial transition from early modern to modern subjectivity, and hence can help us understand more clearly our own patterns of gender construction. Moreover, the striving toward a greater mutuality and reciprocity of thought and feeling between the sexes evident in Carew's lyrics is something we might take to heart. Considering once more "To A. L. Perswasions to love," for example, we find that the poem begins as a typical *carpe diem* exercise warning the young woman she must make use of her fleeting beauty before it fades; yet the argument then turns away from the usual seduction ploy:

> Then wisely chuse one to your friend,
> Whose love may, when your beauties end,
> Remaine still firme: be provident
> And thinke before the summers spent
> Of following winter; like the Ant
> In plenty hoord for time of scant.
> Cull out amongst the multitude
> Of lovers, that seeke to intrude
> Into your favour, one that may
> Love for an age, not for a day;
> One that will quench your youthfull fires,
> And feed in age your hot desires. (49–60)

It is this passage, the most crucial in the poem, that Renée Hannaford glosses over in her reading of Carew's poetic strategies, allowing her to conclude:

> The style of self projected in [the] poem reflects a preoccupation with the manners of a cultural elite; this style of self may serve as a mask or disguise regularly adopted and discarded by Carew's personae, an activity that permeated every moment of the splendid baroque stage that was life at the court of Charles I. Carew's performing speaker strives for poetic *sprezzatura* as well as sophistication in handling a poetic problem to capture audience interest and to swing the focus of the poem away from the subject addressed to the speaker's own artfully fashioned self.[24]

Such a reading emphasizes cultural and social context to the extent that it distorts or misreads the text of the poem itself, and devalues or underestimates not only the emotional reality the speaker acknowledges in the woman addressed, but also the depth of feeling in the speaker himself. For slightly different methodological and ideological reasons Anthony Low also offers a distorted reading of the poem's conclusion: "Carew implicitly presents himself as a client who can help his patroness to what she wants, giving a new twist to the age-old *carpe-diem* theme on which he bases the poem. He also offers a cynically pragmatic version of the perennial desire for eternal love, which here becomes sexual gratification drawn out by mutual convenience into old age."[25] It would indeed be "cynically pragmatic" to regard monogamy and fidelity as "sexual gratification drawn out by mutual convenience into old age," but the cynicism here is Low's, not Carew's. Not simply a sexual opportunist or a witty self-fashioner on display, the male poet expresses a longing for emotional and romantic permanence even as he faces and accepts physical process. The poem becomes not just an honest recognition of time's inexorability but, more movingly, a mature vision of human romantic commitment in the face of change and decay.

Carew's love poetry, therefore, should not be regarded only as a collection of social documents reflecting fashions and mannerisms of a cultural era, but also as the record of the experience and suffering of a man who responded deeply and critically to the conventions of his time, and who in the process has revealed not only his darker emotions for our perusal, but also, occasionally, his brighter dreams. In a "Hymeneall Dialogue" between a "Bride and Groome," for example, the poet seems to cast in miniature a resolution to the interpersonal problems he has been exploring. The Groome states:

> Then I perceive, when from the flame
> Of love, my scorch'd soule did retire,
> Your frozen heart in her place came,
> And sweetly melted in that fire. (9–12)

To which the Bride replies:

> 'Tis true, for when that mutuall change
> Of soules, was made with equall gaine,
> I straight might feele diffus'd a strange,
> But gentle heat through every veine. (13–16)

The Chorus then concludes:

> Oh blest dis-union, that doth so
> Our bodyes from our soules divide,
> As two doe one, and one foure grow,
> Each by contraction multiply'de. (17–20)

This beautiful but mysterious stanza can be elucidated by recourse to Renaissance Neoplatonic thought. Ficino in *De Amore* "considers from several angles the number of worlds enjoyed by a pair of lovers, and in one of these computations declares that their oneness is fourfold, inasmuch as they [each] possess their beloveds, and in the regard of their beloveds repossess themselves."[26] In a union of two lovers who nevertheless recognize and respect each other's integrity and difference, the joy is multiplied fourfold. "Blest dis-union": In a relationship of equal partners experiencing "equall gaine," the difference of bodies becomes a blessing, not a curse.

Unhappily it must be admitted, however, that in the context of Carew's work as a whole such poetic moments are minor consolations, and equality between the sexes only fleetingly envisioned. In contrast to the ideal marriage of "A Hymeneall Dialogue," the poem "A married Woman"—which offers more pragmatically the reconciliation, as Sharpe has observed, of love and passion, appetite and order, through marriage— is an extremely disturbing revelation of Carew's consideration of the proper "manly" regulation of sexuality. Here the male speaker only *seems* to accept responsibility for the disciplining of his own appetite and passions, which threaten to destroy his integrity:

> If I in murder steepe my furious rage,
> Or with Adult'ry my hot lust asswage,
> Will it suffice to say my sense, the Beast
> Provokt me to't? could I my soule devest,
> My plea were good, Lyons, and Buls commit
> Both freely, but man must in judgement sit,
> And tame this Beast . . . (17–23)

Yet the opening of the poem identifies this "Beast" with women, on whom the speaker projects his own failings and indulgences, using the traditional assignation of male reason and female passion as an excuse to control and oppress his imagined wife:

> When I shall marry, if I doe not find
> A wife thus moulded, I'le create this mind:
> Nor from her noble birth, nor ample dower,
> Beauty, or wit, shall she derive a power
> To prejudice my Right; but if she be
> A subject borne, she shall be so to me:
> As to the soule the flesh, as Appetite
> To reason is, which shall our wils unite;
> In habits so confirm'd, as no rough sway
> Shall once appeare, if she but learne t'obay. (1–10)

The argument is, if not historically surprising, psychologically outrageous; the woman is made to pay through subservience, through complete loss of self, for the man's loss of sexual freedom, which can hardly be called self-discipline since the rigor of restraint is narcissistically and tyrannically displaced onto his partner. Perhaps we can be glad that Carew never married if this poem constitutes the best resolution of his psychological dilemma that he could imagine. It might be comforting as well for us finally to dismiss Carew's misogyny as a product of a patriarchy now no longer tolerated or tolerable. As with "A Rapture," however, the psychological dynamic reflects, I suspect, a more universal quandary arising out of our inheritance (to borrow Low's formulation) of "modern individual subjectivity, of the impulse to establish an identity within, yet independent of, the social matrix." The ultimate "moral" of Carew's love poetry may be that whatever reconstruction of romantic ideals we find historically necessary to regulate and order our lives, we must remain eternally vigilant against the tendency to make others pay for the inevitable limitations placed on our own desires.

NOTES

1. Lynn Sadler, *Thomas Carew* (Boston: Twayne Publishers, 1979) 7.
2. Gordon Braden, "Beyond Frustration: Petrarchan Laurels in the Seventeenth Century," *SEL* 26 (1986): 12.
3. Heather Dubrow, *Echoes of Desire: English Petrarchism and its Counterdiscourses* (Ithaca: Cornell University Press, 1995) 6–7.
4. Dubrow, *Echoes*, 12.
5. Anthony Low, *The Reinvention of Love: Poetry, Politics and Culture from Sidney to Milton* (Cambridge: Cambridge University Press, 1993) 147.
6. Renée Hannaford, "Self-Presentation in Carew's 'To A. L. Perswasions to love'," *SEL* 26 (1986): 97.
7. Kevin Sharpe, *Criticism and Compliment: The Politics of Literature in the England of Charles I* (Cambridge: Cambridge University Press, 1987) 115.
8. Sharpe, *Criticism and Compliment*, 121, 119, 120.
9. All quotations from Carew's lyrics are from *The Poems of Thomas Carew*, ed. Rhodes Dunlap (Oxford: Clarendon Press, 1957).
10. Low, *Reinvention of Love*, 145–46.
11. Sadler, *Thomas Carew*, 14–16, offers a brief summary of Carew's "supposed deathbed recantation" during one of his illnesses; see also Dunlap, xxxix–xli. Upon recovery, Carew apparently resumed his "Scandalus life." Sadler also asserts that the Psalms paraphrased by Carew "were probably written during his first siege of syphilis while he was under his father's care. They show no particular personal revelations. Of the nine Psalms he elected to deal with, only Numbers 51 and 119 have any special penitential cast"(16).
12. "To my worthy friend Master Geo. Sands, on his translation of the Psalmes" (93).
13. The fullest account is given in Dunlap's introduction to *The Poems of Thomas Carew*.
14. Dunlap, *The Poems*, 9.
15. Sharpe, *Criticism and Compliment*, 121.
16. William Kerrigan and Gordon Braden, *The Idea of the Renaissance* (Baltimore: Johns Hopkins University Press, 1989) 179.
17. Hannaford, "Self-Presentation,"100.
18. Braden, "Beyond Frustration," 11.
19. Kerrigan and Braden, *The Idea of the Renaissance*, 174–75.
20. Paula Johnson, "Carew's 'A Rapture': The Dynamics of Fantasy," *SEL* 16 (1976): 150.
21. Johnson, "Carew's 'A Rapture,'" 155.
22. Johnson, "Carew's 'A Rapture,'" 155.
23. Braden, "Beyond Frustration," 22.
24. Hannaford, "Self-Presentation," 105.
25. Low, *Reinvention of Love*, 148.
26. Kerrigan and Braden, *The Idea of the Renaissance*, 106–07.

A Garden of Desire, A Meadow of Decay: Masculine Identity Crisis in Marvell's Mower Poems

Edward J. Whitelock

God Almighty first planted a Garden. And indeed it is the purest of human pleasures. It is the greatest refreshment to the spirits of man; without which buildings and palaces are but gross handyworks: and a man shall ever see that when ages grow to civility and elegancy, men come to build stately sooner than to garden finely; as if gardening were the greater perfection.

—Francis Bacon, "Of Gardening"[1]

Alone among Donne's students, Andrew Marvell is a poet of the open air, one who "does not . . . think it necessary to shut his eyes to the outside world in order to develop his inner life."[2] In fact, when Marvell stopped writing poetry in order to focus attention exclusively upon his political career, England would not have a poet so attuned to the delicate balance of outward reflection upon inner life until Wordsworth. But where Wordsworth would become the poet of nature in its sublime wildness, of rivers, mountains, and verdant growth, Marvell was the poet of tamer nature, of garden, meadow, and wood. Wordsworth embarked upon extensive walking tours to encounter his solitude within nature; Marvell needed only a shaded retreat from human cares. Marvell celebrated nature at the periphery of human existence, the boundary areas where human intention mingled with natural lushness.

Marvell's celebration of nature—and of man's place within it—like Wordsworth's later complicated musings, was neither innocent nor idealized. Despite his open appreciation of pastoral beauty and idyllic calm, Marvell was no "easy philosopher, / Among the birds and trees" as he self-deprecatingly calls himself in "Upon Appleton House" (561–62).[3] Gazing upon an ornate knot in a manor garden or sun-splashed workers in a border meadow, Marvell was highly attuned to the social and aesthetic orders that contributed to the scenes before him. Gardens, meadows, and woods represented the peripheries of man's existence within and without nature, and Marvell explored these shaded boundaries for what they would reveal of the human condition. In his four Mower Poems, Marvell undertakes an exploration not only of contemporary attitudes toward man's relationship with nature, but also of man's gendered identity within the landscape. However, for a complete portrait of Marvell's exploration of this topic, this poetic series should be examined in relation to "The Garden" and "Upon Appleton House," poems written during the same period, when Marvell was serving as tutor to Lord Fairfax's daughter, Maria, at the family estate at Appleton.[4] In these poems, Marvell's attentions span the history of gardening in England as he exemplifies and investigates the gendered identity tied to contradictory attitudes of land usage and man's intervention upon nature. This investigation is enacted mostly through the person of Damon, the Mower, who comes to represent a masculine figure of pastoral disharmony, a contrast to Marvell's own position.

Many critics have traced the history of gardening and the varying attitudes toward man's place in nature that shaped Marvell's conceptions as he composed the Mower sequence. Ellen C. Eyler notes that many of the great public figures of the age immediately preceding Marvell's were avid gardeners who encouraged extensive public interest in gardening through their own examples: William Cecil, Walter Raleigh, Francis Carew, and Francis Bacon were all well known for their interest in gardening in addition to their better-celebrated talents.[5] The years leading up to Marvell's birth and childhood saw an explosion of interest and scholarship in English gardening that has not abated even in present times. William Turner, "the father of English botany," published *A New Herbal* in three parts (1551, 1562, and 1568); the first proper book on gardening in England, Thomas Hill's *The Profitable Art of Gardening*, was published in 1563 and went through seven editions; John Parkinson's *Paradis in sole, Paradisus terestrus*, the most popular gardening book of the seventeenth century, was published in 1629.[6] William Lawson's *A New Orchard and Garden* was published in 1618 and went through multiple printings until 1683.[7] Through his European travels and through his access to Lord Fairfax's library during his lodging at Appleton House, Marvell assuredly was familiar with the majority of these works by the time he composed his Mower Poems.

As Paul Shepard notes, the Italian Renaissance garden, the largest single influence upon English gardeners, stressed formal geometry and "severe" design, yet was perceived as natural by its viewers. Wild nature was not yet seen to possess its own order; rather, it contained "the germ of beauty, dormant and imperfect without human help."[8] English gardeners of the sixteenth and seventeenth centuries shared this basic perception while developing their own aesthetic styles. Francis Bacon recommended that the heath, or inner border, of a garden be planted with dense shrubs possessing a "natural wildness," punctuated with flowering plants set "not in any order" to better mimic nature's randomness.[9] When the early modern gardener saw wildness in nature, he was first awed, then moved to tame that wildness and make it serve his own purposes. As in Shepard's analysis of Italian Renaissance gardens, "natural wildness" was seen as an aesthetic effect achieved by a gardener with a careful eye, capable of divining order and beauty from the chaos of unchecked nature. Another early modern aspect of wildness tamed was the rise to prominence of grafting and the active manipulation of natural species, an activity to which Marvell's masculine gardener Damon takes great offense. The Mower sees these practices as impious manipulations of God's grandeur, man overstepping his bounds by seeking to control nature.

And in this Damon has many precursors. Throughout history, the garden represented more than an indicator of man's growing control over nature; it often served as a troubling sign-system of man's precarious moral identity. Regarding Middle Ages attitudes, Shepard notes that "Most Christians treated the environment as an elaborate text composed of fixed lessons in morality," and gardens were particularly troubling texts as they "confronted the individual with the sensual pleasures leading to Hell."[10] Shepard points to the example of an eleventh-century manuscript showing a line of monks ascending a ladder to heaven: One impious monk, who has paused in his climb to pluck a flower, has slipped from the ladder and is falling into the fires of Hell. This is a warning to those who would cling too long to worldly things, even those worldly things of God's creation. Hyman traces this attitude through the Renaissance, where the garden serves as a reminder of man's first disobedience: "The beauty of nature . . . was to the Renaissance poet not so much a source of pleasure as a constant reminder of his former state."[11] Petrarch was so reminded when he climbed Mount Ventoux in Provence in 1336. Addressing his experience at the peak, he said he almost lost his soul "admiring earthly things."[12] Nature, even as it represents the work of God's hand, is an earthly thing; further, to create and covet the beauty of a garden was to flaunt one's attachment to secular pursuits. Such a reminder was foremost in the minds of Puritans of the seventeenth century and their supporters. While Marvell did not see so literal a warning of Hell's gate as did his Middle Ages predecessors when he looked at nature (and man's work upon and within it), he certainly would have been aware of its history as a symbol and would have taken for granted much of the valuations revealed in that symbolic awareness.

One of the primary valuations that has shaped humankind's perception of nature is that of gender. In Western culture, nature is exclusively represented as feminine, which, at times, has led to a troubling relationship between masculinity and nature. Shepard traces the masculine will to control nature through a Freudian reading of humankind's usage of landscape throughout history. Shepard attributes the feminized representation of nature and landscape to a child's first sensory awareness of his/her mother. All human perception of the world and its contents spreads outward from the originary awareness of shelter, food, and warmth provided by a mother. The surrounding landscape is thereby read in terms of mother: "The world is first mother and food."[13] As a man's perception of female shifts from mother to lover in adolescence and adulthood (while the female perception of herself shifts from care-receiver to care-giver), so, too, does his awareness of landscape shift from a feminized valuation in passivity and comfort to a masculine desire for active intervention and control. Where nature was once valued for what it provided to man, it now becomes appreciated in terms of what man can do to it; the value system shifts from passive bounty to active intervention.

Cultural and religious awareness follows this masculine/feminine dichotomy and can be linked to agricultural practices. Shepard notes that in cultures where agriculture was simple or passive—where a community's primary agricultural act was waiting for, followed by the reaping of, nature's bounty—goddesses were worshiped as primary deities. In cultures where agricultural practices were active, however—where tools for more efficient farming were developed or where the landscape itself was changed through irrigation or other intervention—primary gods were male. The history of agriculture is shaped by this psychological distinction in which the masculine identity itself is challenged by a passive, feminized, natural order. Shepard notes that "there is about the birth of plants the appearance of an immaculate conception. The earth needed no men to inseminate it, only the magic touch of women as midwives," and such a natural order is both a threat and an invitation to masculine intervention and dominance: "The necessities of cultivation were inescapably feminine, the whole cycle of vegetative growth, the permanent hearth, the passive waiting and receptivity. . . ."[14] The Mower Poems explore this gendered dichotomy of landscape and agriculture through the masculine presence of Damon and his vocation. Damon comes to embody a masculinity whose self-identity refuses to acknowledge his own masculine domination of a feminized nature, and instead insists upon the veracity of a relationship with nature based upon a mutual passivity as a condition for manhood. However, when confronted with the very real gendered dynamics of feminine sexuality, Damon's passive or "natural" masculine posture is proven ineffective, and the Mower is revealed as an impotent mockery of manhood.

It is interesting that the act of mowing has not received as extensive treatment in relation to Marvell's poem sequence as has the history of gardening. An examination into the entomology of this verb reveals an important distinction for Marvell's Mower series. The *Oxford English Dictionary* provides alternative definitions of "mower" and "mowing" that would have been well-known to Marvell, which would significantly shape his contemporaries' understanding of the poem sequence. In addition to its common definition, a "mower" was also understood in the fifteenth and sixteenth centuries as "one who makes mouths, a jester, a mocker." Similarly, the *OED* cites an alternative definition of the verb "mowing," in varied use from the fourteenth through the nineteenth centuries: "the action of making grimaces, derision." In his *Magnyfycence*, Thomas Skelton uses the verb in this context: "To mockynge, to mowynge, to lyke a jackenapes." Thomas More, in his *Confutation of Tyndale's Answer*, uses the term similarly: "And then should stand up and preache upon a stoole and make a mowyng sermon." The *OED* also cites Ascham from 1568: "to mow with the mouth." Further, Shakespeare uses "mowing" in its variant definition in both *The Tempest* (1611) and *King Lear* (1606). In *The Tempest* II.ii, Prospero makes clear use of the term's alternate definition while complaining of his afflictions: "For every trifle are they set upon me, / Sometimes like apes that mow and chatter at me, / And after bite me. . . ." (8–10).[15] In both *The Tempest* and *King Lear*, Shakespeare uses variations of the phrase "mopping and mowing," meaning to gesture and grimace—a phrase still in contemporary use. In *The Tempest* IV.i, Ariel uses the term "mop and mow" when referring to the rabble that Prospero has instructed her to round up for his purposes (47); in *King Lear* IV.i, Edgar uses the term "mopping and mowing" while posing as "Old Tom" in order to hide his identity from his father, the blinded Gloucester (61). While fading from contemporary usage, so well read a poet as Marvell would surely have been aware of the alternate definitions of the verb "mow" and its variants. Such an alternate meaning would please so subtle and witty a poet as Marvell.

From this additional connotation, Damon, then, can be seen as much of a mocker of men as a mower of grasses. He is at issue with the masculinized intervention upon nature that the garden represents, seeing its formal structure and grafted plant species as impious masculine dominance of nature.[16] The mower claims to represent the older order, a feminized system of passivity of reaping nature's willing bounty, which eschews the contemporary masculine project of methodizing nature. From Damon's perspective, his labor represents a "pure" or prelapsarian interaction between man and feminized nature in which the gendered bodies coexist within a sphere of mutual gratification, untainted by contemporary society's unnatural imposition of an alternative masculinist position. While Damon's criticism branches into three areas of consideration: aesthetic, ethical, and erotic propriety, the Mower's masculine posture is proven insecure at each of these levels, where, ultimately, his mocking proves futile, stemming from his own lack of masculine character, jealousy, and feelings of impotence.

Many critics have looked to Damon's character to infer Marvell's thoughts on man's intervention within nature. Legouis, for example, reads Damon's anti-artifice stance as Marvell's own criticism of contemporary gardening practices.[17] Louis Martz, too, reads Damon's criticisms as Marvell's own, linking Marvell to Damon's concern for "man's general corruption of . . . natural harmonies."[18] Similarly, Frederick Burwick declares the Mower Poems to be "concerned with intrusive forces which disrupt natural order and harmony,"[19] reading Damon's concern as Marvell's; Harold E. Toliver addresses the poems from the same perspective.[20] Damon provides, however, not an idealized pastoral mouthpiece for Marvell's own social and aesthetic philosophy, but rather a rude counterpoint to it. Damon is a fool, unmanned and pathetic. His mocking turns back upon himself the same way his own scythe strikes him down. Damon is both the mower mown and the mocker mocked. Marvell anticipated that his readers would laugh at the brutish impotence of Damon in the Mower series, then turn to "The Garden" and "Upon Appleton House" to glean his, Marvell's, true beliefs regarding man's place in nature, and the propriety of the controls man places upon the natural realm.

Among the Mower Poems, Damon's strongest criticism rests in the aesthetic complaint he outlines in "The Mower Against Gardens"; however, this is also his least sustained complaint, one from which he is quickly distracted. None of the other poems even mentions the subject of man's intervention upon natural order, though the concern is stated so strongly in this first poem of the series that the rest tend to be implicated in its arguments. "The Mower Against Gardens" begins with

Damon's admonition against the worldly masculinity of "Luxurious Man":

> Luxurious Man, to bring his vice in use,
> Did after him the world seduce,
> And from the fields the flowers and plants allure,
> Where Nature was most plain and pure. (1–4)

Here, nature is not only feminine, it is highly sexualized and objectified by "Luxurious Man," who views it solely in terms of promoting his unnatural vice. Unlike the Mower, "Luxurious Man" wishes to seduce what is "plain and pure," thus defiling it by enclosing "within the gardens square/ A dead and standing pool of air" (5–6). Significantly, an early modern connotation of "luxurious" implied lechery, and for Damon, the imposition of "Luxurious Man" on nature is cast as a form of sexual lechery with which the Mower's masculine-self cannot identify. Damon's opening address is clearly designed to position his masculine identity apart from that of "Luxurious Man" as well as those who would celebrate and perpetuate the beauty of a garden, which, through man's active intervention, remains nothing more than an artificial version of nature. In describing this artificial, and hence, unnatural, displacement of feminized nature, Damon's language is ripe with metaphors of licentiousness. The world has been "seduced"; flowers and plants have been "allure[d]"; man has "enclosed" the garden as if locking away a mistress; and nature, "plain and pure," is now "stupefied" (4,8). Further, Damon describes the practice of grafting new or collecting rare species with metaphors of adultery: "No plant now knew the stock from which it came" (23), he complains, because "sovereign . . . and proud" man has "dealt between bark and tree, / Forbidden mixtures" which breed "adulterate fruit" (20–22, 25). Damon compares such created or collected plants to wives in the harem of an immoral Turk, a "green seraglio" complete with "eunuchs too" (27) where the garden becomes emblematic of an immoral, enclosed pleasure palace. Most disturbing for the Mower is "Luxurious Man's" devaluation of the mutual coexistence that signified Damon's own masculine relationship with feminized nature: "Lest any tyrant him outdo;/ And in the cherry he does nature vex,/ to procreate without sex" (28–30). For Damon, the vexing of nature is fully realized in the gardener's tyrannical manipulation of natural order where the garden becomes a perverse manifestation of nature's victimization at the hands of an impious and lecherous form of masculinity.

In the first Mower Poem, Damon is criticizing gardening practices that were becoming prominent during Marvell's time. Hyams notes that from the time of Elizabeth I, English gardeners, often due to climatic reasons as much as temperament, began to favor plantsmanship over design, focusing on the possession and generation of unique and novelty species.[21] By the early seventeenth century, botanical gardens, such as the Oxford Botanical Garden founded in 1621, were becoming a popular repository of rare species.[22] "'Tis all enforced . . ." Damon complains, "While the sweet fields do lie forgot: / Where willing nature does to all dispense / A wild and fragrant innocense" (31–34). Here is the dichotomous gender relationship between reaping and sowing outlined by Shepard. Active farming/gardening is a masculinized treatment of nature; passive consumption, such as the act of mowing grass, which then rejuvenates itself, is a feminine use of landscape. Damon's complaint regarding man's attitudes and practices toward nature, stated in the metaphorical language of masculine dominance and usury and balanced against his strongly implied plea for reaping "willing nature['s]" bounty, demonstrates that his is a feminized valuation of nature. At least, this is how he characterizes himself within his argument.

Damon's criticism in "The Mower Against Gardens" is not just of man's impetuous acts against nature, but also of those that the Mower sees as against God. He refers to the gods of the fields, who, he infers, are locked out of the garden's walls, despite the presence of decorative statues in their image:

> And fauns and fairies do the meadows till,
> More by their presence than their skill.
> Their statues, polished by some ancient hand,
> May to adorn the gardens stand:
> But howsoe'er the figures do excel,
> The gods themselves with us do dwell. (35–40)

Damon is putting his position in the right by aligning himself with the gods of the natural realm. The statues in the garden are a further sign of the garden's artificiality; the real gods dwell elsewhere, just as true nature is not to be found in the garden. The Mower's passive reaping of nature's willing bounty aligns him more harmoniously within nature's frame, and he is rewarded by being accepted into nature's society, dwelling with her gods.

The uneasy distinction between nature as God's realm and the garden as man's stamp upon nature was felt particularly strongly in early modern England. The grand estates with their even grander gardens that were being built throughout the late sixteenth and early seventeenth centuries, were often constructed upon ground that was once owned by the Roman Catholic Church. Under Henry VIII, one-fifth to one-third of real estate in England changed hands within one generation.[23] Hyams notes that "Thomas Cromwell's dissolution of the monasteries, with its consequent enrichment in land and money of the epoch's new men, and the resultant building of fine country houses, meant that there was a call for hundreds of new gardens from people rich enough to spend money on them."[24] Damon's fanciful references to obsolete pagan gods turning their backs on the grand gardens of the privileged can be read as a subtle reminder of this very social condition. Not only were lecherous men profaning nature herself with their adulterous acts upon her pure form, Damon contends, these same men were profaning the former houses of God in order to satiate their immoral desires. For Damon the work of seventeenth-century gardeners is unnatural, unholy, and, ultimately, ethically corrupt.

Would that Damon maintain his focus upon the aesthetic and ethical issues of man's use of nature, his argument might win converts. His concerns, however, branch from these issues into erotic concerns, which distract him from his primary argument and undermine its effectiveness. The remaining three poems in the sequence fail to address ethical or aesthetic issues as the first did; instead, they reveal Damon's own misogynies and inconsistencies, which ultimately cut down his own arguments. While the erotic content is more conceptual in the final three Mower Poems, the focus upon erotic propriety begins in "The Mower Against Gardens" with Damon's sexually-charged metaphors for the landscape and nature. His use of metaphors of licentiousness and adultery refer to man's use of landscape, but Damon also characterizes the landscape itself through sexually-charged metaphorical language. Damon, as Cristine Malcolmson points out, reverses the Cavalier imagery of woman as land into "the Moweresque" imagery of land as woman.[25] In doing so, he offers commentary on the proper attributes of a virtuous woman. The lecherous man profanes nature by primping and preening her properly "plain and pure" (4) form:

> With strange perfumes he did the roses taint,
> And flowers themselves were taught to paint.
> The tulip, white, did for complexion seek,
> And learned to interline its cheek: (11–14)

I have already demonstrated the aesthetic criticism of nature that these lines by Damon represent. They can also be read as a criticism of contemporary, erotic attitudes of what is fair and truly beautiful in women, especially in relation to the crisis Damon undergoes with Juliana's spurned love. Just as Damon criticizes "Luxurious Man" for "making up" nature, so, too, does his criticism reflect upon contemporary women. Damon's references to painted women and false blushes demonstrate his personal distaste for feminine artifice. His is a masculine posture toward the feminine seemingly antithetical to that of "Luxurious Man." The Mower's appreciation of nature and natural beauty is pure and unaffected by the influences of a corrupt society. He would, he infers, spurn the ladies of society with all their airs, preferring, instead, the plain and natural beauty of a country maid.

In this, Damon mirrors the speaker of Thomas Campion's "I care not for these Ladies" from his *A Booke of Ayres* (1601):

> I care not for these ladies
> That must be woode and praide.
> Give me kind Amarillis
> The wanton countrey maide;
> Nature art disdaineth,
> Her beautie is her owne; (1–6)[26]

Campion's speaker celebrates the pastoral maid, unadorned by artificial finery, and shares Damon's distrust of man's intervention upon nature. Campion's speaker goes on to contrast the simple gifts that Amarillis accepts, "fruits and flowers" (12), and a simple bed, "a Bower of willowes,/Of mosse and leaves unbought" (23–24), with the ornate and ostentatious gifts required to win the attentions of the painted and powdered ladies—"But if we love these ladies,/We must give golden showers" (12–13); "These Ladies must have pillows,/And beds by strangers wrought" (21–22). Just as Campion's speaker would woo the willing country maid over the coquettish "Lady," so, too, would Damon passively reap the benefits of an unpretentious, natural woman's attention.

This, at least, seems to be Damon's attitude in "The Mower Against Gardens," but his actions contradict his claims. He does indeed fall in love, not with a wanton country maid, but with a woman more indicative of the perfumed garden and Campion's "Ladies." Unfortunately for Damon, the subject of his amorous attentions is Juliana, who spurns him in the three remaining poems in the series. In "Damon the Mower," Damon offers similar pastoral gifts to Juliana as does Campion's speaker to Amarillis:

> To thee the harmless snake I bring,
> Disarmed of its teeth and sting;
> To thee chameleons, changing hue,
> And oak leaves tipped with honey dew.
> Yet thou, ungrateful, hast not sought
> Nor what they are, nor who them brought. (35–40)

Not only does Juliana refuse these gifts, she is unaware of their significance, their connection to pastoral harmony. Damon's gifts suggest an appreciation of sexuality unbounded by societal convention and a celebration of physical love within nature's realm. However, Juliana either misses or ignores the significance of these gifts. She is not of Damon's world, as her refusal and lack of understanding locates her beyond the pastoral realm and within that of the garden. This separation can be further seen when comparing "Damon the Mower" to Campion's "I care not for these Ladies." Where Campion provides a comfortable bower for his pastoral lovers, Marvell offers Damon no such relaxing shade with Juliana:

> Tell me where I may pass the fires
> Of the hot day, or hot desires.
> To what cool cave shall I descend,
> Or to what gelid fountain bend?
> Alas! I look for ease in vain,
> When remedies themselves complain.
> No moisture but my tears do rest,
> Nor cold but in her icy breast. (25–32)

The sexual imagery of this passage, too, is charged but, ultimately, for Damon, impotent. The heat of Damon's passion wilts the meadow grass, but there is no shade for shelter. The "cool cave" and "gelid fountain" represent entries into Juliana's body, through her vagina or eyes, both of which are closed to Damon. Where Amarillis, the "wanton countrey maide" ultimately gives in to passion, Juliana, the only remedy for Damon's passion, "complain[s]" and refuses him. Again, there is no shade of passionate repose for Damon; the only coolness is in Juliana's response to his attentions. Marvell is very specific in determining the separation between Damon and Juliana. As a character, she does not fit into the tradition of pastoral verse, and as such, does not play by its rules. Playing by those rules, Damon is cast into a crisis regarding his relationship with both Juliana and feminized nature, and, ultimately, his own masculinity.

Unable to win the love of Juliana, Damon is reduced to a series of boasts in "Damon the Mower," boasts intended not so much to catch Juliana's attention as to question why she refuses him. In these boasts, Damon again aligns himself with the gods of the meadows, claiming himself as a favorite son; compares himself to shepherds and boasts of his superiority; and stares into the blade of his scythe and convinces himself he's not all that bad looking. These boasts are intended to comfort his own masculine pride; they have no chance of changing Juliana's mind, for, as with his gifts, they privilege valuations that she does not share. Juliana is not of the pastoral realm; she is of the garden. She represents a femininity with which Damon's seemingly pure masculinity cannot contend. Unlike "Luxurious Man," Damon is incapable of stamping his masculine imprint upon her with his gifts and wooing, and when she crosses into the path of the Mower's attention, she mows him down both metaphorically and literally. In stanza 10, Damon, distracted, cuts his own ankle with his scythe and falls to the ground bleeding. Furthermore, both "The Mower to the Glow-worms" and "The Mower's Song" testify to the extent of Juliana's metaphorical mowing. Distracted by the allure of the "painted beauty," Damon's masculine labor is forgotten as the Mower falls into idleness. Juliana thus becomes a representative of Eve, the first female in a garden and the cause of man's fall from that perfect realm.

Anne Barthoff notes that "In the order of nature as Damon has known it, human passion is an intrusion."[27] Burwick shares this view, saying, "The primary paradox of the Mower Poems is that sexual passion is seen as an intrusion into the natural order."[28] This paradox is of Damon's own creation. Where Eve is an agent of active temptation, Juliana's work upon Damon is passive. She has not approached Damon with any promises of passion; she has offered him no apple that he hasn't already plucked for himself. Further, Adam's is a fall from grace, but Marvell's character never possesses a sense of grace from which to fall. Damon's literal fall, when he clips his ankle with his scythe, is the least significant aspect for Marvell. More importantly, Damon falls to idleness, and from his own claims of pastoral innocence and security when he falls for Juliana. Damon's pure and "natural" masculinity is revealed to be too passive for the adequate display of masculine power. Unlike "Luxurious Man," who can "seduce" the woman of the garden, Damon can only furtively desire the love of Juliana. But he is no victim; his fall is not, in the end, Adamic. Damon chooses to fall before the scythe has clipped his ankle. His criticisms of garden and courtly love ring hollow because, ultimately, his criticism comes not from a sense of enlightened propriety, but from the jealousy of exclusion. He is bitter and would trade all that he claims to be his principles for entrance into that society. Marvell's Damon is a hypocrite; his arguments and actions undermine themselves.

Damon's arguments fall apart on four levels. First, amid his criticisms of the garden as unnatural, as the impure stamp of man's hand upon nature, he is unable to see his own stamp upon nature. The pastoral community he would celebrate is as much a result of man's hand upon nature as are gardens and manors, and it too leaves its mark. Next, when Damon allows himself to desire Juliana, he becomes distracted from both enjoying and upholding his responsibilities to the pastoral lifestyle he claims as superior. Ultimately, Damon turns his back on this lifestyle, and thereby is demonstrated a hypocrite. He becomes guilty of the very accusations he levels at the garden-world that Juliana represents, as his claims of masculinity ring hollow. Marvell creates in Damon a character locked in the midst of a crippling crisis of masculine identity. The Mower's love for Juliana signals his rejection of the "pure" masculinity that his title promotes, and posits him within the carnal world of "Luxurious Man." However, Damon's inability to win Juliana's love demonstrates his failure to comprehend and master the masculinity of the garden-world. As such, Damon is left impotent, stranded between two conceptions of masculine selfhood, either of which he is powerless to claim. It is this masculine identity crisis that first inspires Damon's criticisms, but ultimately cuts down both them and the Mower himself.

Damon is incapable of acknowledging or understanding his own masculine imposition upon nature, even as he criticizes the world of gardens and their intervention upon nature's purity. The fields that he mows were not fields in their natural state. New manors and gardens were being built during Damon's time for all to see, so it is easy for him to point to the changes they imposed upon the countryside. But before them, property was cleared by earlier hands, the monks of the former monasteries, and still others before them. The field in which Damon stands as he levels his criticism of gardens and gardening is itself a stamp of the hands that leveled and worked it before him; he has no historical perspective. Further, while aligning himself with the gods of the meadows, he is incapable of understanding that his work upon the field is a control upon nature's natural process of growth, decay, and regeneration. The fauns and fairies, he notes, till more by presence than skill. This is a reference to nature's cycle. But Damon's mowing interrupts that cycle: He cuts the grasses before they flower and seed, thereby quickening their regeneration so they can be sown again, allowing more hay per field to be reaped. His is an interference upon nature's cycle for the betterment of human existence, not nature herself. That Damon does not realize this begins the undermining of his character that Marvell would have his readers sense.

To further undermine his own arguments and character, Damon becomes distracted from the very duties and pleasures that he claims make him an exemplary citizen of nature. When Juliana comes, she, as Toliver says, "annihilates both green shade and green thought."[29] Yet it is not Juliana's intent to distract Damon; he distracts himself through his own feelings of desire for her. Ultimately, Damon chooses this distraction over nature's calm guidance. In "The Mower to the Glow-worms," Damon acknowledges nature's calming presence and guidance to the pastoral field worker in the form of fireflies whose lights he contrasts with human follies. Where the artificial lights of fireworks are used to celebrate the great men of the age, the sparkling glow of the fireflies is nature's homage to the common man, celebrating the simplicity of pastoral life: "Shining unto no higher end / Than to presage the grass's fall" (7–8). This is nature in harmony, and Damon carefully locates his own place within its great cycle. Compounding this, Damon compares the fireflies' lights, their "officious flame," to guiding lights that would help a field worker who has lost his way in the dark. Damon, certainly, has lost his way; yet, despite his acknowledgment of nature's guiding presence, he knowingly follows a false guide, the "foolish fires" of his passion for Juliana: "For she my mind hath so displaced / That I shall never find my home" (15–16). Damon acknowledges nature's guidance, then chooses to ignore it.

Damon is in his home, the fields, when he makes this claim. He is not, then, lost so much as he has decided that he is unhappy with his present state. By denying the assistance of the fireflies, he makes and acknowledges a conscious decision to turn his back upon the pastoral realm. Despite the claims he presents with such assuredness in "The Mower Against Gardens," he quickly surrenders that belief. He allows his passion for Juliana to distract him from nature. The extent of Damon's distraction and his ultimate defection is clarified in "The Mower's Song." Referring to his hopes, which he once found mirrored in the beauty of nature, the "meadows fresh and gay," the "greenness of the grass" (2–3), Damon now proclaims:

> But these, while I with sorrow pine,
> Grew more luxuriant still and fine,
> That not one blade of grass you spied,
> But had a flower on either side; (7–10)

By allowing the grasses to flower, Damon has allowed their growth cycle to end: Once a plant has flowered, it goes to seed and ceases producing new growth. The grass must be mown before it flowers, so that it is forced to grow anew, to be mown again, producing a bounty throughout the growing season. However, distracted, Damon has fallen to idleness, shirking his responsibility of reaping nature's willing bounty. Thus, there will be no more hay produced by this field this season. Further, in a direct counterpoint to Damon's opening statement of "The Mower Against Gardens," Marvell here shows Damon entertaining "luxuriant" hopes. Damon is now guilty of the very licentiousness and folly for which he criticizes those of the garden realm. Damon's lecherous thoughts take on an even graver moral significance in the comparison: Where the gardeners utilize their lustful thoughts in acts upon nature, Damon is paralyzed by his own. His actions cease as he becomes impotent in the face of his lustful desires.

It is in this mind-set that Damon begins to superimpose his own values upon nature, to read nature not from the perspective of harmony that he claims for himself, but from a humanized, profaned perspective. Humankind has always read nature as a metaphor of its own condition, but Damon, ultimately, is unable to uphold the distinction between a literal and a metaphorical reading of nature. Where his arguments would portray an enlightened love of nature, his perceptions and actions betray him as insecure and profane. When viewing the field at the opening of "Damon the Mower," Marvell's Mower sees not the realm of fauns and fairies but a reminder of his own folly:

Hark how the Mower Damon sung,
With love of Juliana stung!
While everything did seem to paint
The scene more fit for his complaint.
Like her fair eyes the day was fair,
But scorching like his amorous care.
Sharp like his scythe his sorrow was,
And withered like his hopes the grass. (1–8)

Nature, here, reflects Damon's mood, a reflection Damon takes literally. Distracted, frustrated, and full of self-doubt, Damon is incapable of seeing anything free from the distortions of his own state of crisis. The sun's heat, from which there is no shade, is the unquenchable heat of his frustrated passion. Nature's beauty reminds him of Juliana's beauty: His lust for Juliana has overtaken his love of nature. The grass is wilted like his hopes, and more. Marvell here clues his readers to Damon's impotence, which ultimately leads to violence against himself and nature.

As Damon takes his metaphorical reading of nature literally, nature seems to mock him at every turn, and he feels betrayed. "Unthankful meadows," he asks in "The Mower's Song," "could you so / A fellowship so true forgo" (13–14). However, his perceptions are warped by frustrated sexual desire. He attributes his own weaknesses of character to the natural realm that he claims to defend in "The Mower Against Gardens." But where he claims to represent a feminine perspective in that poem, here he imposes, first, masculine desire, then, the brunt of his own crisis of masculinity upon the natural realm. It is as if the meadow owes him something for his earlier defense of its sanctity. He lashes out, angry and insecure, and offers, in "The Mower's Song," a coward's surrender:

But what you in compassion ought,
Shall now by my revenge be wrought:
And flowers, and grass, and I and all,
Will in one common ruin fall. (19–22)

Because he cannot win his prize, Juliana, he has lost his direction, his vocation, and his manhood. He decides to destroy as he perceives himself being destroyed. If he cannot possess Juliana's beauty, he will destroy the beauty of the meadow; if Juliana mows his passion, so will he mow the meadow, in spite and anger. Where his arguments begin with a defense of the meadow in response to the garden, his actions end with the destruction of the meadow in response to his inability to possess the garden. The heat of his anger and his frustrated passion must consume both Mower and meadow. Damon is unable to see that it is his own insecurities that cut him down, just as his own blade does. Paralyzed by desire and fear into nonaction, when Damon finally does act, his actions can only be violent.

Marvell provides numerous cues for readers to question Damon's sense of masculinity, multiple hints of the nature and extent of his gender crisis. Marvell saturates "Damon the Mower" with images of impotence. In the face of heat, already identified as passion for Juliana, Damon notes withering grasses, mute grasshoppers, and lame frogs, all drained of their powers by that heat. His own response to the heat is to escape it; as noted earlier, he has no resource for quenching his passion. Hyman has identified the phallic representation of the snake "that glitters in its second skin" (16) and which is later "Disarmed of its teeth and sting" (36) as symbolic of a sexual act having taken place, with the "second skin" being the surrounding membrane of Damon's lover's vagina and the "Disarmed" snake representing his post-coital flaccidity.[30] I offer a variant interpretation here, demonstrating Marvell's intentions of portraying Damon as impotent. When Damon refers to "the snake, that kept within," he is assuredly referring to his own genitalia, which is, unlike the other meadow creatures, shielded from the sun in the shade of his trousers. The "second skin" represents his own foreskin, from which the head of the penis would emerge in a state of sexual excitement, just as a snake would from its own burrow. The reference to glittering represents the first tremblings of such sexual excitement. But, when confronted with Juliana, all Damon has to offer is a snake "Disarmed of its teeth and sting," limp. He is impotent before her, incapable of consummating his lust. Since he cannot demonstrate his masculinity in the physical act of procreation, he resorts to hollow boasting in an effort to restore his sense of manhood.

Each of the Mower's boasts, from stanzas six through nine, demonstrate the extent of Damon's masculinity crisis and, ultimately, turn back upon themselves, destabilizing his previous, secure masculine posture. In stanza six Damon's boasting backfires through Marvell's usage of feminine imagery. Damon is again portrayed as passive, being perfumed with dew by the morn and licked of his sweat by the sun; evening bathes his feet in "cowslip-water," a woman's bathing tonic. In stanza seven Damon demonstrates his insecurity by trying to compare himself favorably to shepherds. Damon is aware of the hierarchy of field workers, and of his own low place within that social order. He tries to accommodate for his physical deficiency by making a claim of material wealth. But his equation is faulty; he would value hay over wool. This is a witty response, but ultimately an unsatisfactory one. The shepherd clothes people; the mower feeds animals. He even resorts to comparing his own mowing abilities to those of the shepherd's sheep. Kermode and Walker note that Marvell's opening of stanza eight is translated almost word for word from Virgil's *Eclogue* ii.25; but where Virgil's Corydon looks into a calm sea at his reflection, Marvell's Damon uses his scythe blade.[31] This transformation signals Damon's removed perspective from nature, despite his claims of leading fairy dances within the same stanza. Marvell takes Virgil's structure and replaces a natural image, the sea, with a man made tool, the scythe. Damon must look to man, not nature, to see himself. A careful reader of Marvell's time would quickly catch this pun. Finally, in stanza nine, Damon admits to his warped perspective, acknowledging that his passion for Juliana has impeded his ability to share in or enjoy the pastoral life and pleasures he once did.

Such a realization should allow Damon a more balanced perspective, but his accident with the scythe blade follows immediately upon this moment of true self-awareness. Damon returns to his work, sadder but wiser, seemingly nearing a sense of self-acceptance. It is at this moment, when Damon's conscious mind overtakes his unconscious insecurities, that he is cut down by his own hand. Just as his failure to win the love of Juliana signals his inability to claim a masculine prerogative of "Luxurious Man," so, too, does Damon's self-inflicted wound signal a failure on the Mower's part to live up to a masculine ideal. In this symbolic castration, Damon demonstrates the futility and frustration of his masculine identity. Though desirous of the garden's sensual pleasures, Damon recognizes that the passivity which characterized his "Mower masculinity" is an inadequate substitute for active, masculine energy. Though Damon may rail against the vices of "Luxurious Man," Marvell undermines the Mower's words with his own actions, cuing the careful reader to see Damon the Mower as a fool. Marvell himself mocks Damon in the two poems written in temporal proximity to the Mower sequence. Ultimately, these poems counterpoint that sequence, revealing Marvell's true philosophy of man's place in nature. At key points in "The Garden" and "Upon Appleton House," Marvell presents parallels to the Mower Poems that are to be read as counterpoints. These can be seen as indicative of Marvell's own attitudes toward gardening and man's place in nature. Marvell proves himself a man of his time, sharing and demonstrating contemporary attitudes of masculinity and land usage. Damon, the character, the imagined speaker of the Mower Poems, is proven a comic foil, the counterpointed fool to Marvell, the poet who speaks in his own voice in "The Garden" and "Upon Appleton House."

"The Garden" presents an almost point-by-point refutation of Damon's complaints in "The Mower Against Gardens." The opening stanzas of "The Garden" directly counterpoint the opening claims of "The Mower Against Gardens." Where Damon sees the garden as artifice, as a representation of the world of men, Marvell celebrates the garden as a natural retreat from that harried world:

Fair Quiet, have I found thee here,
And Innocence, thy sister dear!

Mistaken long, I sought you then
In busy companies of men.
Your sacred plants, if here below,
Only among the plants will grow.
Society is all but rude,
To this delicious solitude. (9–16)

Marvell reflects upon the false value of the rewards that men seek for their actions, the wreaths and garlands of ceremony that pale in comparison to nature's own "garlands of repose" (8). It is important to recognize here that, for Marvell, nature is represented by the garden itself; he is not attuned to subdivisions in the way that Damon differentiates garden and meadow. Marvell's border is not one of degrees of nature; rather, it is a border between man and nature. When Marvell steps into a garden, he has crossed the border between the "busy companies of men" and nature's realm. There is no question in Marvell's mind regarding the authenticity of the natural realm of the garden.

Where Damon criticizes the garden as artificial for its strict design, its grafted and imported plants, Marvell praises that design and bounty in stanza five, noting in particular the variety of fruits within his immediate reach: apples, grapes, nectarines, peaches, and melons. Legouis notes that none of these fruits is native to England and would not have grown there without man's intervention,[32] the grafting and collecting that Damon holds contemptible. Marvell here offers another specific counterpoint to Damon's arguments, celebrating the ingenuity of men who would create so beautiful and bountiful a garden repose, a *natural* repose in Marvell's valuations.

The subject of beauty offers another of Marvell's counterpoints to Damon's complaints. As noted earlier, Damon describes the garden in terms of a pampered, painted woman, unnatural and lacking virtue. In stanza three of "The Garden," Marvell, too, offers a comparison between woman and garden, but in his estimation, the garden's beauty exceeds that of the most beautiful woman: "No white nor red was ever seen / So amorous as this lovely green" (17–18). Marvell's specific mention of colors offers direct counterpoint to Damon's complaints of doubling pinks and blushing whites. Damon is incapable of seeing beyond his own metaphor; his perception is stunted. Marvell demonstrates his own farther reaching sensibilities by offering up the same metaphor of womanly beauty, then surpassing it in his appreciation of natural beauty. This is further emphasized in Marvell's playful nod to the lover's practice of carving names upon a tree. Marvell would, as demonstration of his perceptive abilities, inscribe the tree's own names upon themselves as a tribute to natural beauty, which surpasses all other forms: "Fair trees! Wheres'e'er your barks I wound, / No name shall but your own be found" (23–24).

Damon's short-sightedness, his lack of an enlightened perspective, is further enhanced in stanzas six and seven of "The Garden." Where Damon is demonstrated as bounded within his own mistaken perceptions, distracted from the higher work of the mind by the profane urges of the body, Marvell shows himself achieving a transcendent state within the natural confines of the garden: ". . . the mind, from pleasures less, / Withdraws into its happiness" (41–42). Marvell is not so easily distracted as is Damon, who consistently demonstrates himself as a primarily physical being. Marvell, on the other hand, is attuned to the ways that the physical world can be made to serve the betterment of one's mental powers. For Marvell, "Luxurious Man" can be seen not so much as a lecherous violator of feminine nature's beauty, but as a partner in the enhancement of nature's own powers to peacefully elevate man's corporeal substance to a state of metaphysical transcendency. The garden represents such a place of repose. Marvell borrows from Spencer the figure of the soul as a bird, rising from his body to a median place between the created and perfect world,[33] a transcendent appreciation of nature's grandeur. Here is Marvell's "green thought in a green shade" (48), counterpointed to Damon's own green thoughts. Marvell speaks of the fertility of the mind, stimulated to a transcendent state, approaching but not overtaking the fertility of nature. Damon, too, speaks of "green thoughts" at the conclusion of "The Mower's Song":

> And thus, ye meadows, which have been
> Companions of my thoughts more green,
> Shall now the heraldry become
> With which I shall adorn my tomb; (25–28)

Damon's "thoughts more green" are not transcendent but physical thoughts. Damon's green is not the green of fertility in an intellectual sense, but the green of physical desire and jealousy. And again, Damon is proven infertile, impotent in both desire and thought, for Damon's release is not the transcendence of the mind rising above its body, but the death of the body itself and the erasure of mind. Marvell's is a contrast, not a surrender to, but a victory over the body's distractions:

> The mind, that ocean where each kind
> Does straight its own resemblance find,
> Yet it creates, transcending these,
> Far other worlds, and other seas,
> Annihilating all that's made
> To a green thought in a green shade. (43–48)

In the garden, a physical place, Marvell becomes attuned to the powers of his mind and is reminded of the limitations of the physical realm. The powers of intellect surpass the powers of the physical world, reminding Marvell of the smallness and finiteness of the physical world and senses, ultimately erasing that world of its significance. Damon's is a literal annihilation of body and mind; Marvell offers a figurative erasure of the physical in order to better appreciate his mental and spiritual powers.

Marvell's references to Eden amplify this transcendence of the physical realm.

His somewhat misogynistic pining for an Eden without Eve—"Two paradises 'twere in one / To live in paradise alone" (63–64)—can be read in terms of his will to transcend the distractions of the physical world. Crewe reminds that "to recall Eden is also to recall Eve's role in its loss,"[34] but Marvell doesn't infer blame upon Eve for tempting Adam to seek knowledge of good and evil. Rather, Eve represents to Marvell the distractions of the flesh. Legouis has demonstrated the consistent tendency throughout Marvell's poetry to subordinate love of women to both love of God and love of nature,[35] while Carey has noted Marvell's association of sex with faithlessness and cruelty, bound to his "awareness of reality as a restriction, a trap."[36] A paradise where the desires of the body distract from the glories of the intellect is less a paradise. For Marvell, the danger of Eve's temptation is not in her beguiling Adam to question, but in her reminding Adam of his presence within a physical body.

Such an erasure of bodily distractions is amplified in Marvell's references to Ovid's *Metamorphosis* in stanza four:

> When we have run our passion's heat,
> Love hither makes his best retreat.
> The gods, that mortal beauty chase,
> Still in a tree did end their race.
> Apollo hunted Daphne so,
> Only that she might laurel grow.
> And Pan did after Syrinx speed,
> Not as a nymph, but for a reed. (25–32)

In Marvell's version, Apollo's ultimate prize is not Daphne, but the laurel, Pan's is not Syrinx, but the reed. Marvell appends foreknowledge of the end result into the lover's thwarted chases, inferring that their intentions were always of a higher order, their desires were of the aesthetic and ideational powers and not the flesh. This is, of course, a false reading, a deliberate inversion of Ovid's stories. Both Daphne and Syrinx are transformed into plants through the intervention of the gods in order to protect them from the wanton desires of their pursuers. Daphne cries out for rescue moments before her transformation: "'Help me, dear father; if the river-gods / have any power, then transform, dissolve / my gracious shape, the form that pleased too well!'"[37] Similarly, Syrinx, trapped in her escape from Pan, "begged / her sister water nymphs to change her shape." That Apollo declares the laurel sacred and Pan makes a flute of the reeds are both acts of contrition. Their physical desires frustrated, they settle for a version of intellectual harmony. Marvell's inversion of their intentions demonstrates his own valuations of mind over body.

This valuation is further refined in "Upon Appleton House," which also references counterpoints to Damon's claims that demonstrate Marvell's acceptance of man's stamp upon nature. The poem is written in honor of Thomas, Lord Fairfax, whose family was awarded the property, originally owned by a Cistercian priory, during the dissolution of 1542.[38] Throughout the poem, in direct contrast to Damon's questions of ethics, Marvell demonstrates his acceptance of both the dissolution of monasteries and man's rightful interventions upon natural order. Stanzas 11–35 offer a heroic history of the property and its acquisition by the current Lord Fairfax's ancestor. The nuns of the former convent are portrayed as devious and inconstant in their luring of the virgin Thwaites, where the first Lord Fairfax's actions do not desecrate holy ground. Instead, they are seen as timely and necessary as he rescues a damsel from injustice: "He would respect / Religion, but not right neglect:" (225–26). Marvell does not question the appropriateness of the Fairfax's presence upon the property, demonstrated especially, as Crewe has noted, in the house's changed name: Originally "Nun Appleton House," Marvell drops the reference to its previous use as a nunnery.[39]

Further, Marvell's imagery throughout the poem demonstrates his comfort with the landscaping and gardens Fairfax has added to the property. In honor of Lord Fairfax's military successes, Marvell described the garden itself in martial terms, describing its flowers rising to attention in Fairfax's presence, and Fairfax as a soldier/gardener. "His warlike studies could not cease," Marvell says of Fairfax in stanza 36:

> But laid these gardens out in sport
> In just the figure of a fort;
> And with five bastions it did fence,
> As aiming one for every sense. (284–88)

Marvell compliments Fairfax's balanced taste as a gardener here, while paying witty tribute to his service as a soldier. Marvell continues to play with martial images in his description of the garden: The scent and color of plants are flags raised in salute (293–99); the flowers are planted in "regiments" that display their colors in homage to Fairfax "as at parade" (309–12); the bees are sentries at the watch in the garden (313–20). The garden and its plants exist, in Marvell's descriptions, to honor Lord Fairfax and his wife. Relatedly, Marvell utilizes the natural realm outside of the garden to show similar respects to Maria, Fairfax's daughter and Marvell's pupil. In Damon's valuation, such comparisons, utilizing nature to demonstrate human glory, are profane. But, for Marvell, such connections represent the height of wit and honor both nature and man.

In a brilliant use of metaphorical language, Marvell goes on to describe Fairfax's military career by utilizing images of gardening. In his military career, Fairfax "did, with his utmost skill, / Ambition weed, but conscience till" (353–54), Marvell proclaims, intimating that the care Fairfax demonstrates within his garden upon retirement represents the same balanced care he accorded his duties. Through this comparison, Malcolmson notes, Marvell is defending the rights of property owners in general, celebrating Fairfax in particular as an enlightened and successful guardian of his land.[40] The poet even makes direct reference to the Levellers, who argued for an abolition of social rank and equality of Parliamentary representation, and against whom Lord Fairfax had seen action, in stanzas 56–57, comparing them, unfavorably, to the mowers of a field.

Marvell here provides yet another clue to his true feelings regarding his character, Damon the Mower. Marvell utilizes the mowers of "Upon Appleton House" in his extended metaphor of military service as a pattern of gardening. The mowers represent common foot soldiers, whom Marvell holds in low esteem. In fact, Marvell makes a particular point in pausing to demonstrate their lack of enlightenment, devoting stanzas 47–55 to a description of the mowers/soldiers in the meadow/field:

> With whistling scythe and elbow strong,
> These massacre the grass along;
> While one, unknowing, carves the rail,
> Whose yet unfeathered quills her fail.
> The edge all bloody from its breast
> He draws, and does his stroke detest,
> Fearing the flesh untimely mowed
> To him a fate as black forebode. (393–400)

Marvell identifies the common foot soldier as an indiscriminate tool of necessity, a violent figure. In Marvell's image, the work of soldiers is clearly represented, cutting down an enemy's flesh as one mows grass. The flightless nestling that is the unfortunate victim of the uncareful mower represents the inevitable victimization of the countryside, the lands bordering a battle. Marvell amplifies the image of pillaging in stanza 53:

> Where, as the meads with hay, the plain
> Lies quilted o'er with bodies slain:
> The women that with forks it fling,
> Do represent the pillaging. (421–24)

But Marvell works a double intentionality here. These lines also provide a direct reference and counterpoint to Damon and the Mower Poems, particularly "Damon the Mower." When Marvell refers to the Appleton House mower, seeing blood upon his scythe and fearing it is his own—"Fearing the flesh untimely mowed"—he draws direct reference to Damon, who does, indeed, mow himself down. Damon, then, shares in the negative characterization that Marvell presents of the mowers of Appleton House. This is a direct, intentional cue as to Marvell's true feelings regarding his Mower, Damon, and all that the Mower claims. For a soldier to fall to a self-inflicted wound is the height of shame. In the masculine order of military service, this is to be unmanned. Damon is just so, unmanned by his own hand. His fall is an act of self-mutilation, a castration. His is both a fall from a claimed grace within nature and a fall from his own sense of masculine identity.

But Marvell falls, too, in both "The Garden" and "Upon Appleton House," in what is the most direct and damning counterpoint to the Mower Poems.

Surrounded by a cornucopia of bounty and beauty in stanza five of "The Garden," Marvell's physical senses are overcome: "Ensnared with flowers, I fall on grass" (40). This is a direct counterpoint to "Damon the Mower": "And there among the grass fell down, / By his own hand, the Mower mown" (79–80). Where Damon's fall is the end result of his distractions of the flesh, his attachment to the physical world, Marvell's is a fall away from the physical distractions of the flesh and into a spiritual revery within nature. Marvell's fall is followed immediately by his "green thought in a green shade," the erasure of physical distractions, and by his borrowed image of his soul as a bird taking flight from his body. This is no Adamic fall from grace; indeed, it is a representation of an Adam in Eden before his own fall, in harmony within his garden. Marvell repeats this fall in "Upon Appleton House," calling out to the surrounding woods of the Fairfax estate:

> Bind me, ye woodbines, in your twines,
> Curl me about, ye gadding vines,
> And, oh, so close your circles lace,
> That I may never leave this place:
> But lest your fetters prove too weak,
> Ere I your silken bondage break,
> Do you, O brambles, chain me too,
> And, courteous briars, nail me through. (609–16)

Marvell calls for himself to be bound within nature, in language that evokes images of crucifixion. The inference is masterful. The fall into revery described in "The Garden" now takes on a deeper significance of transcendence. More than bondage within nature's realm, Marvell seems to call for his own death and resurrection within nature, an ultimate sloughing off of the deadening weight of his body. Marvell would leave his body to rot, to feed the plants that bind it down, so that his spirit could rise, unfettered, into a harmonic convergence within nature.

Damon, in his own fall, calls for the plants of the field to cover him as a memorial, a reminder of his own presence upon and within nature. This is the final indication of his own lack of enlightenment, of the hypocrisy of his claims. Damon, who complains of man's mark upon nature, is concerned that his own presence will leave no trace of its being, no monument. Marvell asks for no such memorial for his own body. Marvell would be integrated into nature, his body dissolved, melted into its loam and verdant growth. Marvell demonstrates, through counterpoint, the superiority of his own claims and the hypocrisy represented by those of Damon. In "The Garden" and "Upon Appleton House," Marvell offers an alternative position to Damon's masculine passivity where man's active imprint upon nature signifies not only masculine power, but also man's appreciation of the transcendent potentiality of feminized nature. For Marvell, the methodization of nature was a necessary element for the development of a true and active masculinity, one symbolized by the martial skill and efficiency of Fairfax, and the poet's own metaphysical examination of man's relationship with nature.

Marvell was aware of and comfortable with man's stamp upon nature. Man's stamp, his presence, was an intrinsic part of nature. His questioning of that presence was never intended to exclude one from the other; rather, Marvell sought to acknowledge the interrelation of the two, and found beauty in those borderlands between the human and natural realm, where that interrelation achieved harmonic balance, the garden. The Mower Poems, as a group, represent imbalance and offer a point of view counter to Marvell's own. Marvell's portrayal of that viewpoint is enacted through a profane character, Damon, intimating his own true feelings. Marvell intends the careful reader of the Mower Poems to see in Damon a fool, to laugh at the Mower's impotence, and to recognize in his fall the crumbling of an unenlightened viewpoint. Marvell mows his Mower down, mocks him, in order to strengthen through counterpoint his own true philosophies of man's place within nature as he presents them in "The Garden" and "Upon Appleton House."

NOTES

1. Francis Bacon, *Works*, eds. James Spedding, Robert Leslie Ellis, and Douglass Denon Heath, 11 vols. (1870; New York: Garrett Press, 1968) 6: 485.

2. Pierre Legouis, *Andrew Marvell: Poet, Puritan, Patriot* (Oxford: Oxford University Press, 1968) 42–43.

3. All quotes from Marvell's poems come from *Andrew Marvell*, eds. Frank Kermode and Keith Walker (Oxford: Oxford University Press, 1990).

4. Frank Kermode and Keith Walker note the uncertainty in specifying exact chronology of all but Marvell's occasional poems—such as "An Horation Ode" or "The Character of Holland"—in their "Introduction" to *Andrew Marvell*, ix–x. It is generally accepted that Marvell wrote the Mower Poems, "The Garden," and "Upon Appleton House" during his stay at Lord Fairfax's estate.

5. Ellen C. Eyler, *Early English Gardens and Garden Books* (Ithaca: Cornell University Press, 1963) 44.

6. Eyler, *Early English Gardens*, 5–13.

7. Christopher Thacker, *The History of Gardens* (Berkeley: University of California Press, 1979) 129.

8. Paul Shepard, *Man in the Landscape: A Historic View of the Esthetics of Nature* (New York: Knopf, 1967) 79.

9. Bacon, *Works*, 6: 490–91.

10. Shepard, *Man in the Landscape*, 69.

11. Lawrence W. Hyman, *Andrew Marvell* (New York: Twayne, 1964) 20.

12. Quoted in Roger Shattuck, *Forbidden Knowledge: From Prometheus to Pornography* (New York: Harcourt Brace, 1996) 31.

13. Shepard, *Man in the Landscape*, 98.

14. Shepard, *Man in the Landscape*, 101.

15. All quotes from Shakespeare's works are from William Shakespeare, *The Riverside Shakespeare*, ed. G. Blakemore Evans (New York: Houghton Mifflin, 1997).

16. Jonathan Crewe, "The Garden State: Marvell's Politics of Enclosure," *Enclosure Acts: Sexuality, Property, and Culture in Early Modern England*, eds. Richard Burt and John Michael Archer (Ithaca: Cornell University Press, 1994) 278. Crewe says that, from the Mower's vantage point, the history of gardens is from the beginning "one of bad masculine origin."

17. Legouis, *Andrew Marvell: Poet*, 44. Legouis states that Marvell shares Bacon's viewpoint, expressed in "Of Gardens," here.

18. Louis Martz, *The Wit of Love* (London: University of Notre Dame Press, 1969) 178.

19. Frederick Burwick, "What the Mower Does to the Meadow: Action and Reflection in Wordsworth and Marvell," *Milton, the Metaphysicals, and Romanticism*, eds. Lisa Lowe and Anthony John Harding (Cambridge: Cambridge University Press, 1994) 176.

20. Harold E. Toliver, *Marvell's Ironic Vision* (New Haven and London: Yale University Press, 1965) 103.

21. Edward Hyams, *A History of Gardens and Gardening* (New York: Praeger, 1971) 145.

22. Thacker, *The History of Gardens*, 127.

23. Eyler, *Early English Gardens*, 2.

24. Hyams, *A History of Gardens*, 144.

25. Cristine Malcolmson, "The Garden Enclosed / The Woman Enclosed: Marvell and the Cavalier Poets," *Enclosure Acts: Sexuality, Property, and Culture in Early Modern England*, eds. Richard Burt and John Michael Archer (Ithaca: Cornell University Press, 1994) 255.

26. Quoted from *The Anchor Anthology of Sixteenth-Century Verse*, ed. Richard S. Sylvester (Gloucester: Peter Smith, 1974) 528.

27. Anne E. Barthoff, *The Resolved Soul: A Study of Marvell's Major Poems* (Princeton: Princeton University Press, 1970) 133.

28. Burwick, "What the Mower Does," 180.

29. Toliver, *Marvell's Ironic Vision*, 112.

30. Hyman, *Andrew Marvell*, 20–22.

31. Kermode and Walker, *Andrew Marvell*, 295.

32. Legouis, *Andrew Marvell: Poet*, 45.

33. Kermode and Walker, *Andrew Marvell*, 299.

34. Crewe, "The Garden State," 270.

35. Legouis, *Andrew Marvell: Poet*, 34.

36. John Carey, "Reversals Transposed: An Aspect of Marvell's Imagination," *Aspects to Marvell: The York Tercentenary Lectures*, ed. C.A. Partidges (London and New York: Routledge, 1978) 152–53.

37. *The Metamorphosis of Ovid*, trans. Allen Mendalbaum (San Diego: Harcourt Brace, 1993).

38. Kermode and Walker, *Andrew Marvell*, 301.

39. Crewe, "The Garden State," 283.

40. Malcolmson, "The Garden Enclosed," 261.

"The blushing shame of souldiers": The Eroticism of Heroic Masculinity in John Fletcher's *Bonduca*

Goran Stanivukovic

At the beginning of *Bonduca*, John Fletcher's solo play written sometime between 1609–14, the British warrior-queen Bonduca calls the defeated Roman soldiers "*Romane* Girls" (1.1.11), saying that their "bodies sweat with sweet oils, loves allurements,/Not lustie Arms" (1.1.9–10), associating their defeat with effeminacy and emasculation.[1] Repeatedly, in *Bonduca* the loss of heroic comportment is associated with male anxieties over effeminization; erotic transgressions, effeminacy, and homoeroticism are linked with the rejection of the masculine ideal promoted by the heroic code and heroic masculinity, and manly virtue is often expressed in terms that describe the beauty of the male body. In this chapter, I examine the ways in which heroic masculinity, modelled on the classical concept of heroic virtue (*virtu*) and the Roman ideal of military honour (*Romanitas*), are disrupted by erotic transgressions that include effeminization and homoeroticism, by immoderate behaviour involving feasting, and by violence against women. The implication of my argument about masculine erotics in *Bonduca* is that the Roman heroic-culture provides Fletcher with a convenient context within which to explore homoerotic desire and construct an alternative male erotic identity to the traditional heterosexual model. Since in Roman heroic-culture, passionate male bonding is not seen as an erotic vice, Fletcher draws on it to allow for the representation of homoeroticism in the play. In *Bonduca* the topos of the warriors' camaraderie on the battlefield (where almost all of the action takes place) and in the privacy of the camp, represents an appropriate vehicle to display homoeroticism, because this type of bonding constitutes the main axis of power in an exclusively all-male world. This topos of the soldiers' bonding is a form of heroic friendship, one of the six "cultural scenarios" that, according to Bruce Smith, early modern writers explored when writing about male-male erotics in less disturbing terms than were defined in legal and religious tracts against sodomy.[2] Looking at male-male desire as a sign of erotic identity that is different from, what one might call, the normative, heterosexual masculinity of the classical heroic code, I want to resist the limited view that Fletcher's characters are "never individuals, but at best types."[3]

In the relatively small body of criticism on *Bonduca*, no attempts have been made to seriously explore the construction of masculinity and male erotic identity within the military world.[4] Sandra Clark, for example, focuses primarily on the emasculation of women in the play and neglects the connection between military virtue and honour, and the construction of homoerotic masculinity.[5] The early modern culture defined heroic virtue and honour according to the Roman models of Cicero and Seneca, and also by following Machiavelli's concept of *virtu*, or the manly virtue. *Virtu* is a complex term that involves, on the one hand, Spartanlike military valour and a sense of duty, or, as Machiavelli says, "good discipline and a sense of security born of many victories."[6] On the other hand, *virtu* also implies moderation and humbleness. As Bonduca's first daughter suggests to Petillius: "Hunt Honour, and not Nations with your swords,/Keep your mindes humble, your devotions high; / So shall ye learn to the noblest part, to die" (4.4.131–33). Masculine conquest and honour are also linked to the idea of a heroic death. So, when Penyus is about to commit suicide by taking poison, Petillius scolds him: "'Tis [taking poison] equal ill; the death of rats, and women,/Lovers, and lazie boys, that fear correction./Die like a man" (4.3.139–41). (I will return later to the erotic subtext to this episode.) The concepts of heroic virtue and *Romanitas*, therefore, represent signs around which masculinity is organized; as such, any aberration from these clearly defined signs represents a transgression of the masculine norm.

Yet honour, as Cicero puts it, is "a slypper place."[7] It is created by both the subject and the impression of others on the subject's actions. The subject never has the full control over the concept of honour. Honour is not a fixed concept because it is defined both as the subject's inward condition of moderation and humbleness and as his outward manifestation of power and self-control. Thus, speaking of heroic virtue, Petillius wonders what happens when "we [soldiers] slip a little/Out of the way of vertue, are we lost?" (4.3.77–79). To this Penyus replies:

> examples that may nourish
> Neglect and disobedience in whole bodies,
> And totter the estates and faiths of armies,
> Must not be plaid withal; (4.3.91–94)

Here the neglect of honour is associated with the anxiety over the unruly (male) body, and unstable masculinity endangers the stability of the state. The protection of the commonwealth, as Junius suggests, is an honourable duty for a soldier: "Gentlemen, can ye forsake me in so just a service,/A service for the Commonwealth, for honour?" (3.2.4–5). It is this other side of heroic masculinity, where masculinity slips out of its prescribed norm, that fascinates Fletcher in *Bonduca*. Looking at this "other side" of heroic masculinity, where norm crosses with transgression, enables us to explore the real nature of this "new," alternative early modern male identity. Witness Swetonius's praise of the British general Caratach:

> . . . he's a Souldier
> So forg'd out, and so temper'd for great fortunes,
> So much man thrust into him, so old in dangers,
> So fortunate in all attempts, that his meer name
> Fights in a thousand men, himself in millions,
> To make him Romane. (1.2.255–60)

Here the Roman military honour, *Romanitas*, is associated with masculinity forged in combat. The linkage of *Romanitas* with the British militant masculinity represents an aspect of Renaissance England's understanding of *Romanitas* as "the recreation of Rome as England's imperial ideal."[8] Fletcher, however, subverts "[t]he vertues of the valiant *Caratach*" (1.2.254) in Swetonius's portrait, by using Caratach's speech, which mixes military and erotic agency, to precede Swetonius's speech. Hear Caratach:

> I love an enemy: I was born a soldier;
> And he that in the head on's Troop defies me,
> Bending my manly body with his sword,
> I make a Mistris. Yellow-tressed *Hymen*
> Ne'er ty'd a longing Virgin with more joy,
> Then I am married to that man that wounds me:
> And are not all these *Romane*? (1.1.58–64)

In this fantasy of cross-gendering, Caratach imagines himself as a sexually "conquered" woman, and the imagined passive homosexuality substitutes masculine conquest. Caratach subjugates his "manly body" to the phallic power of the desired enemy, alluded to by the reference to the sword as the archetypal symbol of masculine sexual prowess. What makes Caratach potentially a sodomite in his erotic imagination is his loss of control over his heroic body, articulated as a desire to be sexually used as a woman. As Bruce Smith reminds us, ". . . in early modern English society, a man can say without shame that he desires to conjoin his body with the body to another male. . . . What he can*not* say without shame is that he wants to be so desired."[9] But Caratach says so. His heroic rhetoric also celebrates masculine virtue in the context of the nuptial union ("I am married to that man that wounds me"), which is reinforced by the references to the "yellow-tressed *Hymen*." One might argue that Caratach's subordination to the Roman enemy functions not only as a prelude to his own surrender to Swetonius, but in the play in which heroism and eroticism are interwoven, Caratach's sexual subjugation also suggests the failure of heroic masculinity (the surrender of the Britons to Romans), and it puts into question the integrity of British nationalism. Furthermore, Caratach's heroic masculinity is symbolically eclipsed by the reference to the wound. Caratach's wound represents an erotic wound, caused by penetration that signals an unheroic and unmanly conduct, which implicitly subverts masculine virtue. Writing about the symbolism of the wound in connection with virtue in Roman plays, Coppelia Kahn says that the wound is "a persistent but unsuccessful attempt to fix, stabilize, delimit masculinity as a self-consistent autonomy free from the stigma of the feminine."[10] Here, though, "freeing from the stigma of the feminine" suggests the embracing of the pleasure of the masculine. Yet Caratach's (homo)erotic fantasy turns into a heroic story of "[t]en yeers of bitter nights and heavie marches" (1.1.65), that promotes the endurance of heroic masculinity. This reordering the boundaries of heroic virtue and honour through the eroticisation of male bonds has larger implications for the construction of male erotic identity. *Bonduca* suggests that homoeroticism imagined between men of equal power and status, between two generals (Caratach and Swetonius), for example, may not be disruptive. Homoerotic desire is disruptive when it is organized around the uneven social and sexual power relations, as examples of the relationships between masters and servants in the seventeenth-century comedy show.[11]

What enables this inscription of erotic desire into heroic action is Caratach's belief that speech does not necessarily imply agency. Note the following exchange between Bonduca and Caratach:

> *Bonduca:* My valiant Cousin [Caratach], is it foul to say
> What liberty and honour bid us do,
> And what the gods allow us?
> *Caratach:* No, *Bonduca,*
> So what we say, exceed not what we do.
> Ye call the *Romanes* fearful, fleeing *Romanes,*
> And *Romane* Girls, the lees of *Caesars* pleasures:
> Does this become a doer? are they such? (1.1.32–39)

By questioning the possibility that this discursive cross-gendering could be inscribed in heroic identity, Caratach implicitly queries the very essence of masculinity, a confusion that might have lead John Dryden to consider Fletcher's drama as "soft and womanish."[12] However, Caratach's questioning of the relationship between language and agency opens up the possibility to articulate erotic desire without eroding heroic integrity. Thus, in Andrew Hickman's words, *Bonduca* "finally destroys any faith that we may still retain in the successful application of ideal standards of honour to practical situations."[13] Thus, Fletcher's *Bonduca* itself becomes an agent of change in the conceptualizing of a new masculine subject in the early modern period, which infuses the language of male-male desire. Here is how Caratach admires Swetonius, general of the Roman army:

> Now I see the Body,
> Observe 'em, *Nennius*; by—a handsome Body,
> And of a few, strongly and wisely joynted:
> *Swetonius* is a Souldier. (3.3.1–4)

This is an example of Caratach's "camp" style, the "elaborate style . . . [which] while seemingly superficial, reveals to the initiated an unspoken sub-text."[14] What is hidden behind Caratach's admiration of the heroic male body ("a handsome

Body . . . strongly and wisely joynted"), reminiscent of the stylized representation of ideal men in early modern books of anatomy, paintings, and sculptures, is his homoerotic imagination. At the end of the speech, Caratach says, "I'll make a relique of thee [Swetonius], for young Souldiers/To come like Pilgrimes to, and kisse for Conquests" (3.3.24–27). The imagined statue of Swetonius, his petrified masculinity, legitimates Caratach's admiration of the male form and becomes a fetish of male worship. Caratach's fetishistic attitude toward masculinity transforms his rhetoric of admiration for the Roman into a homosocial yearning for the union with another man.

Death, too, enables homoerotic fantasy. In 5.1., Caratach stops the funeral procession of Penyus with the following words:

> What noble body that is which you bear
> With such a sad and ceremonious grief,
> As if ye meant to woo the world and nature
> To be in love with death? (5.1.33–36)

In Caratach's rhetoric of mourning, the recollection of virtue becomes a vehicle through which he articulates his desire for Penyus:

> Thou hallowed relique, thou rich diamond
> Cut with thine own dust . . .
> thus I bow
> To thy must honour'd ashes; though an enemy,
> Yet friend to all thy worths: sleep peaceably;
> Happiness crown thy soul, and in thy earth
> Some Lawrel fix his seat, there grow, and flourish,
> And make thy grave an everlasting triumph. (5.1.56–63)

The style of Caratach's eulogy, in which the heroic male body becomes the object of worship, can best be described in Judith Butler's words as "a hyperbolic display of death," a theatrical articulation of suffering that acts out the prohibited desire.[15] The fetishized body of a hero functions as a signifier for the unsanctioned male-male desire. In the Jacobean tragedy's preoccupation with death, "the death/desire dialectic," according to Jonathan Dollimore, "is present not just as a theme, but as a principle of dramatic structure and psycho-social identity," and so death "is itself the impossible dynamic of desire."[16] In Caratach's rhetoric of heroic virtue, which juxtaposes loss and emotional ecstasy, death does not cancel desire; rather, it provides Caratach with the terms to openly speak about what would otherwise be construed as illicit desire.

The linkage of death and masculinity seemed to have preoccupied Fletcher when he was at work on *Bonduca.* Evidence of Fletcher's revisions of the foul-papers in preparing the fair-copy indicate that Fletcher added the "masculine" content to the scene which precedes Penyus's death. When Petillius advises Penyus to commit suicide, the original foul-papers read at one point:

peni: I am resolved to goe. of a most base death.
fitting the basenes of my faulte.
petill: by no meanes: that were abominable.
and wolld still showe you poorer and poorer.[17]

In the final revision of the foul-papers, however, the same scene reads as:

Penius: I'll take a fitter poison.
Petillius: No,
'tis equal ill; the death of rats and women,
lovers, and lazie boys, that fear correction.
Die like a man. (4.3.129–33)

The shift from poison to sword is meant to assure a heroic suicide, worthy of a Roman soldier. Dying by the sword, by the archetypal masculine symbol of sexual prowess, means dying in manly fashion, "dying well," as Penyus says in 2.1.48. Dying by poison effeminates and represents a way lesser, unmanly creatures like rats, women, lovers, and lazy boys die. The phallic symbolism of the sword dominates the scene in which Petillius helps Penyus to choose the proper weapon for his suicide:

Petillius: Die like a man.
Penyus: Why my sword then.
Petillius: I, if your sword be sharp, Sir,
There's nothing under heaven that's like your sword;
Your sword's a death indeed.
Penyus: It shall be sharp, Sir.
Petillius: Why *Mithridates* was an arrant asse
To die by poison, if all *Bosphorus*
Could lend him swords;
your sword must do the deed: (4.3.141–50)

The double meaning of the heroic and phallic in this exchange turns sword into a phallic fetish ("There's nothing under heaven that's like your sword"), makes the sword-penis an object of erotic titillation ("if your sword be sharp," "it shall be sharp," "your sword must do the deed"), and, by associating phallic erotics with death ("your sword's a death indeed"), binds it with desire. The phallic symbolism of the sword introduces male-male erotics in this homosocial dialogue, turning the rhetoric of honour into a vehicle that enables the circulation of homoerotic desire in the play. This scene prepares us for Caratach's emphatic praise for Penyus, culminating in Caratach's rhetorical question "To be in love with death?" where the invocation of death becomes the route to speak about the unspeakable desire, here and elsewhere in *Bonduca*.

Hengo's death is also central to the ways male erotics reorder the boundaries of heroic virtue and honour in *Bonduca*. Caratach's nephew Hengo represents a symbol of hope for the heroic masculinity destabilized in in the play. Hengo's masculinity and his honour are not compromised by any form of transgression with which most of the other soldiers, including Caratach, are implicated. Unlike Caratach, whose inclination toward excessive, illicit desire subverts his heroic masculinity because it removes him from the heroic into the erotic sphere, Hengo is associated only with the yearning to fight for British victory. His masculinity is constructed solely in relation to soldierly virtue as a form of masculinity that subordinates eros to heroic conquest. Thus the pairing of Caratach with Hengo not only sharpens the contrast between the compromised and the uncompromised heroic masculinity, it also makes Hengo's youthful masculinity a potential object of Caratach's illicit desire.

While Hengo wants to put his virtue in the service and defence of his country ("I see no reason/But, to preserve my Countrey and my self,/I should march fourty," 4.2.23–25), he lacks the strength to do so ("O that I had a mans strength" 4.2.48). The murder of Hengo in 5.3., however, eradicates the possibility that heroic masculinity forms part of the heroic order. The character of Hengo may well have been inspired by James's son, Prince Henry, and Hengo's death evokes Henry's. With Henry's death, there also died a hope for the monarchy, sunken in debauchery and looseness under James I, to become again, in Trevelyan's words, "vigorous, popular . . . perhaps even warlike."[18] James himself, in fact, advises Henry how to establish discipline among his soldiers, and in *Basilikon Doron* (1599) says:

> Chose old experimented Captaines, and young able souldiers: be extremely straite and seuere in Discipline, as well for keeping of order, (which is as requisite as hardinesse in the warres) for punishing of sleuth, (which at a time may put the whole armie in hazard) . . . [K3r][19]

And, worst of all, James warns Henry to beware of the "horrible cryme . . . of Sodomie" [F3r-v].Yet most of the soldiers in *Bonduca* are quite the opposite from the ones James advises his son to surround himself with. Hear Petillius to Junius:

> there's the money,
> And there's the warre; square dealing: this but sweats thee
> Like a nesh nag, and makes thee look pin buttock'd:
> The other runs thee whining up and down
> Like a pig in storm, fils thy brains full of ballads,
> And shews thee like a long Lent, thy brave body
> Turn'd to a tail of green-fish without butter. (4.1.17–23)

Petillius's criticism of the soldiers' sybaritic conduct, evoked here in the images of softness and fluidity mixed with corruption, embodies what Alan Sinfield calls "unmasculine *relaxation*—loosening, softening, languishing, letting go."[20] Regulus also links the soldier's lack of valour with emasculation when he says that "The toughnesse of his [soldier's] courage turn'd to water;/See how his manly heart melts" (2.1.105–06). The decline of heroic comportment converges with different forms of the soldiers' immoderate conduct, especially feasting, and represents in

Petillius's terms, "mans unmustiness" (2.1.85). Petillius calls the British soldiers "eating Rogues" (1.2.162), saying that "their stomacks/Are like a widows lust, nere satisfied" (2.1.77–78), and that they "Live by meat,/ By larding up of [their] bodies" (1.2.143). Here food consumption suggests corporeal deformation through, for example, *larding*, which stands for amplifying and expanding. This deformation of heroic body represents a further sign of the deterioration of the ideal of honour.

Food is further associated with erotics in the play's frequent references to *meat*, a word whose meaning, according to Gordon Williams, "floats between person and sexual parts."[21] The erotic connotation of *meat* and eating is in Renaissance drama more specifically associated with female genitalia and consummation of the female body. For example, in Ben Jonson's play *Every Man in His Humour* (1598), Kno'well uses his own erotic experience with the mistress to induce his son to "Taste of the same provoking meats" (2.3.36).[22] And in his play *The Humorous Lieutenant* (1619), Fletcher employs *meat* in the same context that links female sexuality with prostitution, so Leucippe says, "Hang her, she is mustie:/She is no mans meat" (2.3.36–37).[23] While in the early modern literature *meat* tends to be associated with loose female sexuality, in *Bonduca* Fletcher exploits the erotic symbolism of *meat* in connection with male erotics.[24] In 2.3., the stage direction "*Enter [Servant] with wine and meate*" introduces the atmosphere of a licentious feast, through the connotation of "wine and meate" as a variation of "meat and drink," with "an amorous carouse."[25] And the only two participants in this titillating banquet are Caratach and Judas. In this scene of private bonding between him and Judas, Caratach's frequent ordering of "more meat" introduces a sense of erotic urgency, of sexual appetite, and, potentially, of sodomy and the erosion of the virtuous code of masculine moderation. Here, boys stand between the men, as Judas suggests saying to Hengo, "Away Boy, Away, this is not boyes play" (2.3.71). The linkage of the consumption of meat with the experience of male bonding also resonates in the exchange between Hengo and Caratach, where Caratach attributes Hengo's dream of betrayal ("I dream'd we were betraid," 5.1.16) to his inexperience:

> *Caratach:* Tis but thy emptiness that breeds these fancies;
> Thou shalt have meat anon.
> *Hengo:* A little, Uncle,
> And I shall hold out bravely. (5.1.119–22)

There is, on the one hand, irony in this assumption that immaturity can somehow be compensated by eating meat, that eating meat makes one a man. On the other hand, in the larger linkage of *meat* with illicit and loose sexuality, the exchange of the word *meat* introduces the idea of sexual consummation of the body in this dialogue. And in the play, in which numerous images of food and eating are associated with immoderation and male-male erotics, the phrase "holding out bravely" fuses the idea of the heroic to the erotic subtext of this dialogue.

Feeding provides, however, only a larger context for other forms of behaviour that link the lack of self-control with lust and emasculation. The soldiers who are, as Decius says, "full, and lusty" (1.2.161) and "lewd and lazy" (1.2.143) have transgressed the bounds of moderation and of heroic self-control due to their being in love. The Renaissance believed that love emasculates, and the fear of emasculation haunts the imagination of Fletcher's soldiers. In Petillius's song, love undercuts honour, and lovers are seen as soldiers' enemies: "*Fools, boyes, and lovers must not come near the Regiments, for fear of their infections; especially those Cowards they call Lovers*" (2.2.57–59). Petillius himself admits his heroic failure when, shortly before the battle with the Britons, he lies in his tent "most lamentably loving,/To the tune of Queen *Dido*" (2.1.10–11). Dido evokes here the luring power of female eroticism to subvert the masculine conquest (just as the Carthaginian queen did to Aeneas), which threatens stable masculinity. For Penyus, love and desire are "mans shames" (2.1.85), and the implication throughout the play is that soldiers in love have lost their essential masculinity. Emasculation and effeminacy, like Caratach's sodomy, suggest, in David Kuchta's terms, the misappropriation of "the symbols of the warrior class."[26] Petillius expresses the anxiety over the erosion of masculinity through love: "I am in love: I would give an hundred pound now/But to lie with this womans behaviour. O the devil" (4.4.120–21). This falling away from the heroic norm, from restraint, moderation, and commitment to heroic actions, not licentiousness and carnal pleasures, are signs of the corporeal transgression, which are, as Kuchta suggests, symbolically linked with homosexuality and effeminacy.[27] Regulus, for example, articulates this anxiety about failed heroic masculinity in following terms: "The gods make sharp your swords, and steel your hearts;/We dare, alas, but cannot fight our parts" (2.1.129–30).

Masculine anxiety over effeminizaton culminates in an extraordinary scene of violence in which Fletcher pits the hatred of Bonduca's two daughters for Roman soldiers against the Roman soldiers' hatred of them. So, to Junius's "I hate thee, that's my last" (3.5.39), Bonduca's second daughter replies by speaking about the British overpowering the Roman army:

> Let's prick our answers on our arrows points,
> And make 'em laugh a little. Ye damn'd Leachers,
> Ye proud improvident fools, have we now caught ye?
> Are ye i'th'noose? Since ye are such loving creatures,
> Wee'll be your *Cupids:* Do ye see these arrows?
> Wee'll send 'em to your wanton livers, goats. (3.5.40–45)

And Bonduca's first daughter:

> O how I'll trample on your hearts, ye villains,
> Ambitious salt-itcht slaves: *Romes* master sins,
> The mountain Rams topt your hot mothers. (3.5.47–49)

Not only do the warrior-women threaten masculinity by love ("We'll be your cupids . . . "), they have also appropriated the phallic rhetoric of male seduction ("[to] prick," "arrows points," "The mountain Rams topt your hot mothers"). This appropriation of the signs of male erotics by women symbolically disempowers the soldiers of their heroic and erotic power; it destabilizes their masculinity. Significantly, when Bonduca's second daughter says that they "will have vengeance for our rapes" (3.5.69), Caratach's aggressive reply, "You should have kept your legs close then" (3.5.71), brings to the surface his perverse misogyny.

Caratach's misogynistic denial of the world of women, and his almost murderous affirmation of rape, suggests a denial of reproductive, heterosexual masculinity. Coupled with his suppression of emotions (except for Hengo), Caratach's antifeminist attitudes signal his homoerotic desire, especially since the alternative world of pleasure for him is invariably centered around male-male erotics.[28] That Caratach is ambiguously located between the world of ideal honour and the world of masculine transgression, and that his perception of the heteroerotic world is articulated in an aggressive denial of women, suggest that honour and heroic valour are, for Fletcher, no longer stable signs of an ideal masculinity. Instead, by representing masculinity that is simultaneously heroic and homoerotic, *Bonduca* "allow[s] for the possibility that eroticism between men has varying political valences in different contexts."[29] One might argue, then, that such masculinity may be seen as a sign of the growing individualism when ideas about sex and the state, and marriage and society, were intricately connected with James's absolutism and the Jacobean nationalism, and were shaped by the growing scepticism and the transformation of values in Jacobean England. Fletcher's drama then participates as an agent of change in the emergence of the "new," individualistic, masculine subject.

Similarly in Petillius's tirade against women, masculinity that links unrestrained sexuality to rough sex converges with violence:

> Love no more great Ladies,
> Thou canst not step amisse then; there's no delight in 'em;
> All's in the whistling of their snatcht up silks;
> They're only made for handsome view, not handling;
> Their [women's] bodies of so weak and wash a temper,
> A rough-pac'd bed will shake 'em all to pieces;
> A tough hen puls their teeth out, tyres their souls; . . .
> And take the skin off where they are tasted; shun 'em
> They live in cullisses like rotten cocks
> Stew'd to a tendernesse, that holds no tack: (4.1.31–40)

The bizarre association of the female body with the image of a chicken flayed and cooked until its meat dissolves, links feeding with men's violence against women and the desire to erase all traces of women from the homosocial world of the play. By eradicating women from the world of men by symbolically dissolving female bodies, Fletcher leaves the world of *Bonduca* entirely to men. Given the violently misogynist treatment of women and their complete erasure from the play, including Bonduca's own heroic suicide, one finds it difficult to accept Ronald Huebert's view that "In *Bonduca* . . . Fletcher promotes the feminist question to a level of greater dignity."[30] If the play promotes any question, it is the masculinist one. In fact, Fletcher's treatment of women makes *Bonduca* a typical Jacobean tragedy in which women are ultimately victimized.

The homoerotic symbolism and imagery in *Bonduca* enables us to see the extent to which Fletcher dramatizes in contesting and often ambivalent terms the concepts of a heroic past, of Roman honour, and of masculine virtue. In doing so, Fletcher does not just resist "the simplistic dichotomy of Roman honour versus British dishonour," as Paul D. Green suggests.[31] Rather, Fletcher's homoerotic style suggests the erosion, or at best reshaping, of the Roman ideals of honour and manliness. In a period increasingly focused on a civic ideal rather than the militant masculine ideal when soldiers became gentlemen, the homoerotic basis of Roman masculinity also suggests that Fletcher's times did not necessarily look at Rome as an ideal of "moral austerity," but, rather, that the early modern period attempted to challenge that austere morality, and to construct a masculinity that is independent of it.[32] Something of this new power of dramatic art to tease artistic and moral conventions is suggested in Fletcher's poem "Upon an Honest Man's Fortune," dated 1613, around the time when *Bonduca* was written, and was printed together with the play *The Honest Man's Fortune*: "You that can look through heaven . . . /Find out new lights, and give them where you please,/To those men honours, pleasures, to those ease."[33]

Different ways in which the code of masculine honour converges with male eroticism create a queer milieu in *Bonduca* within which male-male erotics is negotiated. The initial victory of the Britons and the heroic celebration of Caratach at the end of the play represents an ironic attempt to reclaim the British heroic masculinity that is contested and challenged throughout the play. By making the "sodomite" General of Britons, now defeated and literally subjugated to Roman power, "the only Souldier" (5.3.192), and by assuring that "The Vertues of great *Caratach* be sung" (5.3.203), the end of *Bonduca* legitimizes and celebrates a masculine code of honour that has been identified with illicit homoerotics, thus making *Bonduca* an erotic performance for and about men.

The association of homoerotic desire with military honour, and the emphasis on the display of the male body on the stage, suggests that, in *Bonduca*, normative masculinity, a measure of a man's worth, converges with socially perceived sexual transgression. This convergence invites the question of the role of homoeroticism in the representation of masculinity in the seventeenth-century tragicomedy. In *Bonduca,* masculinity is not necessarily dependent on heteroerotic desire; the soldiers link the anxiety about male effeminacy with uncontrollable heteroerotic love, which is why the play promotes male bonding as an appropriate avenue for masculine representation. And further, as Caratach's attitude toward women shows, heteroerotic desire induces disgust, thus he substitutes heteroerotic love with his yearning for men. Ultimately, both homosociality and homoeroticism imply masculine desire for "manhood." In that sense, *Bonduca* dramatizes what Mario

DiGangi perceptively calls "orderly" and "disorderly" male homoeroticism, both of which are characteristic of Fletcherian tragicomedy.[34]

Yet, while DiGangi locates these two different forms of homoeroticism as separately manifested in several plays by Fletcher, in *Bonduca,* both orderly and disorderly homoeroticism exist simultaneously, expanding the significance of homoeroticism in early modern drama. Orderly male homoerotisim, which does not imply anxiety about homoerotics, was, as DiGangi suggests, "often manifested through military friendship."[35] In *Bonduca*, orderly homoeroticism is implicated in the homosocial camaraderie of Julius, Petillius, Judas, and the other soldiers. Disorderly male homoeroticism, which disrupts heteroerotic normativity, is exemplified in Caratach, whose aggressive attitude toward women symbolizes his rejection of procreative order. In a play in which there is no marriage at the end to affirm heteroerotic order (replaced by the celebration of male bonding), the potential for disruption in the heteroerotic norm is unanxious because of the context in which it occurs. Thus the social impact of homoeroticism, which typically helps us to evaluate early modern attitudes toward sodomy, is erased from *Bonduca* as Caratach's homoeroticism bears no adverse consequences to the play's celebration of his masculinity and his public reputation as a hero.

This integration of the homoeroticism in the representation of heroic masculinity suggests that in the seventeenth century, homoeroticism became a possibility in the construction of masculine identity. Indeed, this might be related to the changing attitudes toward heroic masculinity; changes which, as I have suggested, were manifested in the social deflation of the idea of militant masculinity and in the representation of aristocratic indulgence in excess. Moreover, as gay historiography has already documented, in the seventeenth century, homosexual identity as a form of marginalized subjectivity had already begun to emerge.[36] *Bonduca*, therefore, dramatizes this critical moment in the early modern history of masculinity, a moment at which the new male subject was constructed at the point of intersection of the changing term of social power, gender, and sexuality.

NOTES

1. Unless otherwise stated, throughout the essay I quote the text of *Bonduca* from *The Dramatic Works in the Beaumont and Fletcher Canon,* ed. Fredson Bowers, vol. 4 (Cambridge: Cambridge University Press, 1979). In the quoted text of the play, I retain the italics used in this edition. For the dating of *Bonduca*, I rely on Gordon McMullan's *The Politics of Unease in the Plays of John Fletcher* (Amherst: University of Massachusetts Press, 1994) 267.

2. Bruce R. Smith, *Homosexual Desire in Shakespeare's England: A Cultural Poetics* (Chicago: University of Chicago Press, 1991) 74–76.

3. Marco Mincoff, "Fletcher's Early Tragedies," *Renaissance Drama* 7 (1964): 85.

4. Marie H. Loughlin, in *Hymeneutics: Interpreting Virginity on the Early Modern Stage* (Lewisburg: Bucknell University Press, 1997) 13–27, offers a succinct critique of the ways critics have failed to engage in depth with the subjects of body and sexuality in the Beaumont and Fletcher canon. Loughlin refers to Sandra Clark's book *The Plays of Beaumont and Fletcher: Sexual Themes and Dramatic Representation* (New York:

Harvester/Whetsheaf, 1994) as the first major study of Eros in the plays of Beaumont and Fletcher. Homoeroticism hardly features as a developed subject in any of the studies that Loughlin discusses, and then it is only perfunctorily discussed in Clark's book.

5. See Clark, *The Plays of Beaumont and Fletcher*, 85.

6. Niccolo Machiavelli, *The Discourses*, ed. Bernard Crick (Harmondsworth: Penguin, 1970) 495.

7. *Marcus Tullius Ciceroes thre bookes of duties, to Marcus his sonne* [De officiis], trans. Nicholas Grimalde (London, 1558) I. 65, sig. D5[r]. For a more extensive discussion of the Ciceronian concept of honour, see Geoffrey Miles, *Shakespeare and the Constant Romans* (Oxford: Clarendon Press, 1996) 22–29.

8. Jonathan Goldberg, *James I and the Politics of Literature: Jonson, Shakespeare, Donne, and Their Contemporaries* (Stanford: Stanford University Press, 1989) 165.

9. Bruce R. Smith, "L[o]cating the sexual subject," *Alternative Shakespeares 2*, ed. Terence Hawkes (London and New York: Routledge, 1996) 101.

10. Coppelia Kahn, *Roman Shakespeare: Warriors, Wounds, and Women* (London and New York: Routledge, 1997) 168.

11. For the sodomitical relationship between masters and servants in the seventeenth-century city comedy, see Mario DiGangi, "Asses and Wits: The Homoerotics of Mastery in Satiric Comedy," *English Literary Renaissance* 25:2 (1995): 179–208.

12. John Dryden, "The Grounds of Criticism in Tragedy: The Preface to *Troilus and Cressida*" (1679), *Dramatic Poesy and Other Essays* (London: J.M. Dent, 1950) 133. Although here Dryden describes Fletcher's poetics as womanish, in his "An Essay of Dramatic Poesy" he expresses a different view where, comparing Shakespeare's and Fletcher's plots to those in the French neoclassical plays, he refers to Beaumont and Fletcher's "more masculine fancy."

13. Andrew Hickman, "*Bonduca*'s Two Ignoble Armies and *The Two Noble Kinsmen*," *Medieval and Renaissance Drama in England* 4 (1989): 167.

14. David Bergman, "Strategic Camp: The Art of Gay Rhetoric," *Camp Grounds: Style and Homosexuality*, ed. David Bergman (Amherst: University of Massachusetts Press, 1993) 99.

15. Judith Butler, *Bodies that Matter: On the Discursive Limits of "Sex"* (London and New York: Routledge, 1993) 233.

16. Jonathan Dollimore, "Desire Is Death," *Subject and Object in Renaissance Culture*, eds. Margareta de Grazia, Maureen Quillingan, and Peter Stallybrass (Cambridge: Cambridge University Press, 1996) 373.

17. Here both the foul-paper text and the one in Fletcher's fair-copy are quoted from Grace Ioppolo, "'The Final Revision of *Bonduca*': An Unpublished Essay by W.W. Greg," *Studies in Bibliography* 43 (1990): 74.

18. G. M. Trevelyan, *England Under the Stuarts* (London and New York: Methuen, 1965) 106.

19. *Basilikon Doron* (Edinburgh: By Robert Waldergraue, 1599) I have silently changed the long "s" in the original.

20. Alan Sinfield, *Faultlines: Cultural Materialism and the Politics of Dissident Reading* (Berkeley: University of California Press, 1992) 131.

21. Gordon Williams, *A Dictionary of Sexual Language and Imagery in Shakespearean and Stuart Literature*, vol. 2 (London and Atlantic Heights, N.J.: The Athlone Press, 1994) 868.

22. Ben Jonson, *Every Man in His Humour*, ed. Martin Seymour-Smith (London: A. C. Black, 1979).

23. Quoted from *The Dramatic Works in the Beaumont and Fletcher Canon*, ed. Fredson Bowers, vol. 5 (Cambridge: Cambridge University Press, 1982).

24. For further examples of the erotic meaning of *meat,* see Williams, *A Dictionary*, vol. 2, 868–69.

25. Williams, *A Dictionary*, vol. 2, 869.

26. David Kuchta, "The Semiotics of Masculinity in Renaissance England," *Sexuality and Gender in Early Modern Europe: Institutions, Texts, Images*, ed. James Grantham Turner (Cambridge: Cambridge University Press, 1995) 239.

27. Kuchta, "The Semiotics of Masculinity," 239.

28. For the relationship between sodomy and nonprocreative sex, see Jonathan Goldberg, *Sodometries: Renaissance Texts, Modern Sexualities* (Stanford: Stanford University Press, 1992) 158ff.

29. Jeffrey Masten, *Textual Intercourse: Collaboration, Authorship, and Sexualities in Renaissance Drama* (Cambridge: Cambridge University Press, 1997) 48.

30. Ronald Huebert, "'An Artificial Way to Grieve': The Forsaken Woman in Beaumont and Fletcher, Massinger and Ford," *English Literary History* 44 (1977): 604.

31. Paul D. Green, "Theme and Structure in Fletcher's *Bonduca*," *SEL* 22 (1982): 308.

32. Green, "Theme and Structure," 308.

33. *The Works of Beaumont and Fletcher*, ed. Alexander Dyce (London: Edward Moxon, 1843) 453.

34. Mario DiGangi, *The Homoerotics of Early Modern Drama* (Cambridge: Cambridge University Press, 1997) 149.

35. DiGangi, *The Homoerotics*, 149.

36. Recently, Masten, DiGangi, and Gregory W. Bredbeck, in *Sodomy and Interpretation: Marlowe to Milton* (Ithaca: Cornell University Press, 1991), have addressed this issue.

"A place privileged to do men wrong": The Anxious Masculinity of *The Maid's Tragedy*

Lisa Hopkins

Beaumont and Fletcher's *The Maid's Tragedy* (1619), their only tragedy to feature a cross-dressed heroine, plots an image of masculinity uneasily positioned at the interstices of machismo, homoeroticism, and the fear of effeminisation, with an anxiety heightened even beyond that which, Mark Breitenberg has argued, attends early modern masculinity.[1] The men in this play aspire to success both in love and war; they find the latter easy to achieve, but the bedroom proves a far more problematic arena for them. The chaos this produces ultimately compromises male valor and masculine identity, and effectively lays bare the fact that the male networks in this society are actually structured and underpinned by the possessing and "othering" of women. I propose to examine the play's representations of manhood by considering the terms used to describe the two sexes, the language of the body rather than of the tongue to which some characters resort as an attempt to impose essentialist meaning, and the use of brother-sister pairings to delineate the boundaries between the genders. Ultimately, I shall argue, the text's attempts to separate masculinity from femininity are radically compromised at every turn.

The frontispiece to the 1619 edition of *The Maid's Tragedy* shows an unusual and rather disturbing image. Two figures are shown in poses that clearly indicate that they have just been dueling; indeed, one has wounded the other who has blood gushing from the breast. Both figures are wearing doublet and hose, and thus appear to be men, though only one has a moustache. However, one is labeled "Amintor" and the other "Aspatia". The image thus hints at an interchangeability between men and women, a difficulty of distinguishing the boundaries between the sexes, which resurfaces at numerous points in the text. At one point Melantius demands of his sister, "Do you raise mirth out of my easiness? / Forsake me then, all weaknesses of nature / That make men women!"[2] Earlier, Melantius has commented upon the striking resemblance between Aspatia and her brother:

> She has a brother under my command
> Like her, a face as womanish as hers.

But with a spirit that hath much outgrown
The number of his years. (1.1.108–11)

This idea of the indistinguishability between the sexes recurs in Aspatia's successful impersonation of her brother: In a prelude to the moment illustrated in the frontispiece, she tells Amintor, "till the chance of war marked this smooth face /With these few blemishes, people would call me / My sister's picture, and her mine" (5.3. 37–39). Significantly, Amintor is unable to penetrate the disguise.

The destabilization of traditional gender norms becomes a keynote of the first act masque, which Sarah P. Sutherland calls "a spectacular anomaly among masques in Renaissance tragedy."[3] Its unusual position in Act One means that it will obviously not be available later to act as an emblem and seal of harmony, while its content offers a suggestive guide to the gender contestations to come. The masque, too, involves a brother-sister pairing; between Cynthia, the moon, and her brother, the sun. Like Aspatia's likeness to her absent brother, this linking, too, symbolically unsettles conventional gender distinctions. Night invokes Cynthia with the words, "Appear; no longer thy pale visage shroud, / But strike thy silver horns quite through a cloud" (1.2. 122–23). Cynthia's possession of horns, albeit a standard part of her iconography, links her primarily to the cuckolded Amintor, whose own pastoral antecedents further link him to the world of classical deities.[4] Cynthia further goes against gender convention when she claims sovereign authority over a male god:

Rise, rise, I say,
Thou power of deeps, thy surges laid away,
Neptune, great king of waters, and by me
Be proud to be commanded (1.2. 170–73)

She is also notably insubordinate to her own absent brother:

Whilst our reign lasts, let us stretch our power
To give our servants one contented hour,
With such unwonted solemn grace and state
As may for ever after force them hate
Our brother's glorious beams, and wish the Night,
Crowned with a thousand stars and our cold light (1.2. 146–51)

Though Cynthia must eventually retire, acknowledging "I must down / And give my brother place" (1.2. 270–71), and does resemble Evadne in her ambition (though that in itself is defined and demonised as unwomanly), overall, the brief impression she creates allows the masque to blur the notion of secure and separate gender identity early in the play.

As well as brother-sister pairings, *The Maid's Tragedy* also offers two pairs of brothers, Diphilus and Melantius, and Lysippus and the King. Ostensibly, brother-brother relationships operate much more to endorse the status quo of masculine identities than to threaten it. This is especially true in the case of Lysippus and the King, since the existence of a younger royal brother means that the succession is secured, and that despite the removal of one monarch, the system itself survives intact. However, an early exchange between Melantius and Diphilus reveals much about how brotherhood works within the world of the play:

Melantius: I thank thee, Diphilus; but thou art faulty:
I sent for thee to exercise thine arms
With me at Patria; thou cam'st not, Diphilus;
'Twas ill.
Diphilus: My noble brother, my excuse
Is my king's strict command, which you, my lord,
Can witness with me. (1.1. 28–33)

Melantius speaks here with the full privilege of an elder brother's authority over a younger within a social system based on male primogeniture. He feels no hesitation about sweeping away the social niceties of greeting and publicly reprimanding Diphilus for a perceived failure in valor—a failure manifested, suggestively enough, at a location named "Patria," a variant of the more normal "Patras," which neatly encodes an invocation of patriarchal authority. Diphilus, who throughout the play is unquestioningly loyal to his brother, shows no resentment at this treatment, but despite this apparent submissiveness his reply actually wreaks considerable ideological damage: For "king" he opposes "Patria," thus opening a disjunction between the theory and the embodiment of patriarchal authority through the implication that "fatherland" [patria] and "king" are separate and distinct, a division that will eventually tear Rhodes apart. Since, as Robert Y. Turner points out, "the only speaking character without a name is the King,"[5] we are even more fully aware that it is ideological issues and abstracts of patriarchy and patronage that are at stake here, rather than a simple clash of personalities.

Within the course of the play, it is the interaction of men who are not brothers that may more overtly threaten subversion of patriarchal social and political structures, since the strong emotions generated between men not contained within any familial or kin relationship may easily tremble on the brink of homoeroticism. This is most particularly the case between Melantius and Amintor, whose affection is expressed in terms so extravagant as to border on the comic:

Melantius: Melantius calls his friend Amintor. [*Embracing him*]
O,
Thy arms are kinder to me than thy tongue.
Speak, speak!
Amintor: What?
Melantius: That little word was worth all the sounds
That ever I shall hear again. (5.3. 256–61)

Melantius's rapture at the word "What" may well be thought excessive here, and we may also take note of some of the vocabulary used in Melantius's earlier description of their friendship:

> When he was a boy,
> As oft as I returned (as, without boast,
> I brought home conquest) he would gaze upon me
> And view me round, to find in what one limb
> The virtue lay to do those things he heard;
> Then would he wish to see my sword, and feel
> The quickness of the edge, and in his hand
> Weigh it; he oft would make me smile at this. (1.1. 49–56)

Amintor's gazing and viewing are sufficiently suggestive in themselves, but the notable and unusual reduction of Melantius's bodily force to the achievements of "one limb" irresistibly evokes the phallus even before the mention of how Amintor would make Melantius smile by feeling his sword. There seems to be a note of deliberate eroticism here as the sword becomes a keynote in the two men's relationship; they take it in turns to draw, flourish, and sheath their weapons, and the language that surrounds such encounters leaves us in no doubt of their erotic subtext.

However, no sooner has Melantius exhibited the strength of his affection for Amintor than, seemingly in a deliberate countermove, he mentions his heterosexual interests:

> But I have a mistress
> To bring to your delights, rough though I am:
> I have a mistress and she has a heart,
> She says, but, trust me, it is stone, no better;
> There is no place that I can challenge in't. (1.1. 148–52)

Despite the extreme exiguousness of her role in the plot, Melantius's mistress bulks large in his thoughts. He is furious when Calianax casts aspersions on her status:

Calianax: It may be so. [*To Diagoras*] Who placed the lady there
So near the presence of the King?
Melantius: I did.
Calianax: My lord, she must not sit there.
Melantius: Why?
Calianax: The place is kept for women of more worth.
Melantius: More worth than she! It misbecomes your age
And place to be thus womanish. Forbear!
What you have spoke I am content to think
The palsy shook your tongue to.
Calianax: Why, 'tis well
If I stand here to place men's wenches.
Melantius: I shall quite forget

This place, thy age, my safety, and through all
Cut that poor sickly week thou hast to live
Away from thee.
Calianax: Nay, I know you can fight for your whore.
Melantius: Bate me the King, and be he flesh and blood
'A lies that says it! Thy mother at fifteen
Was black and sinful to her. (1.2. 59–73)

Melantius's mistress is repeatedly redefined by Calianax during this exchange in increasingly pejorative terms. She goes from "lady" to "woman," from "wench" to "whore" as Calianax assumes the prerogative of applying a social identity to "another man's woman." However, Melantius can retaliate only by equating his mistress with Calianax's mother; more direct redress is denied him by the fact that Calianax himself is not fully seen as manly. Being unwilling to fight and aged, his own status as man remains open to question. Melantius recognizes Calianax's lack of masculine prowess, which proves frustrating to the soldier who knows that to engage such an "unmanly" figure in anything more than a verbal battle would be considered an act of effeminacy.

The potential for questioning one's status as a man is particularly damaging considering the extent by which male camaraderie is structured around a strict cultural notion of the feminine, a point reinforced throughout the play. It is especially there in the ribald jesting underpinned by an agreement to traffic in women:

Diphilus: What odds he has not my sister's maidenhead tonight?
Strato: None: it's odds against any bridegroom living, he ne'er gets it while he lives.
Diphilus: Y'are merry with my sister: you'll please to allow me the same freedom with your mother.
Strato: She's at your service.
Diphilus: Then she's merry enough of herself, she needs no tickling. (3.1. 5–11)

It is there, too, in Amintor's desire for fellowship in cuckoldry —"Gentlemen, Would you had all such wives, and all the world, / That I might be no wonder!" (3.1. 101–03), and later:

Amintor: [*Aside*] Men's eyes are not so subtle to perceive
My inward misery: I bear my grief
Hid from the world. How art thou wretched then?
For aught I know, all husbands are like me,
And every one I talk with of his wife
Is but a well dissembler of his woes,
As I am; would I knew it, for the rareness
Afflicts me now.
Melantius: Amintor, we have not enjoyed our friendship of late,
For we were wont to change our souls in talk.

Amintor: Melantius, I can tell thee a good jest
Of Strato and a lady the last day. (3.2. 46–58)

For Amintor, the only recourse in his desperate misery is to continue to share in the male community, making jokes about women.

Finally, the attempt to bolster male bonding by sharing assumptions about a common superiority over women can also be seen in the gendering of the language of conquest. When Melantius is first reunited with Amintor, his loss of words must be remedied by Amintor's appropriation of female iconography:

Melantius: I might run fiercely, not more hastily
Upon my foe. [*Embracing him*] I love thee well, Amintor;
My mouth is much too narrow for my heart.
I joy to look upon those eyes of thine;
Thou art my friend,—but my disordered speech
Cuts off my love.
Amintor: Thou art Melantius:
All love is spoke in that. A sacrifice
To thank the gods Melantius is returned
In safety! Victory sits on his sword
As she was wont: may she build there and dwell,
And may thy armour be, as it hath been,
Only thy valor and thine innocence!
What endless treasures would our enemies give
That I might hold thee still thus! (1.1. 112–25)

When Melantius's speech becomes disordered, Amintor is able to restore shape and style to it by overwriting his friend's language of love and the heart with a more publicly acceptable allegory of a feminized Victory; however, that "female" victory is safely affixed to Melantius's primary phallic symbol, his sword. As such, the context of the soldiers' embrace can be read simply as a brief interruption of Melantius's martial identity.

All these strategies of masculine empowerment depend, primarily, on a sense of rigid separation between masculine and feminine spheres, and many characters in the play try to enforce this distinction. For example, when Evadne refuses to consummate their marriage, Amintor tries to reason Evadne out of her "perversity" by appealing to what he sees as essential truths about gender:

O, we vain men,
That trust all our reputation
To rest upon the weak and yielding hand
Of feeble woman! But thou art not stone;
Thy flesh is soft, and in thine eyes does dwell
The spirit of love; thy heart cannot be hard. (2.1. 262–67)

Working along similar lines, Melantius, after he mistakenly congratulated Aspatia whom he thought was to marry Amintor, laments that he may have appeared deliberately to target Aspatia:

> I am sad
> My speech bears so unfortunate a sound
> To beautiful Aspatia. There is rage
> Hid in her father's breast, Calianax,
> Bent long against me, and 'a should not think,
> If I could call it back, that I would take
> So base revenges as to scorn the state
> Of his neglected daughter. (1.1. 81–88)

Melantius is anxious to make it clear that he does not consider women appropriate targets of abuse, as again when Calianax says, "O, Melantius, / My daughter will die," and Melantius replies, "Trust me, I am sorry; / Would thou hadst ta'en her room" (3.2. 2–4).

Melantius is also eager to define the parameters of manhood. When Calianax calls Amintor "such another / False-hearted lord as you," Melantius replies, "You do me wrong, / A most unmanly one, and I am slow / In taking vengeance, but be well advised" (1.2. 61–64). Since Calianax can afford only an "unmanly" injury, Melantius's "slow" response effectively differentiates between the masculine status of the two. Unfortunately for Melantius's project, the word "manly" cuts with a double edge here, for if a man can do an unmanly wrong, then in the very act of demarcating what constitutes manhood, Melantius has implicitly conceded that it is not innate within men. For Melantius, it is understood that "maleness" does not equate "manhood," which poses a serious challenge to an essentialist understanding of masculinity as a strictly delineated category of gender. Ultimately, this proves troublesome in his defining proper masculine conduct. Further difficulties bedevil Melantius's other attempts to categorize manliness. After the weeping Amintor confesses that the King is Evadne's lover, Melantius says to him:

> Dry up thy watery eyes,
> And cast a manly look upon my face,
> For nothing is so wild as I thy friend
> Till I have freed thee (3.2. 195–98)

Again, though, the connotations that accrue to manliness here are potentially negative: The question emerges, ought it not to be a state of reason, rather than of wildness? Amintor's tears imply a lack of self-control, an effeminization of his former noble manliness. Equally troubling is Amintor's similar warning to Evadne:

> Do not mock me:
> Though I am tame and bred up with my wrongs,
> Which are my foster-brothers, I may leap
> Like a hand-wolf into my natural wildness,

And do an outrage. Prithee, do not mock me. (4.1. 193–97)

For Amintor, the only alternative to an infantile state of domestication and tameness is a masculinity characterized by a "natural wildness" which is prone to do "outrage[s]."

Melantius, less ready-tongued than Amintor, systematically attempts to circumvent such difficulties with language. Instead of the slippery world of words, he prefers a unitary language of the body, saying, for instance, upon his first entrance:

My lord, my thanks, but these scratched limbs of mine
Have spoke my love and truth unto my friends
More than my tongue e'er could. (1.1. 20–22)

He also reverts to the language of the body when trying to force his sister to confess her relationship with the King:

Evadne.: My faults, sir? I would have you know I care not
If they were written here, here in my forehead.
Melantius: Thy body is too little for the story,
The lusts of which would fill another woman,
Though she had twins within her. (4.1. 28–32)

Here, he is able neatly to co-opt the capacity of the female body to increase during pregnancy as an index of its greater capacity for evil.

The women, however, resist such attempts to define them as essentially separate, choosing instead to appropriate the language of the masculine sphere. From the outset, Evadne is ruthlessly phallic, as when she refuses to sleep with her husband, telling Amintor:

I sooner will find out the beds of snakes,
And with my youthful blood warm their cold flesh,
Letting them curl themselves about my limbs,
Than sleep one night with thee. This is not feigned,
Nor sounds it like the coyness of a bride. (2.1. 209–13)

Even the submissive Aspatia not only criticizes men, but duplicates Evadne's language of snakes, with its suggestions of auto-eroticism and phallic femininity. In order to avoid similar pains, she advises her waiting women:

Then, my good girls, be more than women, wise;
At least be more than I was, and be sure
You credit anything the light gives life to
Before a man. Rather believe the sea
Weeps for the ruined merchant when he roars;
Rather the wind but courts the pregnant sails,

> When the strong cordage cracks; rather the sun
> Comes but to kiss the fruit in wealthy autumn,
> When all falls blasted. If you needs must love,
> Forced by ill fate, take to your maiden bosoms
> Two dead-cold aspics, and of them make lovers:
> They cannot flatter nor forswear: one kiss
> Makes a long peace for all. But man—
> O, that beast, man! (2.2. 14–27)

With her clear echoes of the gender-bending Cleopatra here, Aspatia inverts the usual norms by figuring procreation as decay, men as beasts, and women as capable of transcending and improving their natures.

Also unsettling in *The Maid's Tragedy* is that even when it is not under threat from "mannish" women, the category of manhood can never be entirely stable because it is challenged from within by two anomalous men—Calianax and the King. The age and cowardice of Calianax repeatedly militate against counting him as a man, especially when we are invited to read his challenge of Melantius as being just as futile as Aspatia's challenge of Amintor. Moreover, Calianax is unable to take full part in the male community because he cannot join in the traffic in women. Since there is no one willing to marry his daughter, he has, as it were, no goods to trade in, and our awareness of this structural problem in his situation highlights our sense of the extent to which masculine identity in the play is informed and underpinned by women. That manhood is a state that must be attained is plain in Melantius's remark that "When I was a boy / I thrust myself into my country's cause / And did a deed that plucked five years from time / And styled me man then" (4.2. 161–64). However, the figure of Calianax makes it clear that manhood also has an expiry date, and the disempowerment that he experiences as a result of his daughter's disgrace does further damage to his liminal masculinity, since it not only implicates himself, but also lays bare the extent to which masculine identity is contingent upon a man's ability to successfully possess and control women.

The masculinity of Calianax is so compromised that, like his daughter Aspatia, he is not even considered a viable opponent for a man. In fact, Melantius exclaims:

> Some god pluck threescore years from that fond man,
> That I may kill him and not stain mine honour!
> It is the curse of soldiers, that in peace
> They shall be braved by such ignoble men
> As, if the land were troubled, would with tears
> And knees beg succour from 'em. Would that blood,
> That sea of blood, that I have lost in fight,
> Were running in thy veins, that it might make thee
> Apt to say less, or able to maintain,
> Shouldst thou say more!—This Rhodes, I see, is nought,
> But a place privileged to do men wrong. (1.2. 80–90)

Melantius's last line makes it clear that, for him at least, men are the victims in Rhodes—which has an ironic appropriateness given that Rhodes is famous primarily as the location of the Colossus, a gigantic, celebratory image of manhood that was toppled soon after its erection. If men in Rhodes are victims, it is notable that, in this instance as elsewhere in the play, it is a man who is their oppressor. Even if Calianax is implicitly defined as "not-man" here, that is hardly reassuring, since it suggests that the entire nature of manhood and the extent to which it coincides with biological maleness are open to question and interpretation. Even when Melantius later explicitly defines Calianax as a man, saying to him, "Good my lord, / Forget your spleen to me: I never wronged you, / But would have peace with every man" (3.2. 290–92), the ascription to him of "spleen" emphasizes his advanced years and crotchetiness—and by the time of Pope, at least, would definitively feminize him. As Calianax himself bitterly observes, in this society "Old men are good for nothing" (5.2. 18) and are in danger of being seen as enemies of masculinity in others: When Calianax asks the King, "Why, am not I enough / To hang a thousand rogues?" the latter replies, "But so you may / Hang honest men too, if you please" (4.2. 25–27).

As for the King himself, his position with regard to other men is even more worrying than that of Calianax.[6] Theoretically, he should be the exemplar and arbiter of empowered masculinity, but there is a worrying disjunction between his public position and his private behavior which reminds us that patriarchy, with its insistence on heredity and male primogeniture, has the unfortunate side effect of not always producing the most appropriate individual patriarch. In fact, his main effect is to emasculate the men around him and to render the women mannish. Though the masque may represent Boreas as wild, untameable, masculine sexual desire,[7] the men of the actual play are distinctly tame. Significantly, it is the direct results of the King's plan for hiding his affair with Evadne by marrying her off to Amintor, which emasculates and "tames" the noble man. At an early stage of the play, Amintor muses on Aspatia, to whom he was originally betrothed:

> I did that lady wrong. Methinks I feel
> Her grief shoot suddenly through all my veins;
> Mine eyes run; this is strange at such a time.
> It was the King first moved me to't, but he
> Has not my will in keeping. (2.1. 127–31)

The first five words offer a sentence of great clarity and simplicity, which, even despite its status as an admission of injustice, is, in many ways, reassuring: Amintor's "I" claims agency, grasps and pithily articulates the situation, and differentiates itself securely from "that lady." After this assured opening, however, all such gendered certainties rapidly break down. "Methinks I feel" speaks of an "I" much less sure of events and of its own relation to them; this is a feminized language of emotion rather than a masculine one of action, and it leads the way to Amintor's state of empathy with Aspatia—indeed the parallels between them are so great that it has even been suggested that he, as much as she, is the "maid" of the title,[8] which would lead to an emphasis on male virginity both unprecedented and quasirevolutionary in its implications that men as well as women can be categorized by their sexual status. It also leads to his tears, invariably demonised as feminine in the values of Renaissance drama.

As the plot develops, the pernicious consequences of the King's action multiply, and more traditional gender assumptions are called into question. Because of the King, Amintor experiences a demasculinization as he is made to realize that he cannot enjoy the masculine prerogative of fully "possessing" his new bride. When Evadne refuses to sleep with him, Amintor threatens that if women prove rebellious:

> We will adopt us sons;
> Then virtue shall inherit, and not blood.
> If we do lust, we'll take the next we meet,
> Serving ourselves as other creatures do,
> And never take note of the female more,
> Nor of her issue. (2.1. 223–28)

In his personal misery, what he contemplates is no less than the abolition of the entire system of primogeniture and descent—the very system which, indeed, has produced the King's power.[9] Suggestively, Evadne also strikes a blow at the whole principle of differentiation that has privileged the King:

> *King*: This subtle woman's ignorance
> Will not excuse you; thou hast taken oaths
> So great that methought they did misbecome
> A woman's mouth, that thou wouldst ne'er enjoy
> A man but me.
> *Evadne*: I never did swear so:
> You do me wrong.
> *King*: Day and night have heard it.
> *Evadne*: I swore indeed that I would never love
> A man of lower place, but if your fortune
> Should throw you from this height, I bade you trust
> I would forsake you and would bend to him
> That won your throne. (3.1. 164–74)

The King's invocation of day and night may well recall the Moon's attempt to upstage her brother Day in the masque of Act One, which is recapitulated in Evadne's flat contradiction of the King and her lordly use of "I bade you". His argument is premised on essentialist gender assumptions that have been repeatedly destabilized throughout the play— Evadne is displaying a generic "subtle woman's ignorance," and only certain oaths are suitable for women—but his phrase "A man but me" is fraught with a question with wider and more dangerous implications to patriarchal authority: If the King himself is a man comparable with others, what makes him special?

The question of to what extent the King is a man is repeatedly addressed, even by the First Gentleman, who comments when Evadne leaves the King's room, "How quickly he had done with her! I see kings can do no more that way than other mortal people" (5.1. 118–19). When they are quarreling over whether or not she has slept with Amintor, Evadne tells the King, "I am no man, / To answer with a blow, or, if I were, / You are the King" (3.1. 189–91). Confident in his royal status, the King mistakenly assumes that she could not have confessed the truth to Amintor: "He could not bear it thus: he is as we, / Or any other wronged man" (3.1. 200–201). Amintor, himself, draws upon a similar set of assumptions about the King's masculine status as the First Gentleman when he finally confirms that Evadne has indeed confessed her adultery:

Amintor: I will not loose a word
To this vile woman, but to you, my king,
The anguish of my soul thrusts out this truth:
Y'are a tyrant, and not so much to wrong
An honest man thus, as to take a pride
In talking with him of it.
Evadne: Now, sir, see how loud this fellow lied.
Amintor: You that can know to wrong, should know how men
Must right themselves. What punishment is due
From me to him that shall abuse my bed?
Is it not death? (3.1. 219–29)

Here, words for males cluster tellingly: "my king," "a tyrant," "an honest man," "men," and "this fellow," all counterpointed with "this vile woman." There is a wide degree of social difference plotted between the two poles of "my king" and "this fellow," with its connotations of lower-class status. Amintor asserts what he considers an inherent equality of masculinity between himself and the King that would permit him to address the King in such a manner. However, Amintor is incapable of claiming the redress he feels is owed to him as a man; though a man, the King is still above Amintor, who is left frustrated and unmanned by the King's actions.

Perhaps the most disturbing consequence of the King's actions, however, is the extent to which they not only effeminate men, but make women masculine. This is most obvious in the surprising development of Evadne's character from whore to king-killer. The men may be unable to exercise their phallic power or wield their swords against the King, but Evadne experiences no such difficulties, making the men appear even more ineffectual and feminized by comparison. However the precise reasons why it has to be Evadne rather than Melantius or Amintor who kills the King are repeatedly mystified. The point is first mooted by Melantius:

Evadne: No, I feel
Too many sad confusions here to let in
Any loose flame hereafter.
Melantius: Dost thou not feel, amongst all those, one brave anger
That breaks out nobly and directs thine arm
To kill this base King?
Evadne: All the gods forbid it!
Melantius: No, all the gods require it:
They are dishonoured in him.
Evadne: 'Tis too fearful.
Melantius: Y'are valiant in his bed, and bold enough
To be a stale whore, and have your madam's name
Discourse for grooms and pages; and hereafter,
When his cool majesty hath laid you by,
To be at pension with some needy sir
For meat and coarser clothes:
Thus far you knew no fear.Come, you shall kill him.
(4.1.139–53)

At the outset of this exchange, Evadne seems, for the first time in the play, to have been chastened into a "proper" femininity. Melantius, however, instantly undercuts this apparent reversion to a norm: The words "brave," "nobly," "valiant," "bold," and "knew no fear" all work to make Evadne occupy a subject position described previously and elsewhere in the play as exclusively masculine. He apparently assumes, whether disingenuously or not, that Evadne will *want* to kill the King. When she demurs, he tells her simply that "all the gods require it". In succeeding discussions Melantius's logic becomes, if anything, even less clear, as when he tells his sister:

This must be known to none
But you and I, Evadne, not to your lord,
Though he be wise and noble, and a fellow
Dare step as far into a worthy action
As the most daring, ay, as far as justice.
Ask me not why. Farewell. (4.1. 171–76)

Nor is an explanation vouchsafed to Amintor in a later exchange where the emasculation of the cuckolded Amintor effected by the King becomes increasingly obvious:

Melantius: [*Aside*] He'll overthrow
My whole design with madness. [*To him*] Amintor,
Think what thou dost. I dare as much as valor,
But 'tis the King, the King, the King, Amintor,
With whom thou fightest. (*Aside*) I know he's honest,
And this will work with him.
Amintor: [*Letting fall his sword*] I cannot tell

> What thou hast said, but thou hast charmed my sword
> Out of my hand, and left me shaking here
> Defenceless. (4.2. 308–16)

Whatever the motivations for Melantius's decision to make Evadne his tool, it seems to have remarkably beneficial effects. As she becomes full of remorse for her affair with the King, Evadne embarks on a positive orgy of self-abnegation, lamenting, "sure, I am monstrous, / For I have done those follies, those mad mischiefs, / Would dare a woman" (4.1. 182–84). Her rehabilitation, though, is by no means easy. Amintor is incredulous in the face of her protestations:

> Can I believe
> There's any seed of virtue in that woman
> Left to shoot up, that dares go on in sin
> Known, and so known as thine is? O, Evadne,
> Would there were any safety in thy sex,
> That I might put a thousand sorrows off
> And credit thy repentance; but I must not. (4.1. 206–12)

His desire to trust and to seek "safety" in her quails before his residual belief in Evadne's transgressive masculinity: He credits her with "seed," which he images as "shoot[ing] up." Appropriately, therefore, Evadne's renewed assurances of transformation continue to draw very strongly on the language of more traditional gender stereotyping:

> I do not fall here
> To shadow my dissembling with my tears
> (As all say women can) or to make less
> What my hot will hath done, which heaven and you
> Knows to be tougher than the hand of time
> Can cut from man's remembrance; no, I do not. (4.1. 220–25)

She falls, she weeps, she accepts the truth of general misogynist discourse, she suggests a binary opposition between men and women, and she implicitly aligns Amintor with the perspective of heaven. She follows this with even more extravagant gender-based self-reproach:

> All the creatures
> Made for heaven's honours have their ends, and good ones,
> All but the cozening crocodiles, false women.
> They reign here like those plagues, those killing sores
> Men pray against; and when they die, like tales
> Ill told and unbelieved they pass away
> And go to dust forgotten. But, my lord,
> Those short days I shall number to my rest
> (As many shall not see me) shall, though too late,
> Though in my evening, yet perceive I will,

Since I can do no good because a woman,
Reach constantly at something that is near it. (4.1. 245–56)

In these devastating lines, Aspatia's earlier alignment of men with beasts has been completely inverted; now it is women who are no better than animals.

This imagery, though, is rapidly destabilised as both the masculine and feminine spheres are implicated with beastlike descriptors. In keeping with his earlier talk of hand-wolves, Amintor exclaims:

What a wild beast is uncollected man!
The thing that we call honour bears us all
Headlong unto sin, and yet itself is nothing. (4.2. 317–19)

And as she looks upon the King, Evadne, too, sees men as animalistic:

'A sleeps: O God,
Why give you peace to this untemperate beast
That hath so long transgressed you? I must kill him,
And I will do't bravely: the mere joy
Tells me I merit in it. Yet I must not
Thus tamely do it as he sleeps: that were
To rock him to another world. (5.1. 24–30)

Other things are also going on in this speech. Especially notable is Evadne's invocation of the ultimate patriarchal authority, God. Originally, Melantius had spoken of "the gods," as was indeed made necessary by the prohibition on mentioning the Deity's name on stage; the prohibition is here violated, a fact underlined by the King's reference to pagan rather than Christian gods— "I'll be thy Mars; to bed, my Queen of Love" (5.1. 50)—so that we are fully aware of the extent to which Evadne conceives of her actions as identical with patriarchal imperatives. Moreover, her image of "rock[ing]" the King may sound maternal and hence feminine, but her reluctance to kill the King while he is asleep not only clearly recalls *Hamlet* (1600)—already an obvious influence on the characterization of Aspatia, though she, in pointed contrast, is identified not with Hamlet himself but with Ophelia—but also serves to align her specifically with the Prince, and thus to masculinize her once more. Indeed, she explicitly disclaims a female identity:

King: How's this, Evadne?
Evadne: I am not she, nor bear I in this breast
So much cold spirit to be called a woman:
I am a tiger; I am any thing
That knows not pity. (5.1. 64–68)

And the extent to which she has violated the codes of feminine behavior is further emphasized by the First Gentleman's instinctive reaction to the murder scene: "This will be laid on us: who can believe / A woman could do this?" (5.1. 128–29).

Moreover, it is not only Evadne who is challenging the boundaries of masculinity. Aspatia, too, has a date with destiny as she assumes the disguise of a man, her brother, and seeks out Amintor. Initially, she presents this behavior as a normal function of her femininity:

This is my fatal hour. Heaven may forgive
My rash attempt, that causelessly hath laid
Griefs on me that will never let me rest,
And put a woman's heart into my breast. (5.3. 1–4)

And she continues to subscribe to a theory of radical gender difference, although one that privileges women over men:

How stubbornly this fellow answered me!
There is a vile dishonest trick in man,
More than in women. All the men I meet
Appear thus to me, are harsh and rude.
And have a subtlety in everything,
Which love could never know; but we fond women
Harbour the easiest and the smoothest thoughts,
And think all shall go so. It is unjust
That men and women should be matched together. (5.3. 21–29)

However, she goads Amintor into fighting her by appealing, successfully, to traditional notions of male honour:

Aspatia: Thou art some prating fellow,
One that has studied out a trick to talk
And move soft-hearted people; to be kicked, [*She kicks him.*]
Thus to be kicked! [*Aside*] Why should he be so slow
In giving me my death?
Amintor: A man can bear
No more and keep his flesh. (5.3. 91–96)

Nevertheless, the inherent transgressiveness of her male attire cannot simply be talked away, and the implicit challenge posed to masculinity by her ability to ape it is underlined when Amintor finds himself confronted by not one but two armed women: "*Enter EVADNE, her hands bloody, with a knife*" (5.3. 105 s.d.).

The male characters' response to the women's violence is both unexpected and unanimous. Initially, Amintor makes some attempt to reassert gender norms: He says to Evadne, "I dare not stay; / There is no end of woman's reasoning" (5.3. 165–66). But when he sees her stab herself, he discards gender roles altogether and says, "I have a little human nature yet / That's left for thee, that bids me stay thy hand" (5.3. 170–71), and gender identity is also considerably downplayed as he contemplates his own death and says, "There's man enough in me to meet the fears / That death can bring, and yet would it were done!" (5.3. 183–84). Even more suggestive of masculine behavior transgressing into the traditional sphere of the feminine is Melantius's attempted suicide. Initially, Melantius's heroic identity appears to remain comfortably intact, as he exclaims, "I never did / Repent the greatness of my heart till now; / It will not burst at need" (5.3 270–72). Almost immediately, however, things start to look different:

Melantius: I am a prattler; but no more. [*Offers to stab himself.*]
Diphilus: Hold, brother!
Lysippus: Stop him!
[*Diphilus and Strato hold Melantius.*]
Diphilus: Fie, how unmanly was this offer in you!
Does this become our strain? (5.3. 276–79)

Unmanly? Perhaps only in a play where two women have usurped the male prerogative of violence to wield their own weapons could so surprising an association be made. Far more conventionally unmanly is the method Melantius next proposes for his death:

Is not my hands a weapon sharp enough
To stop my breath? Or if you tie down those,
I vow, Amintor, I will never eat,
Or drink, or sleep, or have to do with that
That may preserve life: this I swear to keep. (5.3. 286–90)

There seems something almost luxurious about the quality of Melantius' death-wish, as he virtually suggests to those around him that they should tie down his hands, and then resolves on self-starvation—a method of suicide that elsewhere in Renaissance drama is the exclusive preserve of female characters. With Melantius's action the inversion is complete: Masculinity, unable to sustain itself in the face of the female invasion of its traditional territory, has, it seems, decided to colonize that of femininity instead.

NOTES

1. Mark Breitenberg, *Anxious Masculinity in Early Modern England* (Cambridge: Cambridge University Press, 1996) 1.

2. Francis Beaumont and John Fletcher, *The Maid's Tragedy*, ed. T.W. Craik (Manchester: Manchester University Press, 1988) 4.1. 93–95. All further quotations from the play will be taken from this edition and reference will be given in the text.

3. Sarah P. Sutherland, *Masques in Jacobean Tragedy* (New York: AMS Press, 1983) 9.

4. On Amintor as a clear reworking of the composite shepherd / knight hero of romance, see Eugene Waith, *The Pattern of Tragicomedy in Beaumont and Fletcher* (New Haven and London: Yale University Press, 1952) 75.

5. Robert Y. Turner, "Responses to Tyranny in John Fletcher's Plays," *Medieval and Renaissance Drama in England* 4 (1989): 128.

6. For an interesting discussion of the King's personal and political positions, see Rebecca Bushnell, *Tragedies of Tyrants: Political Thought and Theater in the English Renaissance* (Ithaca: Cornell University Press, 1990) 166–67.

7. See Sutherland, *Masques*, 68–69.

8. See, for instance, Philip J. Finkelpearl, *Court and Country Politics in the Plays of Beaumont and Fletcher* (Princeton: Princeton University Press, 1990) 184, 194–95.

9. In *Renaissance Dramatists* (Atlantic Highlands, N.J.: Humanities Press International. 1989) Kathleen McLuskie comments, "In this speech Amintor quite clearly acknowledges the political connection between the sexual control of women and the maintenance of social order. Amintor is evidently appalled at the prospect of such anarchy but the connection itself can be (and has been) seen as evidence of a subversive and radical sexual politics in these plays," 194.

Manliness and Misogyny in Dryden's *Aeneid*

Taylor Corse

In her recent book *Pope, Homer, and Manliness*, Carolyn Williams explores the many different ideas and definitions of manliness that were commonly held in the seventeenth and eighteenth centuries. Her useful survey shows two things: that the concept of masculinity was extraordinarily flexible, and that "maleness" did not "automatically confer manliness."[1] Williams also demonstrates that Pope regarded Homer as a "guide to manliness" and a commentary on the patriarchal world of early modern Britain.[2] Much of what Williams has to say about Pope's *Homer* (1715–1726) is relevant to Dryden's *Virgil* (1697); after all, it is a short span of twenty years that separates the two works. Homer's world, however, is very different from Virgil's, and no one knew this better than Dryden.

Samuel Johnson defines the term "manly" as "Manlike; becoming a man; firm; brave; stout; undaunted; undismayed."[3] This is Johnson's first and, presumably, primary definition, which he illustrates with a quotation from Shakespeare's *Henry VI, Part 2* (1590–1591):

> As did Aeneas old Anchises bear,
> So bear I thee upon my manly shoulders. (5.2.62–63) [4]

Clifford, who speaks these lines, is painfully aware of the difference as well as the similarity between his situation and that of Aeneas in Book 2: Lord Clifford is dead, whereas Anchises is still alive. There is another, more poignant, incongruity at work. Unlike Aeneas, who dedicates himself to rescuing his family and few remaining companions from the ruins of Troy, Clifford is determined to seek revenge on the House of York: "Henceforth I will not have to do with pity" (56). In renouncing "pity," Clifford is behaving like the avenging Aeneas of Books 10 and 12 after the death of Pallas; as with so many heroes, he is also on the verge of losing his humanity. Dryden recognizes this when he says that "Valour, destitute of other Virtues, cannot render a Man worthy of any true esteem."[5]

Johnson's entry indicates how natural it was for educated people, male readers in particular, to use classical epic as a conduct book to regulate and formulate their received ideas about what constitutes "correct" behavior. As a code, however, for right action, right thinking, and right feeling, even so exemplary a work as the *Aeneid* is fraught with complexity, contradiction, and inconsistency. Shakespeare's Clifford, for example, regards himself as an Aeneas of sorts, but an Aeneas without pity or piety. In the same speech he also compares himself to Medea, and this allusion carries as much emotional weight as the other:

> Meet I an infant of the house of York,
> Into as many gobets will I cut it
> As wild Medea young Absyrtus did. (5.2. 57–59)

Abandoned by Aeneas, Dido wishes that she, too, had the merciless will of Medea:

> I should have torn him piecemeal: strowed in Floods
> His scatter'd Limbs, or left exposed in Woods:
> Destroyed his Friends and Son; and from the Fire
> Have set the reeking Boy before the Sire. (4.861–64)

The "manly" courage of a Clifford or a Dido suggests a pathology of extremes—a limitless capacity for love and devotion or for hatred and revenge.

Manly women, in literature, are not always shrews or viragos. Swift's Stella is a case in point:

> Say, Stella, was Prometheus blind,
> And forming you, mistook his kind?
> No: 'twas for you alone he stole
> The fire that forms a manly soul;
> Then to complete it every way,
> He moulded it with female clay:
> To that you owe your nobler flame,
> To this, the beauty of your frame. (85–92) [6]

Swift's ideal woman was, as Milton puts it, "manlike, but different sex" (*Paradise Lost* 8.471).[7] In neither case does being "manly" imply a lack of femininity. Swift, in fact, praises Stella for her androgynous blend of masculine and feminine qualities such as "courage" (66), "wit and sense" (80), "kindness" (95), and "tenderness" (119)—while he chides himself for "lamenting in unmanly strains" (99).[8] In this poem on his sickness, Swift develops the witty paradox of a "manly" woman bringing comfort and strength to an "unmanly" man. Swift is no misogynist.[9] It is Stella's "nobler flame" that distinguishes her from the rest of her sex and from most other men as well. Dryden, on occasion, could also commend the "manly Mind" of an exceptionally virtuous woman.[10] Though the jury is still out on this question, there is evidence to suggest that gender lines—in some respects—were still fairly fluid in the Restoration and early eighteenth-century England.[11]

Dryden's *Aeneid* (1697) shows an opposite tendency; instead of blurring the boundaries between men and women, it makes them even more pronounced. Throughout his translation, Dryden constructs distinct masculine and feminine polarities, even outdoing Virgil in his emphasis on manliness. "Manly," in fact, is one of Dryden's favorite epithets; he uses it twenty-two times, always in a positive context and always in connection with men. Most commonly it refers to someone's countenance or physical bearing. Thus, Turnus appears in battle without any protective headgear: "Nor Casque, nor Crest, his manly Features hide" (11.738).[12] Dryden also uses it to describe more generally such qualities of character as "manly Force" (three times: 1.694, 11.480, 11.983), "manly vigor" (8.675), "manly Courage" (12.166), "manly Mind" (12.1295), "manly Soul" (12.1363), and, oddly enough, "manly modesty" (1.833). Individuals are sometimes summed up with this single, all-encompassing term. Thus Dryden invokes Calliope to "Sing what slaughter manly Turnus made" (9.698); and thus Ascanius is praised for being "manly far beyond his years" (9.417). *Virilis* is the Latin word for "manly." With one exception (9.311), there is no lexical equivalent in the original for any of these epithets.[13] It would be a mistake to dismiss them as a trick of style, a mere mannerism. So many instances—not to mention their kind and quality—suggest that Dryden had a program in mind as he composed his translation of Virgil's *Aeneid.* He wanted, I think, to promote a new ideal of masculinity, partly in response to the "softer" version of heroism expressed in Virgil, and partly in reaction to the "growing feminizing of the psyche" in late seventeenth-century England.[14]

A striking illustration of this ambivalent "ideal" appears in the climactic scene of the poem, the duel of Turnus and Aeneas. Before being wounded, Turnus declares somewhat boastfully: "No threats of thine, my manly mind can move" (12.1295). Events, though, prove otherwise when he sues for mercy; Aeneas wavers for a moment, deciding whether or not to slay his defeated and suppliant enemy:

> In deep Suspence the *Trojan* seem'd to stand;
> And just prepar'd to strike repress'd his Hand.
> He rowl'd his Eyes, and ev'ry Moment felt
> His manly Soul with more Compassion melt. (12.1360–63)

The "manly Soul" of Aeneas is that part of him which longs for revenge and the lifeblood of Turnus. Not many heroes, at least of the Homeric kind, would allow themselves to melt with compassion at such a moment. Dryden, it seems, gives us a more humane-sounding Aeneas than Virgil does: "Now, more and more as he paused, the words of Turnus began to move him" (12.940–41).[15] The "Suspence" (another addition of Dryden's) does not last for long, as Aeneas is "rows'd anew to Wrath" (12.1368) by the sight of the golden belt that belonged to Pallas. That he pauses at all suggests the prospect of a better world—of forgiveness, restitution, and atonement—but our glimpse of it is painfully brief. The heroic code will not permit it. Like Dido, Turnus dies indignant and cruelly disappointed, having expected to find "Mercy" (12.1351), "Pity" (12.1353), and perhaps "Compassion" (12.1363) in the "manly Soul" (12.1363) of the epic hero.[16]

For Dryden, epic and heroic poetry is essentially a masculine enterprise.[17] In his "Dedication of the *Aeneis*" he claims that "A Heroick Poem, truly such, is undoubtedly the greatest Work which the Soul of Man is capable to perform" (5:267). This ringing statement is often quoted to illustrate the profound respect that Dryden had for classical epic. I want to comment on the crucial phrase, "the Soul of Man." The word "man" in the seventeenth century carried a double meaning: specifically "an adult male person" (*OED* 4) and more generally "a human being" or "humankind" (*OED* 1 and 2). That is how Milton uses it in *Paradise Lost* when Raphael gently rebukes Adam for placing too much importance on sensual pleasure, which is not "worthy to subdue / The Soul of Man, or passion in him move" (8.584–85). Dryden, like Milton, is employing both senses; and yet the tonal coloring of the sentence, with its emphasis on heroism, greatness, and performance, suggests that these qualities are primarily (though not exclusively) masculine ones. Other statements from the "Dedication" reinforce that impression. Dryden tells us that the "Design" of such a poem "is to form the Mind to heroick Virtue by Example" (5:267). He is using the word "Virtue" in the comprehensive Renaissance sense of "virtu"—the Italian term for "excellence." And as every Latinist knows, "virtue" derives originally from *vir*, the Roman word for an adult male person.[18]

It is on this sexual-ethical basis that Dryden distinguishes the epic proper from its debased modern counterpart, the loose and episodic Romance "novels" of Ariosto and others: "One raises the Soul, and hardens it to Virtue, the other softens it again and unbends it into vice" (5:267).[19] The opposition between manly virtue (that which "raises" and "hardens" the soul) and effeminate vice (that which "softens" and "unbends" it) is quite explicit. Dryden here recapitulates a commonplace of Renaissance criticism: namely, that epic is "primarily a masculine genre," while romance is a "primarily a feminine genre."[20] Throughout his "Dedication," Dryden conceives of literary, moral, and political issues in sexual terms. In an epic poem, "all things must be Grave, Majestical, and Sublime" (5:267); this pronouncement has widespread implications. The English language, for example, is a manly tongue, more muscular than French, "whose Language is not strung with Sinews like our English" (5:322), and more lofty than Italian, with its "redundancy of Vowels" (5:319). This "Masculine Vigour" (5:322) makes it a suitable medium for such heroic qualities as gravity, majesty, and sublimity. There is sweetness, however, as well as strength in Virgil's Latin; and Dryden is aware that English has its disadvantages, being "clog'd with Consonants" (5:329) and overstocked with "Articles," "Pronouns," and "other Barbarities" (5:330), not to mention its surplus of "Old *Teuton* monosyllables" (5:366). Consequently, it can often sound harsh and rugged. It is amusing to discover that the masculine vigor of our "Mother-Tongue" (5:329) may not, after all, prove supple enough to capture the exquisite music of Virgil, the "Majestick Beauty" of his words and his "Harmonious Numbers" (5:335).[21]

Sexual ambiguity about genre, moral purpose, and language also informs Dryden's conception of character, in particular the character of Aeneas himself. Some readers complain that Aeneas is too tender (that is, too feminine); others consider him too stern (that is, too masculine). Dryden, however, regards him as a perfect blend of "Piety" and "Valor." There is some ambivalence about the term "Piety." On the one hand, it "comprehends the whole Duty of Man towards the Gods; towards his Country, and towards his Relations" (5:288). On the other, it comprehends "Filial Love and tender Affections to Relations of all sorts" (5:286). Pity, as James Garrison reminds us, is closely related to piety.[22] Dryden takes special pains to defend Virgil from the charge of having created an epic hero with the womanly traits of sentimentality and cowardice. To those critics who claim that Aeneas weeps more often than "well becomes a Man of Courage," Dryden responds: "if Tears are Arguments of Cowardice, what shall I say of *Homer*'s Heroe? Shall *Achilles* pass for timorous because he wept? and wept on less occasions than *Aeneas*?" (5:291). Dryden also notes that the "tears of *Aeneas* were always on a laudable Occasion. Thus he weeps out of Compassion, and tenderness of Nature, when in the Temple of *Carthage*, he beholds the Pictures of his Friends, who Sacrific'd their Lives in Defence of their Country" (5:292). In short, there is nothing unmanly about shedding tears; on the contrary, it is a sign of our hero's humanity.

What about Aeneas's behavior toward Dido? It is hard to say exactly what Dryden's attitude is on this vexed and vexing question. Both the introduction and the translation itself show that Dryden is teasingly ambivalent; as an exercise in special pleading, his apology for Aeneas is a masterpiece of irony, wit, and evasion. At first Dryden presents this as a simple gender issue: Men are apt to excuse Aeneas, and women to condemn him: "He is Arraign'd with more shew of Reason by the Ladies; who will make a numerous Party against him, for being false to Love, in forsaking *Dido*" (5:294). Dryden maintains the trial metaphor throughout the "Dedication." This slippery conceit allows him to play the roles of impartial judge, concerned advocate for all parties, and jury, too. It is a fascinating act of multiple impersonation. At first, Dryden seems to side with the ladies, with their "shew," that is, appearance of reason: "And I cannot much blame them; for to say the truth, 'tis an ill Precedent for their Gallants to follow" (5:294). In Restoration terms, Aeneas is a "gallant" (a fashionable gentleman about town, and perhaps a potential rake), whereas Dido is a passionate, generous, but very imprudent woman.[23] Our "Ladies," says Dryden, "may learn experience at her cost; and for her sake, avoid a Cave, as the worst shelter they can chuse from a shower of Rain, especially when they have a Lover in their Company" (5:294). This is the language of Restoration comedy, of *Marriage a la Mode* (1672), *The Man of Mode* (1676), and *The Country Wife* (1675); Dryden is speaking in the witty, cynical, wordly tones of a Dorimant, a Horner, or his own Rhodophil. Not surprisingly, Dryden regards the famous seduction scene as an "intrigue," a code term in Restoration drama for a sexual liaison. As Alithea exclaims in *The Country Wife*, "Why, pray, who boasts of any intrigue with me?"[24] So Dryden remarks: "After the Intrigue of the Cave, call it Marriage, or Enjoyment only, he was no longer free to take or leave; he had accepted the favor, and was obliged to be Constant, if he wou'd be grateful" (5:295). Virgil himself is ambiguous about the liaison of Dido and Aeneas—whether or not to regard it as a lawful marriage. Dido claims it is, but Aeneas insists it isn't.[25] Dryden treats the issue with breezy insouciance ("call it Marriage, or Enjoyment only"); he admits, however, that Aeneas was obligated to Dido for "the favor," another Restoration code word for sexual compliance. In this connection, I am reminded of the eighteenth-century critic John Dennis, who remarks on the consequences of Mrs. Loveit's intrigue with Dorimant:

> which is a just Caution to the Fair Sex, never to be so conceited of the Power of their Charms, or their other extraordinary Qualities, as to believe they can engage a Man to be true to them, to whom they grant the best *Favour*, without the only sure Engagement, without which they can never be certain, that they shall not be hated and despis'd by that very Person whom they have done every Thing do oblige.[26] [my italics]

For Dryden and Dennis, Dido and Mrs. Loveit are cautionary examples and warnings to the "Fair Sex" not to grant the final favor without the security of marriage; otherwise, for all their charms, they will be "hated and despised by that very person," whether an Aeneas or a Dorimant, "whom they have done every Thing to oblige."Rightly or wrongly, Dido certainly believes that she is married to Aeneas. After the intrigue of the cave, she:

> No longer made a secret of her Love:
> But call'd it Marriage, by that specious Name,
> To veil the Crime and Sanctifie the Shame. (4.248–50)

It is Dryden, not Virgil, who calls this a "specious" marriage.[27] The translator makes explicit what is implicit in the Latin: namely, that this is a hypocritical ruse that serves as a "veil" (note the pun) to "sanctifie" an illicit and unholy union. In his preface, however, Dryden takes, or appears to take, the opposite view: "*Virgil* confess'd it was a Lawful Marriage betwixt the two Lovers; that *Juno* the Goddess of Matrimony had ratify'd it by her presence, for it was her business to bring matters to that issue" (5:302). But having granted this much, Dryden then proceeds to retract and retrench: "That the Ceremonies were short we may believe, for *Dido* was not only amorous, but a Widow" (5:302). Some Restoration readers may have recalled the title of a popular play by Thomas Betterton, *The Amorous Widow* (1670), with its central character, Lady Laycock. In any case, Dryden wryly presents Dido as the proverbially lusty widow, thus perpetuating that "enduring stereotype of the early modern widow as a woman who anxiously sought a husband at any cost."[28] Dryden excuses the dissolution of this hasty and unceremonious marriage by appealing to the contemporary custom of divorce among the upper classes: "to leave one Wife and take another, was but a matter of Gallantry at that time of day among the *Romans*" (5:303). If Augustus did so, then why not Aeneas?[29] Once again, the love affair becomes a matter of "Gallantry," something that should not surprise sophisticated people who know the way of the world.[30] Ingratitude and insensibility are the two crimes that Aeneas stand accused of. Dryden admits that "Ingratitude after the last Favor [sexual intercourse], is a Crime that never will be forgiven" (5:297). Such, he implies, is the nature of women everywhere. But Aeneas had two motives to excuse his behavior: one religious and the other political: "an Absolute Command from *Jupiter*," which obliged Aeneas to "search an Asylum for his Gods in *Italy*: For those very Gods, I say, who had promis'd to his Race the Universal Empire" (5:295). As for the other crime, insensiblilty, Dryden reminds us that Aeneas "still loved" Dido and "struggled with his inclinations, to obey the Gods" (5:296). Dryden admits that there was "a fault somewhere; and that *Jupiter* is better able to bear the blame than either *Virgil* or *Aeneas*" (5:296). He realizes that the gods themselves bear much of the responsibility for this tragedy, and his translation (as we shall see) reflects that awareness.[31] The ironic treatment of Jupiter in *Amphitryon* (1690) shows, moreover, that Dryden could be quite critical, as well as devastatingly funny, about such matters.

In the foregoing argument, Dryden borrows many ideas from Jean Segrais, the best contemporary critic of Virgil.[32] His own original insight is the notion that women, especially powerful women, are frightening and dangerous: "the Fair Sex, however, if they had the Deserter in their power, wou'd certainly have shown him no more mercy, than the *Bacchanals* did *Orpheus*" (5:297). We have already seen Dido wishing she had torn Aeneas "piecemeal" (4.861). Like other dangerous women in the poem—Amata and Cleopatra—she is presented as a Maenad, a frenzied follower of Dinoysus:

> Frantick with Fear, impatient of the Wound,
> And impotent of Mind, she roves the City round.
> Less wild the Bacchanalian Dames appear,
> When, from afar, their nightly God they hear,
> And houl about the Hills, and shake the wreathy Spear. (4.434–38)

Dryden enhances her madness when he says that the "Bacchanalian Dames" are even "less wild" than Dido. (Virgil, 4.301–02, says that she rages through the city "like a startled Thyiad.") A modern historian tells us that "one of the reasons why the Bacchanalian rites were suppressed by the Roman Senate in 186 [BC] was because the emotionalism of these 'orgies' was said to encourage sexuality in women."[33] Aeneas deserts Dido largely because he fears her intense "emotionalism" and sexuality. According to Dryden, there were "secret Reasons which *Virgil* had, for thus framing this Noble Episode, wherein the whole passion of Love is more exactly describ'd than in any other Poet" (5:297). These secret reasons are private and personal as well as public and general. They have to do with human psychology, with elemental relations between the sexes, when one party feels more passion than the other. As Dryden puts it, Dido was "warm'd with the graceful appearance of the Heroe; she smother'd these Sparkles out of decency, but Conversation blew them up into a Flame" (5:297). Somewhat later follows the "publick owning" of her passion, and "after that, the consummation" (5:298). As for Aeneas:

> possession having cool'd his Love, as it increas'd hers, she soon perceive'd the change, or at least grew suspicious of a change; this suspicion soon turn'd to Jealousie, and Jealousie to Rage; then she disdains and threatens, and again is humble, and intreats; and, nothing availing, despairs, curses, and at last becomes her own Executioner. See here the whole process of that passion, to which nothing can be added. (5:298)

Aeneas is frightened by the intensity of this passion: "it seems he fear'd not *Jupiter* so much as *Dido*" (5:299). And he has good reason to be scared: "she was Injur'd, she was Revengeful, she was Powerful" (5:299). Sentimental accounts of Dido as a figure of "suffering goodness" gloss over the violent and vindictive side to her character.[34]

Another "secret" reason is political. According to Dryden, Virgil:

> knew he cou'd not please the *Romans* better, or oblige them more to Patronize his Poem, than by disgracing the Foundress of that City [Carthage]. He shows her ungrateful to the Memory of her first Husband, doting on a Stranger; enjoyed, and afterwards forsaken by him. This was the Original, says he, of that immortal hatred betwixt the two Rival Nations. (5:298)

"Disgrace" is a strong word, and Dryden does not flinch in using it. After all, he is dealing with a poem that both celebrates and denigrates an admirable woman. This ambivalence in Virgil calls forth Dryden's own ambivalence as a critic and a translator.[35] Therefore he repeats, with some reluctance, the age-old charge that women are fickle; if Aeneas had not forsaken Dido, "she might have forsaken him," especially since "she had already forgotten her Vows to her *Sichaeus*" (5:299). Dryden then quotes the infamous words of Mercury, *varium et mutabile semper femina* (4.569–70), which he calls "the sharpest Satire in the fewest words, that ever was made on Womankind" (5:299).[36] Despite the rhetoric of distance and disavowal, misogyny rears its ugly head throughout this "Noble Episode."

What is one to make of the foregoing defense? Clearly, Dryden entertains contradictory attitudes about the love affair of Dido and Aeneas. One the one hand, he admires Virgil's skill as a poet of the passions, he sympathizes with Dido's plight, and he is critical of Aeneas's ungallant behavior. On the other hand, he recognizes the destructive consequences of that passion, the self-delusion and frantic jealousy of Dido, the public responsibilities of both rulers, and the moral imperative of duty. Closing his case, Dryden throws up his hands in what seems to me an ironic, if not histrionic, gesture of dismay: "If the Poet argued not aright, we must pardon him for being a poor blind Heathen, who knew no better Morals" (5:303). After so much argument, the trial of Virgil comes to an end with a plea for pardon. Sympathy and judgment pull readers and jurors in different directions, toward emotional identification with the suffering hero and heroine and, at the same time, ethical condemnation of their conduct. Dryden, I believe, is responding frankly and fully to the same "indeterminacy" that modern readers find in Virgil's text;[37] his translation reflects the strain of accommodating such competing and conflicting attitudes. A crucial shift in perspective on Dido and Aeneas occurs in Book 4, when Jupiter looks down on Carthage and sees the two lovers living and working together like man and wife. As Dryden puts it, there "he found":

> The lustful Pair, in lawless pleasure drown'd:
> Lost in their Loves, insensible of Shame;
> And both forgetful of their better Fame. (4:322–25)

This is a harsh verdict, and a rather hypocritical one—coming from the world's greatest womanizer. (We should recall the description of Juturna, the sister of Turnus, who was "once a lovely Maid, / E're to the Lust of lawless Jove betray'd" [12.212–13].) Dryden, in fact, makes Jupiter ("all-judging Jove") out to be far more judgmental than Virgil does, who describes the couple, simply and neutrally, as "lovers careless of their better fame" (*oblitos famae melioris amantis*, 4.221). This statement implies some criticism of Dido and Aeneas, but it does not condemn them as shameless hedonists, who are lawless, lustful, and drowning in sinful pleasures.[38] A few lines later, Dryden describes Aeneas as one who "wastes his Days / In sloathful Riot, and inglorious Ease" (330–31), whereas in Virgil, he merely "loiters or dallies in Tyrian Carthage" (*Tyria Karthagine qui nunc / expectat*, 4.224–25). Clearly, Dryden is striving to magnify Jupiter's disgust and dismay, but are we the readers intended to share his view of the Carthaginian queen and her Trojan consort? Jean Hagstrum has pondered this question carefully:

> Dryden's failure to make of Virgil's famous episode a document of sensibility appears in the animus he shows towards Dido, whose character he weakens after he has so magnificently adorned her love and grief. The reason is obvious, though perhaps unforgivable—he is determined to preserve at all costs the dignity of his hero, his political and civic integrity; and he therefore presents not a faithless deserter of suffering goodness but a pious man who leaves an unworthy, licentious, and suicidal woman.[39]

As we have seen, there is some truth to Hagstrum's assessment; the behavior of the two lovers is presented as "licentious." However, it is going too far to brand Aeneas as a "faithless deserter of suffering goodness," which more accurately describes Ovid's sentimental melodrama (*Heroides* 7) than it does Virgil's tragedy. Dryden, moreover, wants to make this episode a "document of sensibility." In his "Dedication" he frequently plays with the loaded terms "sensible" and "sensibility" in the very sense that Hagstrum uses them: "Capacity for refined emotion; delicate sensitiveness of taste; also readiness to feel compassion for suffering, and to be moved by the pathetic in literature or art.[40] Aeneas, Dryden concedes, "might have shewn a little more sensibility when he left her; for that had been according to his Character" (5.296). Aeneas, however, could not consult his own inclination in this matter; he had to consider too many other things.

One such consideration is his manhood. When Mercury comes to chide Aeneas in person, he rebukes him with the taunting words:

> Degenerate Man,
> Thou Woman's Property, what mak'st thou here,
> These foreign Walls, and *Tyrian* Tow'rs to rear,
> Forgetful of thy own? (4.389–92)

This is much stronger language than Virgil's, which also takes Aeneas to task but does so in milder terms: "Are you, a husband, now laying the foundations of Carthage and building a fair city, unmindful of your own kingdom and your own affairs? (4.265–67) Dryden sharpens the rebuke by adding one epithet ("Degenerate Man") and twisting another ("Thou Woman's Property"). Every commentator agrees that Mercury is being snide and sneering when he calls Aeneas *uxorius*. Dryden notes this in his "Dedication" when he says that the word *uxorius* implies being "not only a Husband" but "a fond Husband" (5:302). In his translation, he goes even further, as if to shock Aeneas into total self-awareness; hence the stunningly rude remark. The Trojan leader has forgotten his mission; moreover, he is no longer his own man. Instead, he has sunk to the lowest degree—being the "property" of a woman. Women, of course, in Dryden's age were the property of men, not the other way around.[41]

Dryden seizes every textual opportunity to exaggerate the "feminization" of Aeneas.[42] What, for example, could be more damaging, to Roman (or English) eyes, than the following picture:

> A Purple Scarf, with Gold embroider'd o'er,
> (Queen *Dido*'s Gift) about his Waste he wore;
> A Sword, with glitt'ring Gems diversified,
> For Ornament, not use, hung idly by his side. (4.384–87)

Dryden makes some subtle and telling changes. He turns the cloak—an upper garment (*laena*) that hangs, in the Latin (4.261–64), from Aeneas's shoulders—into a "Purple Scarf" that he wears, like a sash, about his waist. Dryden also adds a completely gratuitous line about the bejewelled sword, which "For ornament, not use, hung idly by his side." Virgil implies as much, but Dryden makes the suggestion explicit: Aeneas is no longer a warrior and an adventurer, but a city planner with rather dubious taste for gaudy accessories. There is another point to be made: Aeneas has become an ornament himself, the glittering consort of a woman, who makes very good use of him (as a lover, a companion, and a co-ruler). As a "man," however, he is quite useless. Dryden helps us see these implications, which are latent in Virgil.[43] Aeneas reasserts his manhood when he rejects Dido and refuses her entreaties. Virgil uses the image of an oak tree to symbolize his newfound strength and resilience:

As when the Winds their airy Quarrel try;
Justling from ev'ry quarter of the Sky;
This way and that, the Mountain Oak they bend,
His Boughs they scatter, and his Branches rend;
With Leaves and falling Mast, they spread the Ground;
The hollow Vallies echo to the Sound;
Unmoved, the Royal Plant their Fury mocks,
Or shaken, clings more closely to the Rocks:
Far as he shoots his tow'ring Head on high,
So deep in Earth his fix'd Foundations lye:
No less a Storm the *Trojan* hero bears;
Thick Messages and loud Complaints he hears;
And bandy'd Words, still beating on his Ears.
Sighs, Groans, and Tears proclaim his inward Pains:
But the firm purpose of his Heart remains. (4.638–52)

Virgil's similes (4.441–49) often call out the best in Dryden, and this passage shows Dryden at the height of his powers as a poet-translator. In this final contest between Dido and Aeneas, the whirling words of a woman (it is Anna, Dido's sister, who speaks these words) are matched against the immovable will of a man. It is a furious but unequal contest. The masculine firmness of the mountain oak stands up to the feminine storm; in fact, the mighty tree gathers strength as it goes, reaching its roots far down into the earth. This "airy Quarrel" (a beautiful periphrasis) expands in Dryden's version into a "Storm" of "thick Messages," "loud Complaints," and "bandy'd Words"; "Tears," moreover, multiply vainly into "Sighs" and "Groans." Compared with Virgil (where the hero is "assailed on this side and that by endless appeals"), such loquacity borders on comic hysteria.[44] Aeneas, whom Dryden calls a "Royal Plant," is taking on new stature as a king in the making. It is, however, an excruciating process; his "inward Pains" are profoundly real and profoundly moving. Psychologically, this ordeal is far more terrible than the one he endured when Juno stirred up the hurricane that shattered his fleet and scattered it on the coast of Carthage.

In the struggle for self-mastery, Aeneas regains his identity, and Dido loses hers. At one time, however, she was "mistress of herself," an admirable ruler who:

takes Petitions, and dispenses Laws,
Hears, and determines ev'ry Private Cause;
Their Tasks in equal Portions she divides,
And, where unequal, there by Lots decides. (1.713–16)

As Barbara Bono notes, Dido, at this point in her career, is busy "forwarding her own masculine heroic endeavor."[45] A capable lawgiver, a fair and generous queen, she is "the leader of the work, a woman" (*dux femina facti*, 1.364). The juxtaposition and apposition of these two words (*dux femina*) is striking; the effect is lost in any translation, including Dryden's: "a Woman leads the way" (1.502). He does, however, capture brilliantly the beauty of Dido, which, like that of Camilla in Books 7 and 11, draws much of its mysterious power from her status as a chaste woman. Virgil compares Dido to two famous virgins, Penthesilea and Diana.[46] The Amazon queen is depicted on the famous wall painting where she:

> Amidst the Press alone provokes a thousand Foes,
> And dares her Maiden Arms to Manly Force oppose. (1.693–94)

Penthesilea is the last figure Aeneas sees, right before he sets eyes on Dido; Dryden wittily anticipates (in his opposition of "Maiden Arms" and "Manly Force") the war games that will ensue between them.

The picture of Dido and her "num'rous Train" (1.697) is even more engaging:

> Such on *Eurotas* Banks, or *Cynthus* Hight,
> Diana seems; and so she charms the sight,
> When in the Dance the graceful Goddess leads
> The Quire of Nymphs, and overtops their Heads.
> Known by her Quiver, and her lofty Meen,
> She walks Majestick, and she looks their Queen:
> Latona sees her shine above the rest,
> And feeds with secret Joy her silent Breast.
> Such *Dido* was; with such becoming State,
> Amidst the Crowd, she walks serenely great. (1.699–708)

There is a good deal of pathos in the simple words, "Such *Dido* was," for never again will she be so happy, so blessed, so "serenely great," as she is at this moment. Dryden's rendering of this scene is, in his own words, "Grave, Majestical, and Sublime." The simile (1.498–504) is managed with exquisite tact and sensitivity. Dido, moreover, is self-possessed, in control of herself, her surroundings, her people, and her situation. Like Diana, "she walks Majestick, and she looks their Queen." The contrast between this "gracefull Goddess" of a woman and the raging whirlwind of Book 4 is tragic, impressive, and appalling.[47]

Can Dryden give us any insight into the nature of this tranformation—into how it happens and why? I think he can. The malevolent forces of Venus and Juno combine to render Dido a hapless and helpless victim of demonic possession. At the urging of Venus, Cupid fires Dido's heart with love:

> A Love so violent, so strong, so sure,
> As neither Age can change, nor Art can cure. (1.948–49)

For a passion like this, there is no Ovidian *remedium amoris*. Virgil speaks, much less emphatically, of a love that "no divine power can change"—*ne quo se numine mutet*—(1.674). Dryden, with his medicinal imagery, makes us see the nastiness of this sinister operation. Though Dido is clearly attracted to Aeneas, it is Venus who causes the infection and orders Cupid to "infuse thy Venom in her Veins" (1.964).[48] It matters little that Dido may suffer wretchedly and undeservedly; Juno, supposedly her protector, is equally unconcerned. Perhaps the poison works more effectively than either goddess could have imagined. The point is, no one cares; and Dido is completely consumed.

After the last interview with Aeneas, she "Begins at length the light of Heav'n to hate; / And loaths to live" (4.654–55). Why does Dido resolve to die? She herself gives several reasons: guilt for infidelity to the memory of her dead husband, shame for neglecting her empire, wounded pride for being rejected by Aeneas, frustration for not being able to change his mind, sadness for having no children, and regret for falling in love in the first place:

> These dear-bought Pleasures had I never known,
> Had I continu'd free, and still my own,
> Avoiding Love, I had not found Despair:
> But shar'd with Salvage Beasts the Common Air.
> Like them a lonely life I might have led,
> Not mourn'd the Living, nor disturb'd the Dead. (4.793–98)

In some ways, this complaint is more eloquent in Dryden than it is in Virgil; certainly, her self-examination is far more searching and accusatory:

> I was not permitted to live innocently, without wedlock
> and without knowledge of such sorrows. Nor did
> I keep the vows I made to the ashes of Sychaeus. (4.550–52)

No longer the joyful Diana-like figure we saw in Book 1, Dido bitterly laments her lost identity and independence ("Had I continu'd free, and still my own"). She blames herself for purchasing "the dear-bought Pleasures" of sexual gratification (Dryden stresses the sensuality of the marriage bed, *thalami*) at the price of her freedom and sanity. In retrospect, she wishes she had led the "lonely" but carefree life of a chaste huntress, when instead she found "Despair" (something for Christian readers to ponder). Dryden's characteristic blend of sympathy and judgment appears in the "balanced" appraisal of the final line ("Nor mourn'd the Living, not disturb'd the Dead"). The vows made to the ashes of Sychaeus have disappeared, and in their place Dryden has substituted the more general impression of a melancholy mind brooding on death.

Death and sex make strange bedfellows in Dido's eerie and fantastic arrangements for her own funeral. We should remember, however, that in Dryden's age the sexual climax was routinely regarded as a kind of death; take, for example, the bawdy song in *Marriage a la Mode*:

> Then often they died; but the more they did so,
> The nymph died more quick and the shepheard more slow. (4.2.66–67)

It is fitting then that Dryden brings a Gothic imagination to Dido's lurid death scene:

> The cloven Holms and Pines are heap'd on high;
> And Garlands on the hollow Spaces lye.
> Sad Cypress, Vervain, Eugh, compose the Wreath;
> And ev'ry baleful green denoting Death.
> The Queen, determin'd on the fatal Deed,
> The Spoils and Sword he left, in order spread:
> And the Man's Image on the Nuptial Bed. (4.729–35)

In Virgil, Dido adorns the pyre with "garlands and funeral boughs" (4.506–07); in Dryden, she goes all out, collecting "Cypress, Vervain, Eugh" and "ev'ry baleful green denoting Death." This fine excess reveals her morbid fascination with death and her obsession with the man who brought her dormant sexuality to life. The erotic irony of this scene, and of the entire episode, is overwhelming. Dido is preparing for a final consummation on the same "Nuptial Bed" where she and Aeneas played out their love affair. Calling this "couch" (*toro*) her "Nuptial Bed" indicates that Dido still regards herself as married to Aeneas.[49] This is the dress rehearsal for a command performance, and the props for it are the mementos of her "husband"—his clothes, his sword, his picture. When she finally kills herself, the swordthrust is unmistakably phallic: "Deep enter'd in her side, / The piercing Steel, with reeking Purple dy'd" (4.950–51).[50]

In death, Dido regains something of her former dignity and self-respect. Her "Manly Force" is everywhere in evidence as she directs the building of the funeral pyre, as she orders the priestess to proceed with the magic ritual, as she deceives her sister Anna about her true purpose—all this while in the throes of a dreadful frenzy:

> What have I said? Where am I? Fury turns
> My Brain; and my distemper'd Bosom burns. (4.853–54)

Her madness is as great as that which assailed Orestes or Pentheus, and yet she fights it to the very end. She bids her nurse:

> Then cast the *Trojan* Image on the Fire;
> And, as that burns, my Passion shall expire. (4.917–18)

Sympathetic magic will not work, however, and Dido knows it won't. Time, the traditional cure, will prove equally ineffectual:

> A short delay is all I ask him now,
> A pause of Grief; an interval from Woe. (4.626–27)

Venus and Juno have seen to it that relief is out of the question; this love is a disease "which neither Age can change, nor Art can cure" (1.949).

Much as we pity and admire Dido, she is simply too dangerous. As Mercury reminds Aeneas, she is "Fix'd on Revenge, and Obstinate to die" (4.812). Under the circumstances, it would be foolish to stick around. When Aeneas and his crew make their getaway, they are running for their lives: "they run; they snatch; they rush into the main" (4.836). Call it cowardice (and that's what Dido does), we can hardly blame them. As Aeneas sails away, he looks back at the conflagration in Carthage. According to Dryden:

> his presaging Mind
> The Fate of *Dido* from the Fire divin'd:
> He knew the stormy Souls of Woman-kind. (5.5–7)

Virgil draws no such firm conclusion. The Trojans have their doubts and suspicions (5.7), but they (and Aeneas) remain in the dark about Dido's death. Dryden wants to enlighten us, and in so doing he opens himself to the charge of misogyny. With startling clarity, we are made to see how much men fear the terrifying force of female sexuality, "the stormy Souls of Woman-kind." This image is Dryden's, and it is most appropriate to a poem that is teeming with powerful and destructive women—Dido, Juno, Allecto, and Amata.[51]

The female figures who populate this poem are often demonic creatures possessed by fury. The most furious of them all is Juno, the "Queen of Heav'n" (1.3) who inspires other people (Aeolus, Dido, the Trojan matrons in Sicily, Allecto, Amata, Turnus) with her own irrational passions. As Brooks Otis observed, we do not really know "why the goddess should have pursued so conspicuously pious a hero with such implacable hate."[52] The mythological and psychological causes (the judgment of Paris, the love for Carthage) do not fully explain her outrageous animosity; for all her many motives, she remains a case of motiveless malignity. When we consider the great regard that Roman women had for Juno, as the deity whose "chief function was to supervise female lives," her malevolent character is extraordinary.[53] Dryden, with his customary exuberance, exaggerates her female traits and presents Juno as the archetypal figure of the scorned and injured woman—the supernatural counterpart of Dido.

Juno wants a glorious future for Carthage, but she has heard that a race sprung from Trojan blood will one day conquer the Tyrian people and rule far and wide. This prophecy is bad enough, but Dryden makes it absolutely galling:

> Yet she had heard an ancient Rumour fly,
> (Long cited by the People of the Sky;)
> That Times to come shou'd see the *Trojan* Race
> Her *Carthage* ruin, and her Tow'rs deface:
> Nor thus confin'd, the Yoke of Sovereign Sway,
> Should on the Necks of all the Nations lay. (1.27–32)

What in Virgil is a neutral report (*audierat*) becomes in Dryden an "ancient

Rumour," which has been "Long cited by the People of the Sky." The vast extent of the Roman empire (*hinc populum late regem belloque superbum*, 1.21) becomes, moreover, an exasperating "Yoke of Sovereign Sway," which lies on the "Necks of all the Nations." Several questions arise when one considers these changes. Is Dryden merely heightening the already fevered imagination of Juno? Is he showing us how unreasonable and ultimately futile it is for her to resist the decrees of Fate and Jove (*sic volvere Parcas*,1.22)? Or is Dryden introducing what a modern critic calls a "further voice," a voice that calls into question the imperialist message of the poem and the imperial mission of Aeneas?[54] Certainly, those sardonic words of Juno jar strangely with the resounding lines: "From whence the Race of *Alban* Fathers come, / And the long Glories of Majestick *Rome*" (1.9–10). Dryden's version raises another possibility: namely, that the motive for all this strife is sexual. "For what Offence," says Dryden, did the "Queen of Heav'n" begin "to persecute, so brave, so just a Man!" (1.13–14). The verb "persecute" is a remarkable substitution for Virgil's "drive" or "pursue" (*impulerit*, 1.11); it suggests an active, purposeful, and relentless hounding of an innocent victim. What could possibly justify Juno's persecution of Aeneas? This is one of the most troubling questions of the poem, since Aeneas himself has done nothing to offend her. On the contrary, he has done his best to placate and appease her. As it turns out, the grudge Juno really has is with her husband, for his frequent and flagrant infidelities:

> Besides long Causes working in her Mind,
> And secret seeds of Envy lay behind.
> Deep graven in her Heart, the Doom remain'd
> Of partial *Paris*, and her Form disdain'd:
> The Grace bestow'd on ravish'd *Ganimed*,
> Electra's Glories, and her injur'd Bed.
> Each was a Cause alone, and all combin'd
> To kindle Vengeance in her haughty Mind. (1.36–43)

In Juno's "haughty Mind," the future destiny of Rome and Carthage is secondary. What matters most is the past, and Dryden stresses the tenacity of her immortal memory with its "long Causes," its "secret Seeds of Envy," its "deep graven" images of Paris disdaining her beauty and of Jupiter slighting her marriage bed, taking as his paramour (among countless others) a lovely Trojan boy, Ganymede.[55] Dryden adds (and it is a telling addition) that "Each was a Cause alone, and all combin'd / to kindle Vengeance." Virgil simply remarks that "these affairs inflamed her even more" (*his accensa super*, 1.29). Her vengeance is directed at Aeneas, but the real target of her wrath is Jupiter, whom she can only wound indirectly. In that respect, Juno is much like Milton's Satan, who picks on Adam and Eve because he cannot injure his superior foe, God.[56] Dryden makes us understand and appreciate the grounds of her resentment and frustration: "So Fate will have it, and Jove adds his Force; / Nor can my Pow'r divert their [the Trojans'] happy Course (1.58–59). Virgil does not say that "Jove adds his Force"; Dryden, however, does so to emphasize the point that power and authority ultimately lie with men, not women, even if that woman is "the Sister-wife of *Jove*" (1.71). As if to underline her impotence, Dryden has Juno remark upon her own "fruitless Force" (1.72). Thus behind, and combined with, sexual jealousy lurks yet another grievance: anger at the inferior status of women.

I noted earlier that Aeneas "knew the stormy Souls of Woman-kind" (5.7) and that storms are emblematic of women in the way that oak trees are emblematic of men. The first action of Juno, who instigates all the literal and figurative storms in the poem, is to go off in a huff and pay a visit to Aeolus:

> Thus rag'd the Goddess, and with Fury fraught,
> The restless Regions of the Storms she sought. (1.76–77)

Juno is in her natural element—outer and inner weather in a state of constant turbulence; restless herself, she stirs up trouble and turmoil for everyone else.[57] It is a masculine deity, Aeolus, who rules over this realm. He is the first of many monarch figures in the poem, and Dryden presents him as an absolute ruler: "The Tyrant *Aeolus* from his airy Throne, / With Pow'r Imperial curbs the struggling Winds" (1.79–80). This "undaunted Monarch" (1.84) stands high in his hall, "shakes his Scepter" (1.85), and commands his kingdom with "arbitrary Sway" (1.93). Why does Dryden turn Virgil's Aeolus into a tyrant? What further voice is he introducing here? One possible voice is laughter, or at least the smile of grave irony. Aeolus, the "undaunted Monarch," is in fact very easily daunted by Juno, who bribes him with the promise of beautiful girl, Deiopea. He is seduced by a sexual favor—the first in a series of entrapments that include Dido's seduction of Aeneas and Venus's seduction of Vulcan. Aeolus forgets that it is Jupiter, the "Father of the Gods" (1.90), who has granted him this power, but he succumbs anyway.

The transition from king to sycophantic courtier is almost comic in its swiftness:

> 'Tis yours, O Queen! to will
> The Work, which Duty binds me to fulfill.
> These airy Kingdoms, and this wide Command,
> Are all the Presents of your bounteous Hand. (1.112–15)

Juno clearly knows her man, and in subverting his rule she challenges the will of another man, the more powerful brother and husband who rules over her. Dryden brings out the sexual politics of the entire situation. Jupiter, taking the long view, is rather indulgent about his wife's activities:

> Ev'n Haughty *Juno*, who, with endless broils,
> Earth, Seas, and Heav'n, and *Jove* himself turmoils;
> At length aton'd, her friendly Pow'r shall joyn,
> To cherish and advance the *Trojan* line. (1.380–83)

Dryden, unlike Virgil, implies that Juno manages to rattle the supreme confidence of "*Jove* himself"; her "endless broils" suggest domestic turmoil (*fatigat*, 1.280)—trouble at home as well as abroad.

Neptune, her other brother, also realizes what mischief she is up to: "Full well the God his Sister's envy knew,/ And what her Aims, and what her Arts pursue" (1.184–85). He reminds the various blustering winds (and by implication, Juno) that the seas are his "supream Command" (1.191) and that the "liquid Empire" (1.198) belongs to him. Furthermore, he rebukes them roundly for their "bold Attempt" and "Rebel Insolence" (1.189)—stronger terms than Virgil's "great confusion" (*tantas moles*, 1.134) In the famous simile that compares the appearance of Neptune, "the Father of the Flood" (221), to that of an orator calming an unruly mob, Dryden heightens the masculine authority of this "grave and Pious Man" (218) who "sooths with sober Words" (219) and "quenches their [the mob's] innate Desire of Blood" (220). (This Hobbesian sentiment is Dryden's, not Virgil's.) Thus, at the outset of the poem, Dryden takes his cue from Virgil in associating reason, judgment, authority, and stability with men; and passion, violence, disobedience, and instability with women.[58] This is a general tendency, not a hard-and-fast rule. Men can also go beserk, especially in the heat of battle (witness the *aristeiai* of Turnus, Aeneas, Euryalus, Pallas, Lausus, and others); by and large, however, irrationality, is a female principle.[59] Examples abound throughout the *Aeneid.* It is beyond the scope of the present chapter to examine, in greater detail, this dimension of the poem. Suffice it to say that Dryden consistently magnifies and intensifies the hysteria of Virgil's "madding" women, especially Allecto and Amata, who are chiefly responsible (along with Juno) for the outbreak of warfare in Book 7 and for its continuation in later books of the *Aeneid.* What these women lack is the ability to check their emotions; unlike Aeneas, they have not learned the lesson of self-restraint. It is a painful lesson—to judge by his chilling farewell to Dido:

> Here paus'd the Queen; unmov'd he holds his Eyes,
> By *Jove*'s Command; nor suffer'd Love to rise,
> Tho' heaving in his Heart; and thus at length, replies. (4.480–82)[60]

In the "Dedication," Dryden assures us that Virgil made Aeneas "of a piece, always grateful, always tender-hearted" (5:294); in the translation itself, we see another Aeneas, who at critical moments smothers these generous impulses. By turns "hard" and "soft," he is an imperfect and all-too-human blend of physical courage, stoic reserve, and romantic sensibility. Dryden emphasizes this when he says that Aeneas did not suffer "Love to rise, / Tho' heaving in his Heart." The substitution of a rising and heaving "Love" for "pain" (according to Virgil, Aeneas "strove to stifle the pain in his heart") is significant.[61] The *Aeneid* may well be the classic study in western literature of emotional repression and the toll it takes on men and women.[62] Dryden's version shows us how the cult of manliness, virtue, and valor goes hand in hand with that tradition.

NOTES

1. Carolyn D. Williams, *Pope, Homer, and Manliness: Some Aspects of Eighteenth-Century Classical Learning* (London and New York: Routledge, 1993) 10. My own thinking about Dryden's *Virgil* as a guide to manliness owes much to Williams's provocative study.

2. Williams, *Pope, Homer*, 1

3. Samuel Johnson, *A Dictionary of the English Language* (London, 1755).

4. I quote from *The Complete Works of Shakespeare*, eds. Hardin Craig and David Bevington (Glenview: Scott, Foresman, 1973).

5. John Dryden, "Dedication of the *Aeneis*" (5:288). All quotations from Dryden's *Virgil* are from *The Works of John Dryden*, eds. William Frost and Vinton A. Dearing, vols. 5 and 6 (Berkeley: University of California Press, 1987).

6. "To Stella, Visiting Me in My Sickness" (1720). *Jonathan Swift: The Complete Poems*, ed. Pat Rogers (New Haven and London: Yale University Press, 1983).

7. John Milton, *Complete Poems and Major Prose*, ed. Merritt Y. Hughes (New York: Macmillan, 1957).

8. Felicity A. Nussbaum also comments on Stella's "androgynous being" in *The Brink of All We Hate: English Satires on Women 1660–1750* (Lexington: University Press of Kentucky, 1984) 115. For a discussion of other androgynous heroines, see Taylor Corse, "'Heaven's last best work': Pope's *Epistle to a lady*," *SEL* 27 (1987): 413–25.

9. For a judicious assessment of Swift's attitude toward women, see Katharine M. Rogers, *Feminism in Eighteenth-Century England* (Urbana and Chicago: University of Illinois Press, 1982) 58–62.

10. See Dryden's poem, "The Monument of a Fair Lady," line 34: "A Female Softness, with a manly Mind."

11. See the fascinating discussion of the "one-sex model" in Thomas Laqueur, *Making Sex: Body and Gender from the Greeks to Freud* (Cambridge: Harvard University Press, 1990), especially the chapter on "Representing Sex," 114–48.

12. Other similar instances are 2.376, 4.215, 5.410, 6.1181, 7.902, 8.828, 8.905, 10.906, 11.55, 12.93. In his collected poems alone, Dryden uses the term "manly" 70 times—a staggering figure.

13. Virgil uses the adjective *virilis* two other times in reference to the "manly spirit" (3.342) of Ascanius and the "male offspring" (7.50) of Latinus. Dryden, however, does not translate the relevant epithet at 3.440–41. Quotations from the Latin are from *The Aeneid of Virgil*, ed. R. D. Williams (London: Macmillan, 1972).

14. The phrase is Jean Hagstrum's. See *Sex and Sensibility: Ideal and Erotic Love from Milton to Mozart* (Chicago: University of Chicago Press, 1980) 105.

15. Compare Virgil: *et iam iamque magis cunctantem flectere sermo / coeperat* (12.940–41).

16. James D. Garrison, *Pietas from Virgil to Dryden* (University Park: Pennsylvania State University Press, 1992), believes that Aeneas at the end has lost all sense of pity and piety: "The triumph of Aeneas is not the triumph of piety" (247). I, however, think that Dryden's (and Virgil's) response is more mixed and complicated.

17. This "gendered" view of literary genres was well established in the sixteenth and seventeenth centuries. See Linda Woodbridge, *Women and the English Renaissance: Women and the Nature of Womankind 1540–1620* (Urbana and Chicago: University of Illinois Press, 1984) 120.

18. Williams, *Pope, Homer, and Manliness*, quotes from Francis Pomey, *Pantheon Mythicum* (1659): "*Virtue* derives her name from *Vir*, because *Virtue* is the most manly *Ornament*" (44).

19. Montaigne, in his essay "Of Books," makes a similar distinction between the "stately" Virgil and the "flighty" Ariosto. See *The Essays of Montaigne*, trans. E. J. Trechmann, 2 vols. (Oxford: Oxford University Press, 1927) 1:403.

20. See Woodbridge, *Women and the English Renaissance*, 120. For an extensive account of literary detractors of Ariosto, see John Watkins, *The Specter of Dido: Spenser and Virgilian Epic* (New Haven and London: Yale University Press, 1994) 48–61.

21. Dryden appears to have based his remarks on a passage in *The Defence of Poesy*, where Sidney makes essentially the same comparisons between English and other languages (French, Italian, German, and Spanish). Like Dryden, Sidney finds English equally "fit" for "sweetness" and "majesty." See *Sir Philip Sidney's Defence of Poesy*, ed. Lewis Sorens (Lincoln: University of Nebraska Press, 1970) 54–55.

22. See Garrison, *Pietas from Virgil to Dryden*, for a magisterial survey of this important topos.

23. In the comedies, "gallant" almost always signifies "lover." See, for example, Margery Pinchwife's remark in *The Country Wife* (4.4.6–7): "When I think of my *gallant*, dear Mr. Horner, my hot fit comes and I am all in a fever" [emphasis mine]. I quote from The Regents Restoration Drama Series, ed. Thomas H. Fujimura (Lincoln: University of Nebraska Press, 1965).

24. William Wycherley, *The Country Wife* (2.1.45). Compare the following exchange between Doralice and Melantha in John Dryden's, *Marriage a la Mode* (3.2.135–41): "As soon as ever I spied my husband and Melantha come together, I had a strange temptation to make him jealous in revenge; and that made me call 'Palamede, Palamede,' as though there had been an *intrigue* between us." To which Melantha replies: "Nay, I avow there was an appearance of an *intrigue* between us" [emphasis mine]. I quote from The Regents Restoration Drama Series, ed. Mark S. Auburn (Lincoln: University of Nebraska Press, 1981).

25. The relevant lines are 4.170–72, 316, 324, 496 for Dido and 4.338–39 for Aeneas. Technically speaking, Dido and Aeneas were not "formally" married. See Sarah B. Pomeroy, *Goddesses, Whores, Wives, and Slaves: Women in Classical Antiquity* (New York: Schocken Books, 1975) 156; yet Pomeroy (152) notes that the Romans recognized marriage "by *usus* (continuous cohabitation for a year)." Dido, however, like Cleopatra was not a Roman citizen; therefore, these legal regulations do not apply. For a fuller discussion, see R.P.H. Green, "*Connubium* in the *Aeneid*," *Studies in Latin Literature and Roman History* 4 (1986): 393–421.

26. See John Dennis, "A Defence of Sir Fopling Flutter," in *The Critical Works of John Dennis*, ed. Edward Niles Hooker, 2 vols. (Baltimore: Johns Hopkins University Press, 1943) 2:249.

27. Compare Virgil, 4.172: "She calls it a marriage, and with this name she cloaks her crime" (*conjugium vocat; hoc praetexit nomine culpam*).

28. Barbara J. Todd, "The Remarrying Widow: A Stereotype Reconsidered," *Women in English History 1500–1899*, ed. Mary Prior (London: Methuen, 1985) 55. For a more recent discussion of widows in society and literature, see Jon Lance Bacon, "Wives, Widows, and Writings in Restoration Comedy," *SEL* 31 (1991): 427–43.

29. See the chapter on "Unhappy Marriages and Divorce" in J.P.V.D. Baldson, *Roman Women: Their History and Habits* (London: Harper and Row, 1962) 209–23.

30. Compare the remark of Harriet to Dorimant at the end of *The Man of Mode*: "Whate'er you say, I know all beyond High Park's a desert to you, and that no gallantry can draw you farther" (5.2.142–43). I quote from The Regents Restoration Drama Series, ed. W. B.

Carnochan (Lincoln: University of Nebraska Press, 1966).

31. In this respect, Dryden anticipates the ironic views of modern critics like R.O.A.M. Lyne, *Further Voices in Virgil's Aeneid* (Oxford: Oxford University Press, 1987). See Lyne's chapter on "Gods and Men," 60–99.

32. For information about Segrais, see the notes to Dryden's *Virgil* (*Works* 6:946–55, 959–63)

33. See the chapter on "Roman Women" in Michael Grant, *Greeks and Romans: A Social History* (London: Weidenfeld and Nicolson, 1992) 29.

34. See Hagstrum, *Sex and Sensibility*, 110.

35. For an extensive treatment of this idea, see Michael West, "Dryden's Ambivalence as a Translator of Heroic Themes," *Huntington Library Quarterly* 36 (1973): 347–66.

36. Desmond's comment on this passage is pertinent: "Although such an antifeminist statement is not a normative assertion for the entire text of the *Aeneid*, this pithy definition of *femina* nonetheless casts a long shadow over the *Aeneid*: much of the chaos and instability in the cosmos as well as in society is attributed to the feminine" (*Reading Dido*, 43).

37. See, for example, W. R. Johnson, *Darkness Visible* (Berkeley: University of California Press, 1976).

38. Dryden's (or Jupiter's) attitude is reminiscent of Spenser's attitude toward Acrasia's lover in the Bower of Bliss, who cares nothing for "honour" or "advauncement," but "in lewd loves, and wastfull luxuree, / His days, his goods, his bodie he did spend" (*Faerie Queene* 2.12.80).

39. Hagstrum, *Sex and Sensibility*, 110.

40. Hagstrum, *Sex and Sensibility*, 9.

41. For the legal and economic subjection of women, see the chapter on "The Situation of Women" in Katharine M. Rogers, *Feminism in Eighteenth-Century England*, 7–51. By contrast, married women in the late Roman republic and early empire did enjoy the right to "administer their property and to enter into legal transactions." See Yan Thomas, "The Division of the Sexes in Roman Law," in *A History of Women in the West: From Ancient Goddesses to Christian Saints*, ed. Pauline Schmitt Pantel (Cambridge: Harvard University Press, 1992) 135.

42. Taunts of Trojan effeminacy are frequent in the *Aeneid*. See, for example, the stinging remarks of Numanus (9.811–50) and Turnus (12.153–56).

43. For a fuller and more explicit rendering of Aeneas's effeminacy, see Marlowe's *Dido Queen of Carthage* (1587), where Achates rebukes his leader in these terms:

This is no life for men-at-arms to live,
Where dalliance doth consume a soldier's strength,
And wanton motion of alluring eyes,
Effeminate our minds inur'd to war. (4.3.33–36)

In this play Aeneas chides himself for enduring "female drudgery" (4.3.55). I quote from the edition by H. J. Oliver (Cambridge: Harvard University Press, 1968).

44. *Assiduis hinc atque hinc vocibus heros / tunditur* (4.447–48). On the subject of verbal aggressiveness in women, see Woodbridge, *Women and the English Renaissance*, 207–10.

45. See Barbara J. Bono, *Literary Transvaluation: From Vergilian Epic to Shakespearean Tragicomedy* (Berkeley: University of California Press, 1984) 19.

46. Lyne, *Further Voices in Virgil's Aeneid*, points out this connection (136).

47. In a brilliant comment on this passage, Barbara Pavlock, *Eros, Imitation, and the Epic Tradition* (Ithaca: Cornell University Press, 1990), notes that Dido's success as a ruler depends largely on the "repression of her sexuality" (195).

48. The notion of love as poison or disease is a traditional metaphor, popular with the Roman elegiac poets. It was also popular with Restoration writers; see, for example, Dorimant's remark when he finds himself falling in love with Harriet: "I have took the infection from her and feel the disease now spreading in me" (*The Man of Mode*, 4.1.149–50).

49. The motif of the "nuptial bed" has a long history in Christian society. According to Allison Coudert, the metaphor of the Cross as nuptial bed "became increasingly popular from the twelfth century onwards." In popular literature, moreover, "instead of the Cross being the nuptial bed, the nuptial bed was the Cross which husbands bore with the fortitude of so many Christs" (74). Dryden may be suggesting that Aeneas was fortunate to escape this particular cross. See Coudert, "Exemplary Biblical Couples and the Sacrament of Marriage," *Homo Carnalis: The Carnal Aspects of Medieval Life*, ed. Helen Lemay (Binghamton: Center for Medieval and Renaissance Studies, State University of New York Press, 1990) 59–83.

50. Dryden's phrase "piercing Steel" is more emphatic than Virgil's *ensem* (664). The erotic overtones of this scene are discussed by Pavlock, *Eros, Imitation, and the Epic Tradition*, 84.

51. The real-life social counterparts of Virgil's fictive women are well described by J.P.V.D. Baldson in his chapters on "Female Emancipation" and "The Women of Augustus' Court" in *Roman Women: Their History and Habits* (New York: Harper and Row, 1962) 45–62 and 68–96.

52. Brooks Otis, *Virgil: A Study in Civilized Poetry* (Oxford: Oxford University Press, 1963) 228–29.

53. Michael Grant, *Greeks and Romans: A Social History*, 29. For a fuller account, see John Scheid, "The Religious Roles of Roman Women," in *A History of Women: From Ancient Goddesses to Christian Saints*, 377–408.

54. See the chapter on "Gods and Men" in Lyne, *Further Voices in Virgil's Aeneid*, 61–99.

55. Marlowe, in *Dido Queen of Carthage*, "queers" the story by opening the play with Jupiter dandling "that wanton female boy" (1.1.50), Ganymede.

56. For Juno as a prototype of Satan, see K. W. Grandsden, "The *Aeneid* and *Paradise Lost*," in *Virgil and his Influence*, ed. Charles Martindale (Bristol: Classical Press, 1984) 97–99.

57. According to David Quint, Juno "represents a universal feminine principle, and she, like Cleopatra, gives the name of woman to the anarchic forces inherent in the East, in the cosmos, and in the human psyche." See Quint, *Epic and Empire: Politics and Generic Form from Virgil to Milton* (Princeton: Princeton University Press, 1993) 28.

58. For a discussion of mind-body dualism in relation to women, see the essays collected in *Women and Reason*, eds. Elizabeth D. Harvey and Kathleen Okruhlik (Ann Arbor: University of Michigan Press, 1992).

59. See the chapter on "The Hysteria of Women" in Nancy Tuana, *The Less Noble Sex* (Bloomington: Indiana University Press, 1993) 93–107.

60. It is a telling irony that in Book 6 (456–66) Aeneas does speak movingly and tenderly to Dido, but then, however, she is a shade in the underworld.

61. Compare Virgil: *Ille Jovis monitis immota tenebat / lumina et obnixus curam sub corde premebat* (4.331–32).

62. George L. Moss, *The Image of Man: The Creation of Modern Masculinity* (Oxford: Oxford University Press, 1996) remarks that "self-restraint was a key attribute of the masculine stereotype" in the formation of the British empire (15).

Soft Women and Softer Men: The Libertine Maintenance of Masculine Identity

Andrew P. Williams

The Restoration of Charles II effectively ended the rigid governmental application of Puritan morality in England and signaled the beginning of a new age, one marked by a reinvigorated spirit of social freedom. Upon the King's return, John Dryden laments, in "Astrea Redux," the pleasures lost to the past seventeen years: "Youth that with joys had unacquainted been/Envied gray hairs that once good days had seen" (25–26).[1] But with Charles's triumphant return to London in 1660, the good days had indeed returned. The theaters reopened, the court in all its splendor once again became the center of society, and the youth enjoyed a liberty unknown to their gray-haired elders. But with the restoration of the monarchy and Charles's ascension to the throne, a troubling version of manhood and masculine identity reasserted itself upon the national consciousness. The unrepentant libertine, a variant of the masculine ideal founded upon the appropriation of a loose confederacy of egocentric philosophical precepts, established himself as a principal figure of male identity, dominating the literary and dramatic depiction of ideal masculinity from roughly the time of Charles's return to the Glorious Revolution in 1688.[2] This unrepentant, or Hobbesian, libertine, the "first type of rake to pursue his lusts on the Restoration stage," demonstrated a masculine identity significantly different from the reformed or philosophical libertine who came to prominence on the post–William and Mary stage.[3] Unlike the reformed rake of the 1690s and early eighteenth century whose fifth-act rejection of his prior libertinism signaled a tacit acceptance of social conventions and regulations, the unrepentant libertine refused to accept a "reformed" version of his social identity and, instead, held fast to a masculine identity that defined manhood within a relatively rigid sphere of characteristics and social deportment. The unrepentant libertine promoted a masculinity routinely identified with certain generic traits, including a voracious sexual appetite, a permanent state of skepticism, and a code of personal conduct characterized by what Dale Underwood calls "an ethics of sensualism" in which the pursuit of pleasure and power remained paramount to the establishment and maintenance of his masculine identity.[4]

In this chapter I would like to examine the figure of the unrepentant libertine, or rake, in a variety of Restoration-era plays and verse, and the ways in which the maintenance of his masculine identity is contingent upon an "identity-project" that necessitates the public acknowledgment of his sexual presence, as well as the denigration of the feminine. By the use of the term "feminine" I do not wish to simply imply female; instead, I use the term as a gender category that encompasses women and men who, for whatever reasons, have been deemed unmasculine by the prevailing hegemonic masculine identity. My focus is not on libertinism itself as a problematic code of conduct; rather, it is on the social processes by which the libertine establishes and defends this masculine identity. Specifically, I would like to illustrate that the maintenance of his social identity, his "libertine-self," proved contingent upon his successful manipulation of social practices in such a way that the conception of autonomous selfhood became the sole province of the libertine, while those gendered feminine were seen to lack the necessary ingredients for selfhood. Thus, in early Restoration verse and drama, a necessary condition for the identification of the "libertine-self" is the presence of feminine or "soft" individuals; namely, women whose sexual objectification solidified the libertine's claim as a supreme image of masculine identity; and men who did not live up to the libertine's standard of masculine behavior and were characteristically effeminate, weak, "womanly," and, like women, easily dismissable by the more "manly" libertine.

The construction of a masculine identity is, in part, derived from the cultural importance a society attaches to the public behavior of its male members. As such, society and personal identity are univocally connected where individual selfhood remains "symbolic of social practices, not of empirical experiences."[5] Social practices are also indelibly linked with the historical process that shapes and determines gender and gendered identities.[6] R. W. Connell's definition of gender makes this connection explicit: "Gender is a social practice that constantly refers to bodies and what bodies do, it is not social practice reduced to the body . . . Gender exists precisely to the extent that biology does not determine the social."[7] Connell's definition is important, for not only does it allude to the "structuring of social practices" that have historically maintained power relationships between the sexes that subordinate women within weaker, gendered categories, it also emphasizes the connection between gender identity and social identity. Gender identifies "what bodies do" in the context of social practices, thus fusing the inequities of "gendering" masculine and feminine into separate political and economic categories with the formation of gendered, social identities such as masculine self-identities.

The identification of the "libertine-self" constitutes the construction of a social identity, what Rom Harre calls "the attributes one shares with the others that make up some relevant reference class."[8] The development of a social identity such as the "libertine-self" involves an individual undertaking an "identity project" where one identifies and acquires the characteristics and qualities of an existing social identity, and then displays them within the appropriate social context.[9] The process, which can be described as constructing a self-made and supported stereotype for behavior, emphasizes and promotes certain attributes recognizable by society and appropriate for the type of identity being projected.[10] But the acquisition of appropriate personal attributes and social behaviors is only part of the "identity project"; once a social identity is established, as part of the "identity project," the individual must defend it against potential disrupting influences, especially those that might question the validity or appropriateness of one's identification or claim to a particular social identity. Specifically, the maintenance of a social identity within the "identity project" depends upon the ability of the individual "to make public the existence of a social identity corresponding to the personal attributes which are displayed and known."[11]

For the successful construction of a social identity, its corresponding attributes must be manifest in carefully prescribed social situations that contribute to the goals of the "identity project." In the case of the unrepentant libertine, the construction of his social identity required the public display of two primary attributes: the graceful command of social intercourse that can be subsumed under the label of wit, and the public recognition of his rapacious sexual appetite. Wit did not prove to be a problem for the libertine; his command of social practices and manners made him the centerpiece of fashionable society. However, the public recognition of his sexual behavior proved somewhat problematic; short of a public "performance" of his sexual nature, the libertine was left with the problem of bringing into the public sphere the private intrigues of the boudoir. While promiscuity became what Lawrence Stone calls a "hallmark of fashion at court and in high political circles,"[12] the latter half of the seventeenth century did mark the beginning of a growing importance of individual, personal privacy. The identification of the "private sphere," the personal arena for tending to one's bodily maintenance, and the "desire to separate one's body and its juices" from contact with others became a significant factor in interpersonal dynamics. Likewise, sexual behavior became one of the "many aspects of one's personal activities" that became increasingly situated within the private sphere.[13] For the libertine, however, the private sphere did not provide a fixed boundary for his sexual activity; the sexual act may be relegated to the private sphere, but the "conquest" is a matter for the public realm.

Though the self-directed quest for sexual pleasure and power characterized much of the libertine's conception of manhood, unless its acquisition was situated within the public sphere, that pleasure and power was irrelevant to the construction of his identity as a libertine.[14] Though, obviously, not every aspect of the libertine's sexual behavior was played out openly for the viewing and discursive pleasure of the public at large, for many libertines, this is not an inaccurate description. Angeline Goreau succinctly demonstrates the propensity of the "court wits" toward the voguish fashion of composing and making public obscene and often misogynistic verse.[15] Therefore, I use the term "public" more in the context of making a private act known to parties not intimately involved in the act. This act of making the private public proved to be a vital component of the libertine's manipulation of social processes for the purposes of solidifying his masculine identity. While the libertine's "conviction that nothing was real beyond the momentary impulse, the violent electrical charge of pleasure and pain"[16] motivated his pursuit of individual, but temporary, sensual experiences, the transitory nature of his pursuit of pleasure offered no permanency or stability to the construction of a social identity. What was needed was for those private "momentary" impulses to become known, "permanent" elements of the public sphere. Only then could the libertine lay claim to the identity he wished to project, and subsequently enjoy the social and political prerogatives that accompanied this version of the masculine ideal.

Though any cultural moment is marked by competing versions of masculinity, one version of the masculine ideal invariably assumes the hegemonic position where it wields an inordinate degree of social and political power. R.W. Connell defines hegemonic masculinity "as the configuration of gender practices which embodies the currently accepted answer to the problem of the legitimacy of patriarchy which guarantees (or is taken to guarantee) the dominant position of men and the subordination of women."[17] Michael S. Kimmel states it more succinctly: "The hegemonic definition of manhood is a man in power, a man with power, and a man of power."[18] This is a fairly accurate description of the unrepentant libertine. In the plays and poetry of the Restoration, the libertine is inevitably portrayed as an attractive, socially mobile, and aggressive man; he is admired by other men, lusted after by women, and in very rare occurrences in the literature of the first two decades after Charles's return, does he ever fail to acquire exactly what he wants. The libertine towers above all other masculine identities who invariably find themselves unable to fulfill their individual desires. Simply put, the unrepentant libertine surfaces as the hegemonic masculinity because he succeeds on his own terms where other versions of manhood tend to fail.

As a "man of power," the hegemonic masculinity maintains that power through the manipulation of social practices in such a way that competing claims of autonomous selfhood that may threaten the existing gender order are made subordinate. This calls for the hegemonic group to acknowledge the gendered separation of the masculine and feminine in such a way that produces what Elizabeth Minnich calls "a division that is not a dualism but a hierarchical monism."[19] While this gendered division subordinates the feminine on the grounds of biology, versions of masculinity that compete with the hegemonic conception also become stratified within the hierarchy of gender, and are relegated, like females, to a gendered category that is not only separate and unequal to the hegemonic masculinity, but inferior and subhuman, as well.

The emergence of the libertine, or rake, as a hegemonic form of ideal masculinity after the Restoration can be attributed in large part to the "collapse of moral Puritanism as a dominant influence in society," resulting in a greater secularization of social mores and, what Stone calls, a "release of the libido from the age-old restraints of Christianity."[20] The figure of the King himself compounded this upsurge of libidinal energy in the two decades after his return. Handsome, young, and charismatic, the restored monarch and symbol of English patriarchy exuded a vibrant and vital masculinity that proved a significant contrast to the Puritan exemplar of masculine leadership, Oliver Cromwell. Charles's example reflected an ethical posture of moral relativism that saw adultery, promiscuity, and excessive sexual liberty as fashionable accouterments of the complete gentleman.[21] His sexual conquests were both many and matters of public record; he fathered twelve known illegitimate children to seven different women, granting nine dukedoms to six of his bastard sons.[22] This is indeed a vigorous indicator of a libertine attitude toward sexual conquest from the man whom the libertine, John Wilmot, Earl of Rochester, calls "The easiest King and best-bred man alive"(4), and who happened to possess "the sauciest prick that e'er did swive"(16).[23]

Charles's active and open sexuality illustrated a fundamental component of the libertine as a representative of the masculine ideal. Central to the libertine's conception of masculine selfhood is a rapacious and energetic sexual appetite that requires public recognition. Rochester's praise of Charles's "prick" situates the locus of the King's libertine identity not only within the sexual act, but more importantly, in the public declamation of the act, recasting what Calvin Thomas calls "an arguably indifferent bodily organ, the penis, into the primary or transcendental signifier, the phallus."[24] But as a signifier, the phallus is significant only to the extent that it reinforces the libertine's hegemonic masculinity through the public elevation of the sexual organ to a symbolic example of true, powerful manhood. However, this gives rise to a significant problem within the libertine's "identity project." The libertine's phallic power must be demonstrated, it must become part of the public domain, and yet, the phallus is exposed only within the culturally normative confines of the private sphere.[25] There is no place for the phallus public; "it is not permitted to participate in everyday life . . . but furtively, under cover of darkness. Nowhere is phallos [sic] out in the open."[26] But the libertine is forced to bring the phallus "out in the open" in order to claim its power as a manifestation of his own masculine identity. Realizing without the phallus, "all is feminine," the libertine is forced to substitute the actual phallus with logos, the word, which functions as a socially permissible, symbolic phallus. More than the monological boast of sexual prowess or conquests routinely found in the court poetry, the unrepentant libertine creates a social dialogue concerning his sexuality. In regards to his "identity-project," the libertine engages others within society to discuss, assist him, and, most importantly, respond to his recreative sexual acts.

Typical of an exchange of doggerel verses that took place among the members of the "merry gang" of libertines at Charles's court is the correspondence between Lord Buckhurst and George Etherege, both of whom need to publicly proclaim their active and enthusiastic sexual liberty. Buckhurst entreats, "by this letter/to enquire for whores, the more the better:/ Hunger makes any man a glutton" (p.35. 25–27).[27] Etherege replies that he:

> wandered in the spacious Town
> Amongst the bawds of best renown,
> Making enquiry far and near
> To find out fresh and wholesome gear. (p.39. 33–36)

The libertine's vibrant sexuality is an active extension of his manhood where the gluttonous appetite for sex serves to define his conception of masculine-self while it simultaneously denies full selfhood to his "conquest." Encapsulated in Etherege's reply is the rake's undisguised desire to reduce his female partner to nothing more than a sexual organ: "This shows Love's chieftest magic lies/In women's cunts, not in their eyes" (p.43. 15–16). By placing "Love's chieftest magic" within the female genitalia, Etherege demonstrates an oppositional significance of the sexual organs when compared to the libertine's masculine "pintle." In terms of gendered power dynamics, the masculine, for the libertine, is superior in every significant way. Equating masculine identity with the phallus marks a public glorification of the cultural importance of the organ. However, since the feminine is always situated beneath the masculine on the monism of gender, a similar project of equating identity with biology in dealing with the feminine cannot have the same elevating effects. Instead, the equating of the feminine to a biological entity serves to further reduce the gendered status of the female, going so far as to deny the feminine of the gendered identities of "lover," "wife," and even "bawd," and substituting an identity that is solely anatomical and only partially human.[28]

The reduction of the female to the status of subhuman entity constitutes a central strategy in the libertine's efforts to maintain his masculine social superiority. By reducing the female subject to a sexual organ, the libertine views the feminine solely in terms of the utilitarian potential for fulfilling his sexual desires. Women are organic machines and, as such, can be dismissed as convenient cogs in a larger social mechanism. However, the libertine's equation of the feminine subject with her sexual organs also posits the center of the libertine's masculine identity and power within his own genitalia. If the libertine's "pintle" is, as Etherege crudely puts it, "the cunt's delight" (p.2. 43), the male genitalia must function in unison with the female sexual organs in order for the fulfillment of the rake's own sexual conquest. And, as the libertine is aware, any inability, real or presumed, on his part to rise to the occasion constitutes a serious and potentially damning indictment against his masculinity.

The potential for sexual dysfunction exacerbates the inherent state of anxiousness that accompanies the libertine's conception of self.[29] For one whose masculine identity depends heavily upon the public perception of his sexual vigor, the loss, even temporarily, of sexual power constitutes a major setback to the maintenance of his hegemonic status. Rochester's "The Imperfect Enjoyment" illustrates the libertine at his most vulnerable, unable to procreate though a willing mistress beckons: "But I, the most forlorn, lost man alive/ To show my wished obedience vainly strive:/ I sigh alas! and kis, but cannot swive" (25–27). The failure of his organ is a failure of his masculine identity; the libertine's very manhood is called into question where the public disclosure of his shortcomings would be disastrous to his "identity project." Rochester's persona laments, "Thou treacherous, base deserter of my flame,/ False to my passion, fatal to my fame" (46–47).

Rochester's "The Imperfect Enjoyment," like Etherege's poem of the same title and Aphra Behn's "The Disappointment," demonstrates a sexual anxiety that intensifies the public humiliation of sexual inadequacy and hints at an inversion of the gendered monism that sustains the libertine's masculine identity. As the poems demonstrate, sexual dysfunction traps the libertine in an unwinnable situation. He may either accept the blame for his inability to perform, or place the blame on the female whose sexual aggressiveness (or in the case of Etherege's poem, modesty) overpowers his desire. Either way, the libertine is forced to accept the momentary loss of not only his erection, but his hegemonic status as an ideal man as the previously subhuman female assumes a position of sexual control over the male organ and libido. Etherege's libertine concedes, "From my defeat your glory does arise,/ My weakness proves the vigor of your eyes" (45–46). But however the blame is directed, the libertine's "defeat" triggers a reaction marked by a sudden and violent recognition of the fragility of his social position. Realizing the futility of his situation, Rochester's libertine confesses, "Eager desires confound my first intent,/Succeeding shame does more success prevent/ And rage at last confirms me impotent" (28–30). Desire and shame result in a disabling rage. The same is the case with Lysander in Behn's "The Disappointment":[30]

> His silent Griefs swelled up to storms
> And not one God his Fury spares;
> He curs'd his Birth, his Fate, his Stars
> But more the Sheperdess's Charms
> Whose soft bewitching Influence
> Had Damn'd him to the Hell of Impotence. (135–40)

The anger and frustration projected by the libertine is only partly directed at his momentary situation. Damned to the "Hell of Impotence" implies a permanent condition of sexual dysfunction, which is not necessarily the result of a single "Disappointment." The rage of the libertine at his inability to copulate signals a self-conscious admission of his failure to live up to the masculine standard he has identified himself with. He may rage at the gods, at fate, and most of all, at the woman who has witnessed his dysfunction, but the primary locus of the libertine's anger is directed inward. Even a momentary loss of sexual prowess when situated in the public sphere becomes a permanent loss of phallic power for the libertine. He is fully aware that "The Hell of Impotence" marks a fixed reduction in the libertine's hegemonic status, displacing him to a masculinity more indicative of the submasculine fops and fumblers. The libertine's rage in the "Imperfect Enjoyment" poems is a disguised fear; the fear of weakness, age, and the loss of hegemonic power. All that is left for the libertine, as Rochester's "The Disabled Debauchee" indicates, is his displacement as a viable figure of manhood:

Thus statesmanlike, I'll saucily impose,
And safe from action, valiantly advise
Sheltered in impotence, urge you to blows,
And being good for nothing else, be wise. (45–48)

However, while the libertine is aware that the "Hell of Impotency" will effectively deconstruct his masculine self-identity, the rake's sexual pursuit of women remains characteristically aggressive and violent. Regardless of the increased potentiality for disease (pox) and debilitating effects (impotency) of rampant promiscuity that will seriously damage the libertine's social identity, the rake consciously pursues an agenda of sexual conquest that requires, as a condition of manhood, a variety of sexual partners. Libertine masculinity not only systematically dehumanizes women, it also commodifies them, reducing the female subject to a product of limited and temporary value. Like an empty bottle of sack, females are easily discarded by the libertine once their potential for providing sexual pleasure has been realized.

Within libertine masculinity, therefore, the reduction of the feminine subject to a dismissable biological entity stands paradoxically juxtaposed against the libertine's rapacious need for a variety of female sexual partners. However, this apparent contradiction is easily rectified within the libertine ethos, which posits monogamy and sexual felicity as deviant and oppressive constructs that deprive men of their natural sexual liberty. The need for sexual variety, as interpreted by the libertine, is a natural condition of manhood, and, as such, should be satisfied at every opportunity. The image of William Wycherley's Horner juggling sexual partners in the "china scene" of *The Country Wife* (1675) ably demonstrates the libertine attitude toward the pursuit of sexual variety and conquest. Horner is incapable of refusing a sexual tryst even if it may mean the revelation of his potency, which would severely limit his plans for future cuckoldry. However, unlike Horner and his mistresses who are engaged in a game of sexual quid pro quo, the libertine's pursuit of sexual variety is rarely depicted as an inconsequential or mutually satisfying element of the female's sexual experience. In Restoration dramas such as Thomas Shadwell's *The Libertine* (1675)[31] and Nathaniel Lee's *The Princess of Cleves* (1681),[32] the necessity of sexual variety to libertine masculinity is manifested through a calculating and brutal approach to sexual relations that routinely incorporates rape, polygamy, and deceit as wholly permissible avenues toward the "natural" satiation of masculine sexual desire.

Shadwell's *The Libertine* offers a heightened portrait of the personal and social devastation that accompanies the sexual mores of this brand of masculinity. Shadwell's Don John is a hyperbolic illustration of libertine manhood whose pursuit of sexual pleasure is indelibly linked with violence and carnage, yet he remains decidedly open and honest about his conception of the state of masculinity. For Don John, libertinism is the natural condition of manhood:

Nature gave us our Senses, which we please:
Nor does our Reason war against our Sense.

> By Natures order, Sense should guide our Reason (1. 26)

Sense and reason prove compatible within the libertine ethos, allied for Don John in the relentless pursuit of physical, sensual pleasure. "We'll surfeit in delights, And never think ought can be ill that's pleasant" (1. 26). For the libertine, however, the negation of thinking "ill" of anything that brings pleasure amplifies an already skewed moral sensibility allowing Don John to conclude that "there is no right or wrong, but what conduces to, or hinders pleasure" (1. 28). As for women, their bodies bring pleasure, but their chastity and judgment remain impediments. Thus, as Don John illustrates, sexual violence is an appropriate and admirable alternative to the denial of pleasure:

> *D. John*: I could meet with no willing Dame, but was fain to commit a Rape to pass away the time.
> *D. Anto.*: Oh! A Rape is the joy of my heart; I love a Rape, upon my Clavis, exceedingly.
> *D. John*: But mine, my Lads, was such a Rape, it ought to be Registered; a Noble and Heroick Rape. (1. 32)

The libertine expresses a marked indifference toward sexual violence and treats the act of rape as just another routine pleasure to while away his idle time. Don John's violation of the female is in no ways indicative of the conception of the "Pleasing Rape," where the female's protestations are viewed as simply token resistance, and the rape proves a mutually satisfying experience for both victim and rapist.[33] Instead, Don John's deed, committed in a church, denies any semblance of selfhood to the act's victim. Don Antonio, who also committed a rape, at least allows for some portion of feminine identity to his victim. He boasts that after beating "a grave mighty bearded Fool," he "carried away his Mistriss, serv'd her in her kind, and then let her go" (1. 32). Don John's rape, however, was committed because he found no "willing Dame." Though repugnant, the identification of a "willing Dame" does imply some degree of human personage to a sexual encounter. However, Don John's actual sexual encounter, the rape victim, lacks selfhood or indication of a social identity, even those implied by "Mistriss" or "Dame." She is relegated to an anonymous, faceless, biological entity whose existence is verified solely in the terms of her commodification and violation; terms forced upon her and then publicized by Don John.

For the libertine, rape remains an acceptable avenue to the satiety of masculine sexual desire, and a means by which to express not only masculine domination of the feminine, but also phallic power. Rape becomes an extension of what Eugene Monick calls the "shadow of chthonic phallos," which Monick explains is routinely made manifest through violence and sexual degradation:

> The shadow of chthonic phallos can be characterized by its grossness, brutality, and carelessness. It can be characterized by its insatiable desire and possessiveness, by its

unmitigated power needs, by a kind of mad drivenness, by the mayhem of war and ruthless competition it occasions. [34]

However, after the rape has been committed, the expression of phallic power assumes for Don John a nearly mythical status. For the libertine, the rape has transcended momentary physical pleasure, it has become a "Noble" and "Heroick" deed. It is a public testament to the libertine conception of masculinity, which affirms sexual ruthlessness and mayhem, and rejects the potential permanency of affectionate and reproductive sexuality. Rape may be a crime committed in the dark, but for the libertine, it is essential that it be made a matter of public interest. For Don John, the rape should be "Registered" for the edification and pleasure of the masses, and more importantly, the identity of the rapist should be clear. Only then can the act be considered one of phallic/masculine significance and successfully contribute to the libertine's social identity. Similarly, when confronted with six women all claiming to be his wife, Don John exclaims: "Why should I conceal my good actions! In one word I am married to every one of you, and have above four-score more, nor will I ever give over, till I have as many Wives and Concubines as the Grand Signoir" (2. 43).

The pursuit of all that is sensually "pleasant" remains the chief concern of Don John, and any ideology, law, or moral code that promotes the curtailment of that pursuit can be reasonably judged by the libertine as unnatural. Don John goes further to hint that the denial of sensual pleasure is even sinful: "My appetites are all I'm sure I have from Heav'n, since they are Natural, and them I always obey" (1. 28). Obeying the dictates of nature requires the libertine's reduction of the feminine subject to a depersonalized form of selfhood where the female body provides a temporary satiation of his sexual appetite. For Lee's libertine, Nemours, the female body constitutes the primary pleasure of the libertine's sensuous appetite: "Women are the sole pleasure of the world. Nay, I would rather part with my whole estate, health and sense, than lose an inch of love" (2.3.52–54). But, for Nemours, the pleasure of women is strictly dictated in commercial terms; gender dictates an economic inequity where the libertine male interprets the feminine-self as another consumable good. For the libertine, women have value, as Nemours says, "Not to be married to'em, but to serve my turn. What's good in'em never scapes me" (2.3.68–69). Nemours's rejection of marriage displaces the female subject outside the parameters of conventional social dynamics of the early modern period, and relegates all females to the status of prostitute. For Don John and Nemours, women are valuable only to the extent that "what's good in'em" provides momentary pleasure; the rest of the female subject, her autonomous nature and self, is irrelevant and dismissed.

Recognizing that the actual sensual pleasure of the "rape" or "conquest" is momentary, the libertine does strive to establish a sense of permanency to his sexual encounters. While the libertine does not acknowledge or value the independent feminine-self, he does admit to and appreciate the unique quality of individual sexual experiences where variety becomes the cornerstone of the libertine's sexual ethos and identity. Speaking of its effect, Don John accounts it as the most delightful of pleasures: "Use variety as I do, and you'll not be miserable. Ah! there's nothing so sweet to frail human flesh as variety" (2. 40). Though marriage, family, and constancy are out of the question because they result in undesirable masculine identities, "Husband" and "Father," libertine masculinity substitutes these "unnatural" constructs with an emphasis on sexual variety in which each female the libertine has sexual intercourse with becomes an individual signifier of the rake's status as a supreme figure of manhood. Husbands, Don John concludes, are "dull, drudging Animals" (3. 57), but when asked if he is a man or a devil after requesting a "fine young buxom Whore" of the Hermit who has come to his assistance, the libertine boasts, "Men, men, and men of lust and vigor" (3. 55). For the libertine, masculine sexual energy, his "lust and vigor," is defined not in terms of the amount of sexual activity he has—after all, a husband may have sex with his wife as often as a libertine with his variety of paramours—but in the number of "conquests" the libertine can lay claim to. Sexual variety then takes the place of sexual constancy as a barometer of masculine desire and ensures the continuation of not only the rake's sensual pleasures, but his masculine identity as well.

In a similar vein, Nemours declares the importance of sexual variety to the libertine's social identity. Speaking with Tournon with whom he has just had sex, Nemours inquires if she has managed yet another intrigue for him:

> *Nem.*: But come tell me; what, no new game? For thou knowest I die directly without variety.
> *Tou.*: Certainly never woman loved like me, who am not satisfied with sacrificing my own honour, unless I rob my delights by undoing others.
> *Nem.*: Come, come, out with it. I see thou art big with some new intrigue, and it labours for a vent.
> *Tou.*: What think you of Saint-Andre's lady?
> *Nem.*: That I'm in bed with her, because thou dar'st befriend me. (1.2.32–42)

Nemours's pun ("big with some new intrigue") conflates reproductive sexuality with recreational sex where Tournon's procurement of a new intrigue becomes a symbolic pregnancy, and an assignation with "Saint-Andre's lady" the result of Tournon's labor. Thus, for the libertine, the purpose of sexual relations is not procreative; rather, it is an end to more sexual activity, hence creating the potential for a seemingly endless variety of paramours.

From Nemours's example it seems that sexual constancy proves an anathema for the libertine and his social identity. Addressing the issue, Rochester confines constancy to those "unmanly" men who lack the libertine's energy and appetite:

> Old men and weak, whose idle flame
> Their own defects discovers,
> Since changing can but spread their shame,
> Ought to be constant lovers. (9–12) [35]

Only change, variety, can ensure that a man is not identified with the old and weak whose "idle flame" equates constancy with impotency. Thus, the potent man, the "true masculine-self," follows the path of the libertine and spreads his masculine fame by changing a mistress, as Rochester says, "As each kind night returns" (18).

From this perspective, alternate masculine social identities that do not require a variety of sexual partners as a significant referent to a social class are relegated to a lower sphere of manhood. The masculine identities of "Husband" and "Father" carry with them a set of attributes the libertine found antithetical to his conception of hegemonic masculinity. Though the dramas, more often than not, illustrate the opposite, society at large still expected constancy and love as a condition for marriage. Yet for the cynical libertine, husbandly constancy was an outward sign of masculine weakness and loss of phallic power, and love was nothing more than an illusion, "an elaborate myth to cover what was really no more than sexual desire pressing to be satisfied."[36] Though painfully contradictory, the potent, manly libertine viewed sexual intercourse as a recreational and nonprocreative activity. A bastard or two was no problem, but to legitimize one's paternity, to acknowledge the identity of "Father," was an irreparable blow to the libertine's "identity-project." The only good that came from the identities of "Husband" and "Father" was to provide the libertine with a demasculinized conception of the masculine ideal, one by which he could prove his superior masculine status by flaunting his sexual liberties and transforming the social identity of "Husband" to an even lesser, effeminate figure of manhood, "Cuckold."

As descriptors of masculine deportment during the seventeenth century, the terms "effeminacy" and "effeminate" referenced two main strands of connotative associations, physical weakness and delicacy, and some type of nonnormative form of heterosexual behavior.[37] The label "effeminate" did not necessarily imply homosexuality, rather, heterosexual behavior that tended toward the extremes, sexual disinterest (asexuality), and rampant promiscuity (omnisexuality). Susan Shapiro points out that "one recurring type of man against whom the charge of effeminacy is constantly leveled is the exclusively but uxoriously heterosexual, ranging from the dominated milquetoast to the elegant ladies' man."[38] However, though the term "effeminate" was used to describe the "compulsive pursuit of sexual experience," its usage in this context seems to be more a matter of semantics than application in the two decades following the Restoration. From Wycherley's *The Country Wife*, Harcourt defends the "effeminate" pleasures of sex after Horner's disingenuous tirade against women and glorification of the "manly" pleasures of masculine friendship:[39] "For all that give me some of those pleasures you call effeminate too; they help to relish one another" (1.1.239–41). Libertine sexuality certainly falls within the category of omnisexuality, and the libertine would most certainly consider himself a ladies' man, yet it does not seem likely that a libertine would be charged with effeminacy because he had recreational sexual intercourse with a variety of women.[40] In theory, libertine sexual proclivities may be described as "effeminate" in certain early modern connotations of the word, but the libertine or rake was never labeled as "effeminate" by society. This charge was more appropriate for the libertine's antithesis, the fops and lackwits.

While various connotative layers were applied to the term "effeminate," two fundamental elements of its application remained consistent: It was a derogatory charge directed solely toward men—women were "womanly" or "feminine" but never "effeminate,"—and it signified a presumed lack of masculine power. Effeminacy, for seventeenth-century society, represented "an inherent unmanning."[41] Wycherley's Manly (*The Plain Dealer* 1676), clearly makes this connection when he says to the fops Novel and Plausible: "You presume sure upon your effeminacy to urge me, for you are in all things so like women that you may think it in me a kind of cowardice to beat you" (2:1.734–37). The "inherent unmanning" associated with effeminate males represents a loss of masculine power that stretches beyond the masculine identity normally associated with the effeminate, Frenchified fop. The now familiar categories of lackwits, witwoulds, and country fops all succinctly identify other "submasculinites," which were characteristically labeled as "effeminate" during the early modern period.[42] Seventeenth-century satires such as *The Character of a Town Gallant* (1680), *The Character of a Coffee-House, with the Symptomes of a Town Wit* (1673) (whose masculine identity has been "effeminated by the childish Toyings of a rampant imagination"), and *The Character of the Beaux* (1696), all illustrate various subcategories of less than admirable figures of foppish manhood. However, the unmanning associated with the loss of masculine power, and hence privilege, as a result of age or infirmity was also understood by the libertine as a form of submasculine or effeminate masculinity.

At issue is the fundamental connection between the public recognition of socially encoded "manly" attributes and masculine hegemony. While the cultural implications of male effeminacy during the seventeenth century are too widespread to be adequately addressed in this chapter, in regards to the libertine's "identity project," the effeminate man was a valuable element. He served as a convenient comparative signifier for what the libertine was not, socially and sexually inadequate. Since effeminacy was inherently associated with a lack of masculine power or potency, to display power was a sure sign of masculine prowess. As such, exposing another man as lacking the appropriate degree of sexual power or potency also became an effective method for the libertine to display his hegemonic status as a man of power. Manly's recognition of the fops' submasculine status indicates a privilege of the hegemonic masculinity, namely, identifying the parameters for the conferral of masculine selfhood. For the libertine's "identity project," this power was paramount in demonstrating his manhood. Only alongside the "soft" man could the libertine's masculinity be judged against the cultural validity of other masculine identities. In the drama of the Restoration, this comparison inevitably yielded the same result: The libertine was seen to be a man of substance while the nonlibertine, the effeminate man, was considered, in Edward Ravenscroft's words, a "Man of Show."[43]

While libertines are commonly referred to as "Gentlemen of wit and sense"[44] or "Young Gentlemen of the Town,"[45] their submasculine counterparts are routinely described, in addition to the social labels of "coxcomb," "fop," or "lecher," as malformed or incomplete versions of the true, natural man. This is especially true when the man in question does not possess the libertine's propensity for bedroom intrigues. Regardless of a male's projected social identity, sexual inadequacy (or, considering the libertine's need for a variety of partners, inadequate sexuality) is a prime indicator of nonlibertinism and a diminished claim to manhood. For example, in James Howard's *The English Mounsieur* (1663), the rakes Wellbred and Comely accurately expose Mr. Vaine's sexual shortcomings and relegate him to the status of a partial man:[46]

> *Com.*: . . . that fellow is a Coxcomb of great value, his humour is very pleasant, he loves to be thought a debauch, in all kinds, and is none; brags of his great acquaintance with women—and their kindness to him, and yet, knows not one in the whole Town.
>
> *Well.*: Prethee look yonder and behold the approaching shadow of the man we were talking of, substance he has none. (1.1.22–28)

Without the sexual "knowledge" of at least one woman of the town, Vaine's masculine substance lacks corporeality. He is an incomplete shade of the more masculine libertine whose sexual prowess and appetite is considered a natural condition of true manhood. The half men, the shadows of men, lack this vital and natural component of masculine deportment. From *The Country Wife*, Dorilant pointedly includes men past their sexual primes within the ranks of the effeminate and submasculine who lack masculine, sexual power. Addressing Horner on the services they perform for women of quality, Dorilant says:

> *Dor.*: Nay, I dare swear, they won't admit you to play at cards with them, go to plays with 'em, or do the little duties which other shadows of men are wont to do for 'em.
>
> *Horn.*: Who do you call shadows of men?
>
> *Dor.*: Half-men.
>
> *Horn.*: What, boys?
>
> *Dor.*: Ay, your old boys, old *beaux garcons*, who, like superannuated stallions, are suffered to run, feed, and whinny with the mares as long as they live, though they can do nothing else. (1.1.223–33)

From the libertine's perspective, older men are akin to young boys whose full masculine potential have yet to be realized. The "Old Boys" are competent to perform the "little duties" for women, to be their companions, but their presumed inability to perform sexually with the ladies is a public indicator of their loss of masculine power.

The recognition of masculine sexual prowess and potency is a central element to not only the libertine's "identity project," but to the social recognition of a male's claim to complete manhood. In an appropriate twist of comic irony, one of the best examples of the social emasculation and "effeminization" of a masculine figure comes from *The Country Wife* in the form of Wycherley's highly sexually active and successful libertine, Horner. In this play, Horner undertakes the complex construction of two separate and antithetical social identities; the first and primary is the identity of the libertine, which he will share only with a select few, his female conquests and the quack; the second, illusionary identity is that of the impotent eunuch, which he publicly promotes within the masculine community. While Horner's sexual juggling act effectively allows him to maintain two masculine identities at the same time, the public emergence of his "impotent-self" aptly demonstrates the social restructuring of masculine identity as the "former" libertine is reduced to a submasculine status.

Horner's perceived impotency provides the sole grounds for his reduced status within the masculine community. Though he does not exhibit any of the "effeminate" qualities such as cowardice and delicacy, which are traditionally associated with the fops, his "impotency" is enough of an unmanning to demote his masculine identity on the monism of gender to the ranks of the effeminate. Though fellow libertines, Dorilant and Harcourt subtly reinforce their own masculine prowess by identifying their friend's sexual inadequacy:

> *Har.*: Now your sting is gone, you looked in the box amongst all those women, like a drone in the hive, all upon you, shoved and ill used by 'em all, and thrust from one side to t'other.
>
> *Dor.*: Yet he must be buzzing amongst 'em, still, like other old beetle-headed, liquorish drones. (3.2.10–15)

Even when Horner offers an alternative to sex for demonstrating masculine power over women, his more manly companions are quick to point out the weakness of both the plan and the planner:

> *Horn.*: Yes, sir, and I shall have the pleasure at least of laying 'em flat with a bottle, and bring as much scandal that way upon 'em as formerly t'other.
>
> *Har.*: Perhaps you may prove as weak a brother amongst 'em that way as t'other.
>
> *Dor.*: Foh, drinking with women is as unnatural as scolding with 'em; but 'tis a pleasure of decayed fornicators, and the basest way of clencing love. (3.2.33–40)

Dorilant's equating the pleasure Horner claims getting women drunk will provide with "decayed fornicators" further demonstrates the complete lack of masculine power associated with male impotency. Not only is Horner's plan "unnatural" and base, but substituting sexual conquest with drunkenness is seen as a desperate attempt to claim a degree of masculine power that the "unmanned" Horner no longer retains. For the able-bodied libertines, Horner's plan ranks him with the old boys whom Dorilant had previously categorized as mere shadows of men. Perhaps even more damaging to Horner's masculine identity is Harcourt's subtle insistence that the former libertine's impotence may have made him too weak to outdrink a woman.

Harcourt further associates Horner with the "*beaux garcon*" by seeking Horner's help in his plan to seduce Alithea: "But hark you sir, before you go, a little of your advice; an old maimed general, when unfit for action, is fittest for counsel" (3.2.51–54). Like Rochester's "Disabled Debauchee," the man "unfit for action" is relegated to a substratum of the masculine community, a man who lacks the corporeal substance to act and is left with little more to do than watch the intrigues of real men. Even the affected and cowardly fop Sparkish feels himself man enough to claim a prerogative of the hegemonic masculinity and deny full masculine selfhood to the once prominent libertine. Relating a jest he had with "some ladies," Sparkish says to Horner: "Said I to the fourth, 'Did you never see Mr. Horner? He lodges in Russell Street, and he's a sign of a man, you know, since he came out of France'; Heh, hah, he" (1.1.349–52).

The trio of Harcourt, Dorilant, and Sparkish situate Horner's masculine identity within a submasculine or effeminate status, which they recognize as antithetical to their own. It is irrelevant that Horner's impotency is only a ploy; as far as the masculine community is concerned, he has become unmanned, a "sign" or a "shadow" of what was once a man but is no longer. Horner's masculine incapacity has left him, as Sir Jasper says, "an innocent playfellow" (2.1.613). Horner himself skillfully uses the terminology of incomplete manhood in describing his "impotent" masculinity. Speaking to Sir Jasper, he says, "I will not be your drudge by day, to squire your wife about, and be your man of straw, or scarecrow, only to pies and jays, that would be nibbling at your forbidden fruit" (4.3.97–100). Of course this speech is shortly followed by Horner's successful seduction of Sir Jasper's wife, proving to the female community that he is certainly no man of straw. However, for the other men, Horner is a "scarecrow" and his proximity allows them to publicly acknowledge his unmanning, which in turn, reinforces their own masculine claims to power. Even bumblers like Sparkish and Sir Jasper are secure that their manhood is more potent and "masculine" than Horner, whose command of social practice eclipses the pair in every significant way.

The construction of two dissimilar social identities, the masculine libertine and the submasculine eunuch, allows Horner to pursue his sexual agenda with little or no hindrance from other males. It also demonstrates the complexities of comparative masculine identities. Perceived as a eunuch by the masculine community, Horner is effeminized and categorized as a shadow specimen of manhood. As such, he is beneath the other, potent masculine figures on the monism of gender. By acknowledging that Horner's masculine identity lacks the essential element of manhood, namely phallic power, the other men, including the fops, could substantiate their own claims to masculine selfhood by pointing out that they were not like Horner; they could not be called signs, shadows, or innocent playfellows. However, Horner's very real potency firmly establishes his libertine identity within the feminine community, where the rake's masculine status is never in question. When compared to the other masculine figures, Sir Jasper, Pinchwife, and even Harcourt and Dorilant, Horner's masculine-self excels; he has successfully demonstrated not only his sexual prowess, but also his power to manipulate and shape social practices and relationships for his own personal gain. Horner has outwitted the males, making them cuckolds and fools, and has revealed their own limited capacity for comprehending the sexual game of wit being played by the libertine.

The presence of effeminate fops such as Howard's Mr. Vaine and Wycherley's Sparkish, and elderly males such as Mr. Pinchwife, serve primarily as comic foils for the witty intrigues of the manly libertines. Their blocking the desires of the "men of wit" and invariable humiliation constitutes a primary plot element of most Restoration comedies. However, their presence within the same social circle as the libertine also magnifies the social difference between the power holding hegemonic masculinity and the other, lesser forms of masculine-self. Among men, masculinity remains distinct from anatomical maleness, it is a gendered identity that must be earned and proven within the appropriate sphere. In the two and a half decades after the Restoration, that sphere became increasingly connected with the social arenas for fashionable society—the park, the playhouse, the drawing room, and the bedroom—while the timely and effective display of wit emerged as a social barometer of masculine power.[47] While the effeminate or submasculine males proved necessary fodder for the maintenance of the libertine's "identity project," their presence also had the potential to threaten the libertine's hegemonic masculinity with the possibility that the libertine's masculine power might fail him, and that the effeminate male may, in fact, prove to be the better man.

The destabilization of the unrepentant libertine's masculine identity is, perhaps, most clearly evident in Etherege's *The Man of Mode* (1676).[48] With the possible exception of Wycherley's Horner, Dorimant represents the Restoration's most complete and identifiable libertine exhibiting, as Dale Underwood points out, "a Hobbesian aggressiveness, competitiveness, and drive for power and Glory,"[49] while the play's other "man of mode," Sir Fopling, remains the era's unrivaled paragon of foppery. As masculine templates, there seems to be no comparison. Dorimant publicly humiliates Mrs. Loveit, he seduces Bellinda, and he successfully manipulates his social environment for his own ends. However, what he is incapable of doing is establishing his masculine power over the doting and vacuous Sir Fopling.

Though the effeminate fop is laughed at by the members of the witty society, Dorimant seems to be the only serious critic of Fopling Flutter who finds it necessary to target the fop for the type of public ridicule suffered by other effeminate fops such as Howard's Mr. Frenchlove. Perhaps, as Emilia says, it is because the fop "passes for a wit with many" (3.2.292). However, Dorimant's plan to humiliate Fopling with Mrs. Loveit backfires, and instead, it is Dorimant who suffers a loss of masculine power from which he never fully recovers:

> *Med.*: Would you had brought some more of your friends, Dorimant, to have been witnesses of Sir Fopling's disgrace and your triumph.
>
> *Dor.*: 'Twere unreasonable to desire you not to laugh at me; but pray do not expose me to the town this day or two.

Med.: By that time you hope to have regained your credit. (3.3.350–57)

In escaping ridicule, Sir Fopling is momentarily positioned on the hierarchy of gender above Dorimant who becomes, himself, the object of another man's ridicule. The "credit" that Dorimant has lost in his fellow libertine's eyes is his masculine power, his manly prerogative to expose the limitations and shortcomings of other men. And though the loss may seem only a minor setback in a larger plan, it is sufficient enough for Medly to doubt Dorimant's hegemonic status. Medly recognizes that Dorimant can only "hope" to regain his masculine power with a public victory over Sir Fopling. However, Dorimant never fully achieves this. In fact, Dorimant even finds himself questioning his own masculine resolve after seeing Mrs. Loveit with Fopling, asking, "She cannot fall from loving me to that?"(3.3.320).[50]

Dorimant's inability to fully expose Sir Fopling's reduced gender status hints at the libertine's own inability to completely manipulate his social settings for the benefit of his masculine "identity project." Though clearly effeminate, the fop's presence does more damage to the libertine's masculine identity than it does good. Beside the failed plot to ridicule Fopling that results in Dorimant's loss of masculine "credit," it is Sir Fopling who nearly ruins Dorimant's plans to seduce Harriet by refusing to call the libertine by his alias, Courtage, and it is the effeminate fop who "penetrates the metaphors" of the libertines and "discloses their polite secrets."[51] At play's end, Dorimant's attempts to prove his masculine superiority over Sir Fopling ultimately prove futile. The fop escapes the usual punishments designed for effeminate males, banishment from the society or the tricked marriage, and, instead, is left standing at Dorimant's side, joining him in one last comic barb aimed at Mrs. Loveit. Dorimant's inability to reduce the fop's gender status has, in fact, elevated Fopling's masculine status, making his "mode" of manhood a viable alternative to that of the libertine. In fact, while Fopling is accepted into the social circle of the witty society, it is Dorimant who will be leaving the social arena of London society in order to pursue Harriet in the country.

Etherege's Dorimant has traditionally been admired for his attractive rakishness, but his inability to reduce the gendered status of Sir Fopling to a "shadow" of a man, and Harriet to a mere sexual conquest, signals a failure on the part of the libertine to maintain his masculine "identity project." Dorimant has been, in large part, humbled by the soft man and woman; he has lost his masculine "credit" and can no longer lay a complete claim to the prerogatives of the hegemonic masculinity. As such, Dorimant is left to do the only thing the libertine can when he sustains an irreparable blow to his social identity; he renounces it as viable masculinity, and sets out on a different identity project, one that will grant him a new masculine identity, that of the reformed rake. Dorimant's declaration of love and that his "soul has given up her liberty" (5.2.478) may be another self-serving ploy to gain the sexual favors of Harriet, but it also effectively displays his public renegotiation of his masculine identity. His inability to reduce the masculine status of Sir Fopling represents a serious indictment against the libertine's masculine power that cannot be rectified within the libertine ethos. However, by specifically declaring the loss of his soul's liberty, Dorimant rejects the very core of the libertine ethos, and as such, his claim to that particular form of masculinity. He no longer identifies himself within the social parameters of libertinism, saving himself the embarrassment of having his masculinity evaluated by his former peer group.

Dorimant's apparent rejection of the libertine ethos represents a significant shift in the public affirmation of libertine masculinity promoted by fellow libertines. Unlike Dorimant's rejection of "liberty," which clearly signifies a rejection of libertine masculinity, the libertine who is successful in maintaining his masculine credit is not swayed by social conventions or pressures to renounce his previous libertinism and the codes of conduct that governed him. To live by his own code of conduct, to be his own man, seem to be the rake's primary ends within the dramatic depiction of libertine masculinity. Even marriage cannot fully subdue the libertine's incessant drive for autonomous selfhood. From Dryden's *The Wild Gallant* (1663), Loveby's marriage to the financially secure Constance does not negate what he perceives to be his masculine superiority over his wealthy wife. According to John Harrington Smith and Dougald McMillan, Loveby's "rakishness is a masculine trait tending to keep him independent of her, and this too is a prerogative which, as things are managed, he is not compelled to renounce as a condition of having her."[52] In this case, the libertine's particular brand of masculine identity ensures his independence as well as legitimates his financial arrangement through the bonds of matrimony. Similarly, at the conclusion of Wycherley's *Love in a Wood* (1671), Ranger puns, after being asked by Lydia if he could "quit all other engagements and voluntarily turn yourself over to one woman" (5.2. 124–26), that "The end of marriage now is liberty, And two are bound—to set each other free" (5.2. 130–31).

When the libertine's fate does not include marriage, the unrepentant libertine is able to more freely remain true to his conception of masculine selfhood. Even Horner, whose secret has been discovered by the female community, may continue to enjoy his dual social identities as long as he can simultaneously convince the men he is impotent and demonstrate to the women that he is not. Perhaps no more dramatic depiction of the libertine's refusal to compromise or reject his masculine social identity comes at the end of Shadwell's *The Libertine*. Don John, who has raped and murdered with gleeful abandon, finds himself about to be drug into the bowels of hell. Given the chance to repent, Don John's final speech sums up the arrogant defiance of all social and religious convention which characterizes libertine masculinity:

> Were Seas of Sulphur flaming round about me
> And all Mankind roaring within those fires,
> I could not fear or feel the least remorse.
> To the last instant I would dare thy power.
> Here I stand firm, and all thy threats contemn. (5. 91)

Like another exemplar of masculinity whose egocentric search for knowledge and power also secured his damnation, Don John stands Faustlike, incapable of rejecting his masculinity, even at the cost of his soul. Only through the absolute rejection of society and morality can Don John maintain his masculine identity; as ruthless and devastating his libertine nature may have been, unlike other libertines, such as Dorimant, who find refuge in reformation, Don John does not experience a loss of masculine power. In fact, he would literally be damned before he did.

Dorimant's reformation seems to have not only been motivated by his apparent love for Harriet, but also by his masculine failure to subordinate Sir Fopling's masculine status. As such, the reformation is necessary for Dorimant to maintain a viable masculine identity; if he were to continue to pursue a purely libertine self-identity, his failings with both Fopling and Harriet would undermine his credibility. However, in the case where the libertine has not lost his masculine "credit," the libertine's declaration of reformation needs to be seriously evaluated as another, in a long line of manipulative social practices designed to further the libertine's pursuit of power and sensual pleasure. Lee's Nemours who, like Etherege's Dorimant is linked with Rochester,[53] does not suffer the type of masculine defeat that Dorimant did, yet he publicly declares his own rejection of his libertine past: "I see and loathe my debaucheries . . . This, I hope, whenever I die, I will convince the world of the ingenuity of my repentance, because I had the power to go on" (5.3.299–304). Much of the interest in Nemours's last-minute reformation has been focused on the play's concluding couplet as a cynical barb directed at Rochester's own death-bed conversion: "He well repents that will not sin, yet can;/But death-bed sorrow rarely shows the man" (5.3. 305–06). While Lee's skepticism of Rochester's sincerity is evident in the closing lines, they also offer "proof" of Nemours's reformation. Rochester had nothing to lose by reforming; he was past the point of demonstrating any masculine power. Nemours, on the other hand, is still young and able to continue his libertine ways, and as such, his repentance is "well" and true. However, Nemours's rejection of his libertine identity is carefully constructed so as not to exclude a potential for future libertine activity. Nemours counts on the world recognizing the "ingenuity" of his repentance, but that ingenuity can imply both his sincerity and his cunning. As a manipulator of social settings who has just finished boasting that he will bed the Princess in "eighteen months three weeks hence," Nemours's admission that he has the power to continue his libertine ways seems to be an indication that he will. Like Horner's impotency, Nemours's renunciation of his past debaucheries is a facade to ensure the proliferation of his libertine masculinity.

The fifth-act reformation of the libertine, which became a staple of dramatic masculine representation in the years after the Glorious Revolution, signaled a decline in the hegemonic status of libertine masculinity. With the passing of the court of Charles II and the rise of the reform-minded Orange court, the gender dynamics that proliferated the libertine's "identity project" were increasingly becoming the objects of critical scrutiny and social suspicion. By the time Jeremy Collier could pronounce a "fine gentleman" as a "Whoring, swearing, smutty, atheistical Man,"[54] the status of the unrepentant libertine as a hegemonic form of masculinity had been permanently displaced. The soft women and softer men who had once been indispensable to the maintenance of his social identity had eventually proven too powerful for the libertine's continual assertion of his masculine power and prowess. Eventually, the libertine ethos became seen as less a form of masculinity, and more a stage of prolonged adolescence that a man must pass through, and ultimately reject, in order to lay a claim to true manhood. With the approach of the eighteenth century, masculinity became increasingly associated with a man's ability to control the natural impulses the libertine so freely satiated.[55] The emergence of what Harold Weber calls the "philosophical libertine," best exemplified in the comedies of William Congreve, becomes a template for the new, sensitive figures of manhood that will come to dominate masculine representation in the eighteenth century. Ultimately, the unrepentant libertine who so ferociously clung to a perversely misogynistic and egocentric conception of masculine selfhood became himself, in the eighteenth century, a man of reduced gender identification; a masculine figure whose inability, not to fulfill his appetites, but to control them, would render him effeminate. Like the Faustian figure of Shadwell's Don John being drug to hell rather than repent or deny his libertine identity, the masculine social identity of the libertine was inevitably doomed. Age, infirmity, and other "emasculating" weaknesses would eventually catch up to the unrepentant libertine and turn him, like Rochester's "Disabled Debauchee," into an impotent shadow of his former self who, despite his claim to wisdom, in the end remains "good for nothing else."

NOTES

1. *Selected Poetry and Prose of John Dryden*, ed. Earl Miner (New York: Random House, 1985) 12.

2. This year also saw the publication of Shadwell's *The Squire of Alsatia*, which initiated what John Harrington Smith and Dougald McMillan call the "regrettable feature" of the libertine renouncing his rakishness, "a masculine trait," as characterized in the later, reform comedies. *The Works of John Dryden*, vol. 8 (Berkeley: University of California Press, 1965) 238.

3. Harold Weber, *The Restoration Rake-Hero: Transformations in Sexual Understanding in Seventeenth-Century England* (Madison: University of Wisconsin Press, 1986) 52.

4. Dale Underwood, *Etherege and the Seventeenth-Century Comedy of Manners* (New Haven and London: Yale University Press, 1957) 16. For a comprehensive description of the libertine ethos, see chapter two, "The Fertile Ground," 10–40.

5. Rom Harre, "Identity Projects," *Threatened Identities*, ed. Glynis M. Breakwell (New York: John Wiley and Sons, 1983) 38.

6. For a detailed discussion of the social dynamics that impacted the early modern conception of gender, especially masculinity, see Michael McKeon's "Historicizing Patriarchy: The Emergence of Gender Difference in England, 1660–1760" (*Eighteenth-Century Studies* 28. [1995]: 295–322), and Michael S. Kimmel's "From Lord and Master to Cuckold and Fop: Masculinity in Seventeenth-Century England" (*University of Dayton Review* 18.2. [1986–87]: 93–109).

7. R. W. Connell, *Masculinities* (Berkeley: University of California Press, 1995) 71.

8. Harre, "Identity Projects," 45.

9. Michael Ketcham's remarks on the "social self," as evident in Restoration drama, similarly describes the construction of the social identity: "In the comedies, a person is not defined in terms of place but in terms of performance: an individual projects an image of himself that becomes his social self; and he creates a stage space around himself that constitutes the setting for his performance" ("Setting and Self-Presentation in the Restoration and Early Eighteenth Century," *SEL* 23 1983) 408–09. Ketcham's use of the term "stage" or "social space" is similar to my use of the term "social processes." Both "entail conceptual and rhetorical habits which also reflect implicit concepts of the social self" (399); however, my use of the term broadens the discursive arena for the construction of identity beyond Ketcham's emphasis on what he calls "patterns of language" (400).

10. For a discussion of the social identity, see Bernard Williams's "Identity and Identities," *Identity: Essays Based on Herbert Spencer Lectures Given in the University of Oxford*, ed. Henry Harris (Oxford: Clarendon Press, 1995) 1–11.

11. Harre, "Identity Projects," 47.

12. Lawrence Stone, *The Family, Sex and Marriage in England 1500–1800* (New York: Harper Torchbooks, 1979) 329. For a discussion of middle-class sexual proclivities and attitudes toward adultery, see chapter 11, "Gentlemanly Sexual Behaviour: Pepys and Boswell" (340–81).

13. Stone, *The Family*, 171.

14. See Stephen J. Greenblatt's *Learning to Curse: Essays in Early Modern Culture* (London and New York: Routledge, 1990), especially chapter 7, "Psychoanalysis and Renaissance Culture," 131–45. Referencing drama, Greenblatt says: "The social fabrication of identity is, I have argued, particularly marked in the drama where, after all, *identity is fashioned out of public discourse*, [emphasis mine] and even soliloquies tend to take the form of rhetorical declamations" (143).

15. Angeline Goreau, "Last Night's Rambles: Restoration Literature and the War Between the Sexes," *The Sexual Dimension in Literature*, ed. Alan Bold (London: Vision and Barnes and Noble, 1982) 49–69.

16. Warren Chernaik, *Sexual Freedom in Restoration Literature* (Cambridge: Cambridge University Press, 1995) 67.

17. Connell, *Masculinities*, 77.

18. Michael S. Kimmel, "Masculinity as Homophobia," *Toward a New Psychology of Gender*, eds. Mary M. Gergen and Sara N. Davis (London and New York: Routledge, 1997) 228.

19. Quoted in William Doty's *Myths of Masculinity* (New York: Crossroads, 1993) 15.

20. Stone, *The Family*, 327.

21. Goreau points out that, though the King's libertine example did not necessarily promote promiscuity "in the population at large," it did spark imitation from the "court wits" (50).

22. Antonia Frasier, *Charles II: His Life and Times* (London: Weidenfeld and Nicolson, 1993) 230. While detailing an impressive list of major and minor mistresses, Frasier oddly downplays the King's "debauchery," which she argues did "not appear to have been very great" (169).

23. "A Satyr on Charles II," *The Complete Poems of John Wilmot, Earl of Rochester*, ed. David M. Vieth (New Haven and London: Yale University Press, 1968) 60–61. All references to Rochester's poems will be from this volume and cited in text by line.

24. Calvin Thomas, *Male Matters: Masculinity, Anxiety, and the Male Body on the Line* (Urbana and Chicago: University of Illinois Press, 1996) 34.

25. The term "phallus" is used in the context of what Eugene Monick explains as "chthonic phallos," which is absorbed "in the realm of sexuality" as opposed to "solar phallos," which moves toward the spiritual realm. All references to Monick will utilize his spelling of "phallos." For a discussion of the chthonic and solar "phallos," see Monick's *Phallos: Sacred Images of the Masculine* (Toronto: Inner City Books, 1987) 57–60.

26. Monick, *Phallos,* 17.

27. All references to the letters between Buckhurst and Etherege are from *The Poems of George Etherege*, ed. James Thorpe (Princeton: Princeton University Press, 1963) 35–45. Subsequent references will be cited in text by page number and line.

28. It is beyond the scope of this chapter to fully discuss the psychological anxiety associated with the libertine's reduction of the feminine-self to a sexual organ. However, Warren Chernaik's reading of Rochester's "Signior Dildo" adequately sums up a significant portion of the libertine's conception of human sexuality. Rochester understands that men are "subject to physiological limits in their sexual performance, and women, whose unbridled appetites and capacity for multiple orgasms are treated here with a degree of fear and envy" (73). What is significant to the libertine's "identity project" is the fear; fear that his sexual capacity will be perceived as limited.

29. See Mark Breitenberg's *Anxious Masculinity in Early Modern England* (Cambridge: Cambridge University Press, 1996): "Those individuals whose identities are formed by the assumption of their own privilege must also have incorporated varying degrees of anxiety about the preservation or potential loss of that privilege" (3).

30. Aphra Behn, "The Disappointment," *The Works of Aphra Behn*, ed. Montague Summer, vol. 6 (London: William Heinemann, 1915) 178–82.

31. All references to Thomas Shadwell's *The Libertine* are from *The Complete Works of Thomas Shadwell*, ed. Montague Summers, vol. 3 (London: The Fortune Press, 1927) 7–93. Subsequent references will be cited by act and page numbers.

32. All references to Nathaniel Lee's *The Princess of Cleves* are from *Four Restoration Marriage Plays*, eds. Michael Cordner and Ronald Clayton (Oxford: Oxford University Press, 1995) 89–173.

33. The term "Pleasing Rape" is taken from Dryden's *Absalom and Achitophel* (1681): "Doubt not, but when he most affects the Frown/Commit a pleasing Rape upon the Crown" (473–74). For a detailed discussion of this idea as it pertains to libertinism, see Duane Coltharp's "'Pleasing Rape': The Politics of Libertinism in *The Conquest of Granada*," *Restoration: Studies in Literary Culture, 1660–1700* 21.1 (1997): 15–31.

34. Monick, *Phallos*, 94.

35. "Against Constancy," 82.

36. Goreau, "Last Night's Rambles," 53.

37. Susan Shapiro, "'Yon Plumed Dandebrat': Male 'Effeminacy' In English Satire and Criticism," *Review of English Studies* 39 (1988): 400.

38. Shapiro, "'Yon Plumed Dandebrat,'" 402.

39. All references to William Wycherley's *The Country Wife* are from *The Plays of William Wycherley*, ed. Peter Holland (Cambridge: Cambridge University Press, 1981) 227–341. Subsequent quotes from Wycherley will also be from this volume.

40. In addition to Shapiro, Thomas McGeary's "Warbling Eunuchs: Opera, Gender, and Sexuality on the London Stage, 1705–1742" (*Restoration and 18th Century Theater Research* 7 [1992]: 1–22), and Laurence Senelick's "Mollies or Men of Mode: Sodomy and the Eighteenth-Century London Stage" (*Journal of the History of Sexuality* 1 [1990]: 36–67), make similar connections between an overly fervent pursuit of sex and charges of effeminacy.

41. Senelick, "Mollies," 44.

42. For a description of the variety of fops who populated the Restoration stage, see Robert Heilman's "Some Fops and Versions of Foppery" (*English Literary History* 49 [1982]: 363–95). See also Andrew P. Williams, *The Restoration Fop: Gender Boundaries and Comic Characterization in Later Seventeenth-Century Drama* (New York: The Edwin Mellen Press, 1995) 89–164.

43. Edward Ravenscroft, "Epilogue to *The Town Fop: or, Sir Timothy Tawdrey*" by Aphra Behn, *The Works of Aphra Behn*, ed. Montague Summers, vol. 3 (London: William Heinemann, 1915) 94.

44. From Shadwell's *The Virtuoso* (1676), referring to Longvil and Bruce.

45. From Wycherley's *Love in a Wood* (1671), referring to Ranger, Vincent, and Valentine.

46. James Howard, *The English Mounsieur* (London, 1663).

47. For a comprehensive examination of the role of wit on the Restoration stage, see Harold Brooks's "Principal Conflicts in the Restoration Comedy of Manners: The Battle of Sex, and Truewits v. Witwoulds and Lackwits" (*Durham University Journal* 80 [1988]: 201–12), and Thomas H. Fujimura's *The Restoration Comedy of Wit* (Princeton: Princeton University Press, 1952).

48. All references to George Etherege's *The Man of Mode: or, Sir Fopling Flutter* are from *The Plays of George Etherege*, ed. Michael Cordner (Cambridge: Cambridge University Press, 1982) 209–333.

49. Underwood, *Etherege*, 73.

50. Dorimant's frustration echoes the complaint of Rochester in "A Ramble in St. James's Park." After seeing the "proud" Corinna accompanied by three effeminate fops, Rochester exclaims, "Gods! That a thing admired by me/ should fall to so much infamy" (89–90). However, if Corinna would have chosen a more masculine figure to fulfill her carnal desires, "Some stiff-pricked clown or well-hung parson" (92), Rochester's masculine pride would not have been offended: "I the proceedings should have praised" (95).

51. Lisa Berglund, "The Language of the Libertines: Subversive Morality in *The Man of Mode*," *SEL* 30 (1990): 375.

52. *The Works of John Dryden*, vol. 8, 238.

53. Cordner and Clayton, "Introduction" to *Four Restoration Marriage Plays*, xxiii–xxviii.

54. Jeremy Collier, *A Short View of the Profaneness of the English Stage, together With the Sense of Antiquity upon this Argument* (London, 1698) 143.

55. David M. Weed, "Sexual Positions: Men of Pleasure, Economy, and Dignity in Boswell's *London Journal*," *Eighteenth-Century Studies* 31 (1997–98): 217.

Displacing Masculinity: Edward Kynaston and the Politics of Effeminacy

Thomas A. King

RESIDUAL PEDERASTY

In legal, philosophical, and popular representations, the privacy of the modern male subject positions him as the originator of his speech and bodily acts, such that the masculine-self ostensibly possesses a coherence and continuity prior to and uninterrupted by a man's entrance into any specific social space or interaction. By contrast, the official and popular representations of early modern England described male identity as a function of the place(s) the body passed through and occupied. Men's public selfhood had been conceived and practiced through spectacular and discontinuous relations to social spaces, patterned on the courtly body's power to use up, mark, and extend itself across space, producing what French sociologist Michel de Certeau called "place" or the "proper."[1] Occupying distinct social spaces, men positioned themselves more or less closely to the sovereign body, the primary place and the center around which power relations were exercised. The concretion of sovereign power in the body of the monarch and the centralization of aristocracy at court under the Tudors and Stuarts had been effected by making displays of effeminacy, patronage, and what I will describe as "residual pederasty," overlapping exercises of power, setting up positions of domination and submission, and inscribing differences of status among men through mimetic patterns (displays) of sexual entitlement and subordination. Before the emergence of a modern discourse of sex and gender, as Leonard Tennenhouse has also noted, patronage marked the early modern desire for proximity to the sovereign center: "The higher the place, the greater the desire invested in the body that occupies it."[2] A consideration of these spatial practices, these occupations of places close to the spectacular body, is requisite to an analysis of the politics of effeminacy in seventeenth-century London. Having discussed the link between effeminacy and residual pederasty in the early seventeenth century, I will consider the boy actor Edward Kynaston's role in the restoration of pederastic relations during the Restoration.

Understanding the historical shifts in the meaning of "effeminate" has proved problematic for those historians who have attempted to make the term describe a species of person (a subjectivity, more or less related to the modern homosexual male). By focussing on the social spaces within which men's practices of selfhood occurred, I mean to complicate the familiar explanation of changes in the idea of "effeminacy" from a description of the "primarily heterosexual men" in the Renaissance who were overly interested in women, domestic pleasures, and consumption, to the "feminine" self-display of the mid- to late-seventeenth-century "asexual" fops, and, finally, the "feminine identification" of the ostensibly self-conscious "homosexual" men who appeared in the early eighteenth century (the "mollies"). This account anachronistically locates "effeminacy" as describing two or more sexual subjectivities and fails to explain the switch from one sexual type to the next. It also anachronistically describes premodern sexual practices as engaging gendered desires rather than as relations of power establishing lines of status.

Indeed, social changes in categories of maleness across the seventeenth and eighteenth centuries take the form of a chiasmus: The behaviors characterizing "effeminacy" became "privacy," while the spectacularity or publicness of the aristocratic body became "effeminacy" and "queerness." Whereas scholars who read backward from nineteenth-century social formations to the early modern period have described eighteenth-century society as divided between "public men" and "private women," readers of late sixteenth- and early seventeenth-century literature will recognize that the category of the "private man" was, in fact, a new development characteristic of the long eighteenth century. Through the Stuart reigns of the seventeenth century, men's occupation of the home space and their proximity to women was considered "effeminacy." Why should practices considered to indicate a man's lack of suitability for public leadership, indeed a loss of rationality, become the vehicles of the new legitimacy of men in the long eighteenth century? I offer that changes in the meaning of effeminacy follow from a wider remapping of social and body space, which enabled the rejection of traditional patterns of social subjection and the emergence of a public interest in men's privacy. The task of the long eighteenth century was to remap social space so that men's occupation of the home space marked the new legitimacy of their public leadership *qua* men. "Effeminacy" described, through the seventeenth century, not a falsely gendered or sexual subjectivity, but a misoccupation of social space by men whose bodies were cynosures or "gazes," what philosopher Jürgen Habermas has described as the "*publicness* (or *publicity*) *of representation*" borne by the noble body.[3] While the problem of spatial misoccupation remained the constant reference of the category "effeminacy," the remapping of social space in terms of masculine privacy required a shift in the account of those subjects who could be said to be misoccupying certain social spaces.

In this area Habermas's *Structural Transformation of the Bourgeois Public Sphere* has made an important intervention by demonstrating that the *collective* category of "public men," as it emerged in the eighteenth century, marked a historical *discontinuity* from the "public representativeness" of *particular* men (aristocrats) in earlier, traditional society. The public legitimacy of men *qua* men in the eighteenth century was represented as founded on their "privacy," an "audience-oriented" subjectivity originating in the intimate sphere of the conjugal family.[4] The "public man," since the eighteenth century, has been a man working through "the public sphere" to advance men's mutual and collective interest in "privacy." This important analysis begs the question, however, of how men's "privacy" and occupation of the home space became a legitimate sign of their authority. Literary representations of effeminacy and pederasty can help us defamiliarize and therefore historicize this emergence of a "privacy," which was elided with men's interests, represented as originating in the conjugal domain, and naturalized through institutional practices establishing the hegemony of heteronormative gender positions and desires. While the naturalization of men's privacy as heteronormative occurred most markedly in the latter half of the eighteenth century, "privacy" emerged as a form of *political resistance* in the seventeenth century. "Privacy" was a vehicle of men's resistance to traditional social patterns of hierarchy, deference, and subordination. In these terms, "effeminacy," which had been understood as proximity to women's bodies, became "privacy," and the negative implications of the category were applied to those men excluded from the new category of privacy—residually "public" men whose identities were dislocated from the conjugal sphere of domestic relations, whether as aristocratic libertines, Frenchified fops, or sodomitical "mollies." "Effeminacy" thus provided both the terms for denigrating the public representativeness of the courtly aristocracy in the seventeenth century, and material for appropriation and reinvention by those men who resisted the category of "privacy" from above and below. I want now to look at this reversal in more detail.

It is well known that in the English Renaissance a man was considered "effeminate" if he attended too much to women or boys, ease, luxury, and the pleasures of linguistic play or the body. The early modern effeminate desired to be with women and catamites (beautiful boys, often prostitutes); he was associated with domestic comforts and unregulated consumption rather than the austerities of military heroism or the corporeal regimens producing manly virtue.[5] Effeminacy represented, in fact, the present and the future of the aristocratic male; already in Castiglione's *Book of the Courtier*[6] (c.1516; trans. Sir Thomas Hoby, 1561), the male *homosocial* model of the soldier-prince was impossible. The ideal courtier embarked on a new heroic task of appropriating behaviors once thought soft, luxurious, and nonuseful—singing, dancing, painting, trading witticisms, and composing love letters—and practicing them within a *heterosocial* space, producing a courtly body marked by an aesthetic difference, his accomplishments only a technology for displaying *sprezzatura*. This courtly citation of effeminacy, filling the category with new meanings, was a performance practice through which a new courtly elite displayed the difference of their (male *and* female) bodies at the very moment when the legitimacy of a blood difference was being undermined.

As late as John Milton's *Samson Agonistes* (1671), effeminacy was a necessary corollary, for men, of domesticity and too much marital love. Betrayed by Dalila, shorn and blinded, Samson laments:

> To what can I be useful? wherein serve
> My nation, and the work from Heaven imposed?
> But to sit idle on the household hearth,
> A burdenous drone; to visitance a gaze,
> Or pitied object [. . . .] (ll. 564–68)[7]

Improperly carried over into other spaces (the battlefield or throne—as in the plays of Christopher Marlowe), effeminacy invaded aristocratic masculinity and threatened its exercise. These manly or effeminate spaces were both "public"; the man/public, woman/private dichotomy is not helpful here: Effeminate space was not private space. In sum, it was neither women nor men, neither the man given to women nor the man given to boys, who were essentially effeminate, but social spaces and the acts proper to those spaces. This understanding of effeminacy as an exercise of selfhood lacking public utility provided the basis for the seventeenth-century critique of the courtly aristocracy. The dependence of sovereign and court power on spectacularity, and the conspicuous circulation and consumption of commodities and labor became "effeminate" against the development of the utilitarian, rationalist, and critical looks enabling the explosion of technological and bureaucratic power.

On the eve of war, Charles I and his court deployed effeminacy as the symbol of their continued legitimacy. Dancing as Philogenes, the Lover of his People, in the late masque *Salmacida Spolia*[8] (Sir William Davenant and Inigo Jones, 21 January 1640), Charles was represented as a divinely appointed epitome of wisdom, mercy, and patience, which he exercised against popular unrest and aristocratic opposition. The published libretto further represented Charles's power over civil unruliness through an elaborate allusion to the softening powers of the waters of Salmacis, site of the mythological effemination of Hermaphroditus. Classical sources had explained the powers of the waters in diverging ways: Through Ovid's story of Hermaphroditus's curse or Vitruvius's account, in *De Architectura*, of barbarian tribes whose attacks on the Greeks were ended when, drinking of the waters of the fountain of Salmacis, in Jones's translation, "[from] fierce and cruel natures [they] were reduced of their own accord to the sweetness of the Grecian customs" (*Salmacida Spolia*, lines 90–92, page 730).[9] Corresponding to the masque's conventional movement from disorder to order, the latter variant had an obvious appeal. Jones and Davenant's published libretto therefore assigned the power of the waters of Salmacis to Charles I himself: Softening the rough spirit of the age, Charles's legitimacy was his ability to *effeminate* his male subjects and, one version of the story recalling the other, to put them in the place of the boy beloved, Hermaphroditus. Reenacting their submission through their entries and revels, the courtiers performed themselves as the constituent signs of sovereign presence. From the perspective of place, therefore, effeminacy in the seventeenth century cannot be considered separately from another courtly strategy, which I have described as "residual pederasty."

Pederasty entailed the eroticization of patterns of dominance and submission between men, marking positions of status as continuously negotiable in a politically mobile society. Sexual relations with boy pages, servants, apprentices, students, and other social or political inferiors—a status group in which women were included to the extent that their caste did not override their absorption within gender difference—were constitutive of these performative exchanges of submission and empowerment. So, too, were the speech acts that located speaking bodies in proximity to spectacular bodies: compliment, courtesy, and dedication, and also the citational procedures in which one man established his legitimacy by imitating (occupying and being occupied by in turn) the authority of an other (man). Pederastic desire, invested in spectacular bodies occupying places of power and enacted through embodied exchanges among those places, incorporated men, women, and boys into the nodes of its exchanges; it operated internationally (thereby opening up spaces of aristocratic resistance to national publics). Its multiple tactics cannot therefore be restructured (retrospectively) in terms of a single opposition (gender, class, race, nation, sexual orientation); rather, these oppositions were produced by the late seventeenth century as the procedures through which pederastic internationalism would be overthrown. Pederasty was a vehicle of social movement rather than a reflection of personal identity; the place of desire did not express the subjectivity of the embodied agent occupying it. I use the term "pederasty" to signal the eroticization of early modern *subjection,* and thus its difference from a modern economy of heterosexual, homosexual, and bisexual *subjectivities.*[10]

It is frequently noted that the seventeenth-century "bisexual libertine" appeared with his mistress on one arm and his catamite on the other. The term "bisexuality" describes a subjectivity directed erotically toward two objects; it cannot account for pederasty as a performative exchange productive of a social authority or manliness that was not yet modern masculinity, where the latter may be understood as an a priori, a given point of privilege. This was a manliness that by definition could never be finally achieved, but was domain—and context—specific. No man was "phallocized" in essence and consistently with other men; masculine entitlement was always tenuous, limited to certain spaces and times; and what was superordination in one domain was subordination in another. We have neither sufficiently accounted for the normalizing function of pederasty as a means to power nor pondered the problem of its disappearance.[11] I call the pattern of super- and subordination in seventeenth- and early eighteenth-century England "*residual* pederasty" to denote its tactical deployment as a form of counter-resistance to the emergent and oppositional privacy of the men making up the, so-called, liberal public sphere.

By the late seventeenth century, effeminacy described, not an excess of pleasures, but a failure of pleasure, indicating a substantial relocation of the public pursuit of pleasure. The capacity for pleasurable relations with women—once the touchstone of effeminacy—had become the gold standard of "feeling" by the eighteenth century, the foundation of the political rights of private men. Against this, the Restoration libertines could pose, poetically if not practically, as either promiscuous or impotent, both stances readable as refusals of companionate sexuality. In "The Imperfect Enjoyment," John Wilmot, Earl of Rochester, remembered his prowess with common women and with boys:

> Stiffly resolved, 'twould carelessly invade
> Woman or man, nor ought its fury stayed,
> Where'er it pierced, a cunt it found, or made. (41–43)[12]

For Rochester, penetration established asymmetries of power, but intercourse with a woman who expected him to "pay a debt to pleasure too"—who expected reciprocity—led to premature ejaculation and impotency: "But when great Love the onset does command, / Base recreant to thy prince, thou darest not stand" (23, 60–61). We should not, as scholars are wont to do, take these enunciations as confessions of failed authority, indicating "a crisis in masculinity" and a "feminization" of society in the late seventeenth and eighteenth centuries. As redeployments of prior acts of speaking, the enunciation situates the sign in a new field of interaction (power relations). If effeminacy registers failed pleasure, the enunciation of the sign of failure is not (cannot be) an indication of actual failure. Rather, impotency and effeminacy become modes of competing for the social definition of pleasure. To the extent that the phallus organizes the right to enunciation, the linguistic occupation of failure is a stylized but powerful claim to phallic mastery. Here this enunciation organizes a resistance to the privilege increasingly granted in the seventeenth century to companionate, cross-sex relations to organize the field of political legitimacy.

From the opposing perspective, however, effeminacy described a man's failure to derive his public utility from a particular mode of relating to women and to privatized society. The fop, like the eighteenth-century "fribble" (a feeble or incapacitated man) and *petit-maître* (little master), disconnected consumption from a nationalist economy figuring men's privacy around the household and their companionate relations with women and children. By appropriating consumption as a spectacle of their difference from the social practices organizing privacy, these figures represented real resistances to the hegemonic public sphere even as it was emerging. In doing so these literary figures marked, in the text, a challenge to the authority of that public sphere whose emergence, as representative of private interests, granted legitimacy to the text, replacing (if gradually) the necessity of aristocratic patronage. Representing the limits of "the marriage plot"—in the texts they typically refuse to make (hetero)sexual consummation or domestic companionship the endpoint of their relations with women—the fops, fribbles, and little masters must either good naturedly acquiesce to their exclusion from private society or be violently denied the place of public representability they attempt to claim. As the failure/refusal of reciprocal sexual relations with women, "effeminacy" was simultaneously the failure/refusal of men to establish a proprietary relation to the domestic space women (and effeminate men) occupied. Effeminacy was the limit case of domestic and erotic egalitarianism.

Within the regime of courtly pederasty, the seventeenth-century boy players were neither male nor female, but spaces mimetically stamped with content, made usable to the representational authority of aristocracy. To understand the transvestism of the seventeenth-century boy actor simply in terms of modern, binary gender roles is to ignore that rank and nationality, as well as gender, were all part of the play of his corporeal and gestural surfaces. Not only did the boy actor wear the clothes of the opposite sex, he generally wore the clothes of the upper ranks, perhaps in the style of the foreign courts that English courtiers emulated. At any given moment in a performance, any or all of these surfaces could be foregrounded as vehicles of meaning. Leonard Tennenhouse has argued provocatively in a significant critique of depth readings of the body that "some principle other than gender organized the social body image appearing on the Renaissance stage."[13] In his article "Simulating History: A Cockfight for Our Times," Tennenhouse attempted to "reconstruct an earlier moment in the history of the theatre where meaning seems to have resided in surface rather than depth" (139). While I would not suggest that gender was not one of the organizational principles of the boy actor convention, I would agree that the rhetorical signs of gender were one part of a stage image in which, as Tennenhouse pointed out, aristocratic patronage "was embossed" on the surfaces of the actors' bodies through the livery they wore and the coronation and holiday suits they acquired (146). This practice continued through the Restoration. We know, for instance, that Thomas Betterton wore Charles II's coronation suit in a revival of William Davenant's *Love and Honour* (1649),[14] and the Duchess of York made a present of her wedding suit to Elizabeth Barry.[15]

I want to locate the Restoration boy actor Edward Kynaston's transvestism as a displacement of the gendered landscape of the incipient public sphere. Despite (or precisely because of) the emergence of what Katharine Eisaman Maus has called "a model of sexual relations dependent upon polarity rather than upon hierarchy,"[16] Kynaston's appearances in the older repertory revived at the Restoration marked, not his own gendered subjectivity, but the elite status of those men and women attempting, in the few years following the Restoration, to reinstate the authority of the courtier class over and against the leveling, nation-building category of gender.

KYNASTON IN THE RING

In a word, *Kynaston*, at that time was so beautiful a Youth, that the Ladies of Quality prided themselves in taking him with them in their Coaches, to *Hyde-Park*, in his Theatrical Habit, after the Play; . . . Of this Truth, I had the Curiosity to enquire, and had it confirm'd from his own Mouth, in his advanc'd Age. . . .

—Colley Cibber[17]

Until the appearance of Elizabeth Howe's *The First English Actresses*, Cibber's anecdote had gone unremarked except as an amusing note. Howe's explanation is little better: "Kynaston had become a theatrical freak."[18] In describing residual stage transvestism in the Restoration as "a curiosity," Howe has reified the very "realistic" account of gender difference, which was only establishing its hegemony during this period. To suggest that female courtiers displayed Kynaston in the Ring at Hyde Park as a kind of rarity or monstrous spectacle is to suggest that they themselves identified fully with the category of gender. I want to argue instead that Cibber's anecdote suggests that at least some women of quality were able to appropriate Kynaston's performativity as an indication of their own difference from the leveling category of gender. Elite women's appropriation of Kynaston marks not his "freakishness," but the revival of a residual display of status organized around the body of the male youth.

As in the theatres, conspicuous display was the *sine qua non* of Hyde Park. There, in a special "Ring," fashionable Londoners spent spring Sundays circling in their coaches. Elite women in particular seem to have taken advantage of the opportunities the Ring provided for making spectacles of themselves. For example, the bourgeois and Puritan Pepys made quite a few trips to Hyde Park for the sole purpose of catching a glimpse of the idiosyncratic Margaret Cavendish, Duchess of Newcastle:

> That which we and almost all went for, was to see my Lady Newcastle; which we could not, she being fallowed and crowded upon by coaches all the way she went, that nobody could come near her; only, I could see she was in a large black coach, adorned with silver instead of gold, and so with the curtains and everything black and white, and herself in her cap. (1 May 1667) [19]

Cavendish's spectacularity, her skillful command of the field of vision, stated her difference from the gendered performativity of men and women in the hegemonic public sphere; Pepys's writing, by contrast, enjoys the primacy of his looking eye. Meanwhile, the women at court had been appearing in Hyde Park in masculine riding habits, a fashion that had been set by the Queen. Like the Puritan Busy, Pepys complained:

> Walking here in the galleries [at Whitehall], I find the Ladies of Honour dressed in their riding garbs, with coats and doublets with deep skirts, just for all the world like men, and buttoned their doublets up the breast, with perriwigs and with hats; so that, only for a long petticoat dragging under their men's coats nobody could take them for women in any point whatever—which was an odde sight, and a sight did not please me. (12 June 1666) [20]

It seems beside the point to ask whether these women were transgressing gender boundaries; the very question relocates them within that discourse of incommensurate and complementary gender underlying the mode of performativity of the public sphere, that equalization of all men over and against all women.

Recuperating the new gendered account of the spectacle, an account that linked spectacularity and femininity to a residual display of courtly difference, aristocratic women positioned themselves as the symbolic center of a consolidated courtly identity. Women's conspicuous occupation of spectacularity could be a reassertion of the privilege of rank, the mark of their difference from the domesticated femininity, which was increasingly providing a central symbol of privacy and of opposition to courtly alliance.

How did Kynaston's presence contribute to this? Rather than noting a similitude between the kinds of characters Kynaston played and the women who took him to Hyde Park, or suggesting that these women approved of his characterizations, I suggest that what they found useful in the boy actor was his capacity to register opposition to the gendered public sphere, and to its leveling of status. The joint circulation of Kynaston and elite women in the Ring in Hyde Park was another in a long line of contested couplings of the unruly woman and the effeminate man, that hermaphroditical pair who displayed their difference from a *gendered* social order, where "gender" was increasingly understood as a natural category crossing and dissolving status difference.[21] As in King James's edicts against masculine city-wives, the pamphlets *Hic-Mulier* (1620) and *Haec Vir* (1620), or Jonson's "amphibious" couple Mistress and Tom Otter (*Epicoene* [1609?]), this "gender disorder" could be resisted from both directions, claimed as the exclusive property of the court or made the vehicle of criticism of the court's illegitimacy. So Anthony Wood denounced the reappearance of the hermaphroditical couple in 1665:

> A strange effeminate age when men strive to imitate women in their apparrell, viz. long periwigs, patches in their faces, painting, short wide breeches like petticotes, muffs, and their clothes highly scented, bedecked with ribbons of all colours. . . . On the other side, women would strive to be like men, viz., when they rode on horseback or in coaches weare plush caps like monteros, either full of ribbons or feathers, long periwigs which men use to weare, and riding coats of a red colour all bedaubed with lace which they call vests.[22]

At the level of text, it may be difficult to distinguish Wood from the anonymous writer of the *Hic-Mulier / Haec Vir* pamphlets. But despite the continuity of the rhetoric, each appearance of the hermaphroditical couple has its own meanings, meanings derived from the specificity of the performance within the spatial domain its articulates, the previous performance it negotiates or resists, and the new possibilities for or limits on performance it generates. These women could utilize the boy actor's transformation of gender into spectacle to suggest that they themselves were more like men of their rank than they were like women of other ranks. Their similitude with aristocratic men was figured in their conspicuous patronage of a player.

Theirs was not an isolated example of aristocratic women's participation in residual pederasty. Much earlier, Jonson had poked fun at it, in a play that would provide another of Kynaston's star turns at the Restoration. At the very start of

Epicoene,[23] Clerimont has asked his page boy to convey his affections to his mistress, and the boy has resisted because it will get him only "a perfect deal of ill-will" at her mansion:

> *Boy*: . . . I am the welcom'st thing under a man that comes there.
> *Cler.*: I think, and above a man too, if the truth were rack'd out of you.
> *Boy*: No, faith, I'll confess before, sir. The gentlewomen play with me and throw me o' the bed, and carry me in to my lady, and she kisses me with her oil'd face and puts a peruke o' my head and asks me an' I will wear her gown, and I say, "No." And then she hits me a blow o' the ear and calls me innocent and lets me go.
> *Cler.*: No marvel if the door be kept shut against your master, when the entrance is so easy to you— . . . . (1.1.8–19)

Epicoene sets out, I think, to trap certain segments of its audience (citizens, puritans, the upwardly mobile) in their satisfaction in a boy player's successful performance of normative "city" femininity. But from the first lines of the play, the complex sign "*boy*" is foregrounded, over and against one boy page / boy player's imitation of this femininity, as the locus of pleasure for the *privileged*: page, singer, bawd, and as Truewit implies, reading the boy as one of several overdetermined signs of gentlemanly luxury, Clerimont's ingle (1.1.24). The boy's pederastic relations with his own master and other men were expected within aristocratic male homosocialism; the humor here was the boy's own witty grasp of his role in the pederastic economy. The boy is "under a man" in years, height, and authority; but as Clerimont complains, the page is nevertheless "above a man" in that his mistress prefers the boy to him and allows him access that is denied Clerimont. In other words, the boy is an overdetermined sign of gentlewomanly luxury as well. (Indeed men's struggle to gain access to space controlled by powerful women is a central motif in this and other Jonson plays.) Against these more denotative meanings of the dialogue, the sexual connotations shock only from a modern, post-pederastic perspective: The boy is positioned under the man sexually and, what was speakable then if not now, confesses to being above him in the act of sex as well. The sexual jokes fill out the seductive power of the player-boy, trapping the citizen factions of the audience in their own reinscription of aristocratic erotics and recuperating the play's field of possible meanings to the traditional authorities of pederasty.

Within this strategy the play's concern with two crises in adult male authority become clear: The boy has access to spaces that the adult male does not, and cross-dressing the boy fuels the *women's* eroticism. (That this play was written to be performed by the then-popular Children of the Queen's Revels, an all-boy cast, both allowed Jonson to tease out this anxiety and to contain it within a pederastic spectacle of patronage and apprenticeship.) The women's cross-dressing and making a spectacle of the boy for their own pleasure "shuts the door" on the "master's" entrance into their domain. Lisa Jardine misses this point when, reading these lines outside of the context of the play as a whole, she argues that the noble women's crossdressing of the boy "in an idle moment" is meant to "draw attention to his availability as an object of *male* erotic attention."[24] [I suspect that Jardine misconstrues this action as "idle" in order to avoid the suspicion that these women, too, like Ovid's Salmacis, might make the boy a "potentially rapeable" object of erotic attention. Her interpellated "idle" frees women of direct participation in pederasty and allows Jardine to conflate premodern pederasty with modern male homosexuality.] In fact, we hear about noble women's desire for boys again: Among the perils of marriage with which Truewit will haunt Morose in the second act is the prospect that his wife will not care how she wastes his estate, "so [long as] she may kiss a page or a smooth chin that has the despair of a beard" (2.2.107–08). Well after women actors had replaced boy players, the epilogue to Nathaniel Lee's *The Rival Queens* (1677) still imagined that women would prefer male youths to their adult male suitors as erotic objects. Threatening to return to using boy players if elite men continued to recruit women actors as their mistresses, the Epilogue warned:

> If once they come, they'l quickly spoil your sport:
> There's not one Lady will receive your Court:
> But for the Youth in Petticoats run wild,
> With oh the archest Wagg, the sweetest Child.[25]

Like the page boy in Jonson's *Epicoene*, bandied between Clerimont and his mistress, object of erotic play with both, Kynaston's movements among social spaces marked the trajectory of a sex-gender system different from that upon which the emergent public sphere rested. The court ladies' patronage of Kynaston was a conspicuous use of the spectacle of patronage to mark their difference from a discourse of femininity that was supposed to cross all classes and put all women below all men.

DISPOSSESSING THE SPECTATOR

Enabling the formulation of the hegemonic public sphere and its ethic of self-identity, post-Cartesian theories of vision identified the place in which we stand as spectators as exclusively our own, such that seeing, in a sense, *makes* us. In possessing our look, we possess the body-space from which we look and the visual field across which we map our consciousness. We possess ourselves as unique and autonomous subjects; we are vested with subjectivity. We display our membership in the public sphere by performing an equation between our visibility and an underlying truth about ourselves. We guarantee, through our self-presentations, that we are indeed as we appear to be; we are, we say, as you see. The courtly strategy of display had a completely different intention: For if neither the place in which we stand as spectators nor the visual field is our own (if, that is, it is external to us), then the identity of the "I" that is doing the seeing is contingent; an identity given to us from without, it is dependent on sovereign power and changes with the vicissitudes of that power. Conversely, our very visibility, and such external signs as our sex, rank, and occupation, were, in this model, inscribed on us externally, through sumptuary legislation and received assumptions about the use of our bodies. Seeing and the visible, in this model, are resources reserved to an external power; it is not we who make things (including ourselves) visible.

Kynaston gestures from pictorial space to space in an extant engraving from a portrait attributed to the Stuart court painter Sir Peter Lely [Fig. 1].[26] He looks "offstage" to a place that may be that from which the authority to place him originates. He generates the illusion that his meaningfulness is the property of the gaze of an (unseen, but seeing) other. Like Jonson's puppet Dionysius, pointing to the negative space on which mimetic fictions are stamped (but always from without), the subject of this engraving "points to" his capacity for deflecting the narrative a spectatorial mastery would write across his body. Unlike the absent(ed) other, the third man outside the frame of the engraving, the spectator cannot inscribe Kynaston. Simultaneously, however, the subject's own look, his manipulation of two spectatorial looks (mine and the unseen other's) revises his subjection, opening up the (fictive) space of a subjectivity.

Although Lely certainly borrowed from the vocabulary of theatrical gesture, I do not think that Kynaston's portrait documents any specific characterization. Rather, the portrait itself constitutes a performance by setting Kynaston in an immediate relationship to the spectator, making the dynamics of performance and spectatorship the subject of the portrait. The engraving of Lely's portrait that has come down to us figures an agon of spectator and performer, of critical look and mannerist gesture. The contradictory gestures of the portrait point not toward a psychological interiority, a psychic ambivalence, but toward the subject's (Kynaston's) positioning within and negotiation of two competing discourses of spectacularity. The displacement of critical spectatorship was simultaneously a displacing of the hegemonic public sphere of men and women recognizable by their privacy.

The extant engraving shows a youth with long curling hair and large heavy eyes. He gestures theatrically with raised hands and looks out of the frame of the portrait over his right shoulder. Although Kynaston was famous as a player of women's roles, he is not cross-dressed in the portrait. His long hair is not that of a woman, being common to youths and men in the period and prominent in both Lely's "Portrait of a Boy" and in his own self-portrait.[27] Second, Kynaston is shown (like Lely in his own self-portrait and Pepys in the Hayls portrait) in a man's "Indian gown," favored in portraits at this time, rather than a theatrical costume.[28] Third, as he is not explicitly shown in the costume of a female character, neither is he given an equivalently "feminine" status by being depicted as a dependent apprentice or a member of the lower classes—two ways in which it has been suggested that actors were perceived as feminine.[29] That he was portrayed by the court painter Lely testifies to his importance as a player, and, as I suggest, Lely has clearly represented him as an intimate of the court circle. Mezzotints of Lely portraits, sold in bookstores, indicate the courtly appropriation of commodification

Fig. 1. Edward Kynaston by Sir Peter Lely. 1889 engraving by R. B. Parkes, after R. Cooper's copy of Lely's original. Published in the Lowe edition of Cibber's *Apology* (facing 1: 122). Courtesy of Special Collections Department, Northwestern University Library, Evanston, Illinois.

as a means of circulating courtly iconography through the public sphere.

Finally, Kynaston is not necessarily given "feminine" gestures to perform. While Charles Gildon described the "rolling eye" given to Kynaston in Lely's portrait as "strong proof of Wantonness and Immodesty" in women,[30] and Robert Burton had associated it with the dangerous power of artifice,[31] more telling might be John Bulwer's comment, in his manual for orators, that the turning eye, when it became customary in a man, indicated an inherent state of *effeminacy*.[32] If female characterization on stage was achieved to a great extent by the boy's managing of his eyes, Bulwer's claim that the turning eye signaled male effeminacy could be used to link Kynaston's performance of female characters with the much-maligned effeminacy of the Stuart court. However, within the theatrical coding of gesture, the turning eye might signal, not gender, but deliberation, and would be clearly connected to the rhetorically controlled gestural balance of his hands. In sum, gender might not be the most interesting or productive question to ask of this engraving; Kynaston's effeminacy displays the contested authority of a spatial practice.

Still, Lely's portrait is more an act of transvestism; if not a gendered performance, then a status act. Lely gave Kynaston his trademark eye—the sleepy, wanton eye popularized in the portraits of Charles's elite mistress, the Duchess of Cleveland. It appears in Eleanor Gwyn's portraits as well and, not being restricted to women, in the self-portrait of Lely and the portrait of a boy referred to earlier. Richard Wendorf has noted that a contemporary recorded a rival painter's complaint that Lely:

> . . . put something of Clevelands face as her Languishing Eyes into every one Picture, so that all his pictures had an Air one of another, all eyes were Sleepy alike. So that Mr. Walker [the] Painter swore Lilly's Pictures was all Brothers & Sisters.[33]

Similarly, Oliver Millar has quoted a slightly later critique of the "languishing Air, long Eyes, and a Drowzy Sweetness peculiar to [Lely], for which they reckon him a *Mannerist*."[34] This eye is usually discussed—both by contemporaries of Lely and by twentieth-century critics—as a flaw in Lely's technique because it destroys the verisimilitude (identities) of the portraits; the sitters do not possess a unique way of seeing but are all given the same eye.[35] Inverting this criticism, I suggest that this eye signaled a particular courtly attitude of that time. As contemporary descriptions of these eyes as "sleepy," "sweet," and "languishing" suggest, Lely's eyes may have signaled a libertine reaction against the introspection and privacy promoted by Puritan ideology. There is no fervent self-inspection going on in Lely's portraits; there is no desire to fix one's self into a posture betraying privacy or self-possession. The choice of the word "sweet" to describe these eyes is particularly interesting because it was a word specifically chosen by Cavaliers to describe the ideology of the pre-civil war aristocracy. Resistance to anticourtly ideology is signaled in Kynaston's (and Gwyn's) portraits by a cross-status transvestism of the eyes. Not only do the sleepy, rolling eyes and the rhetorical

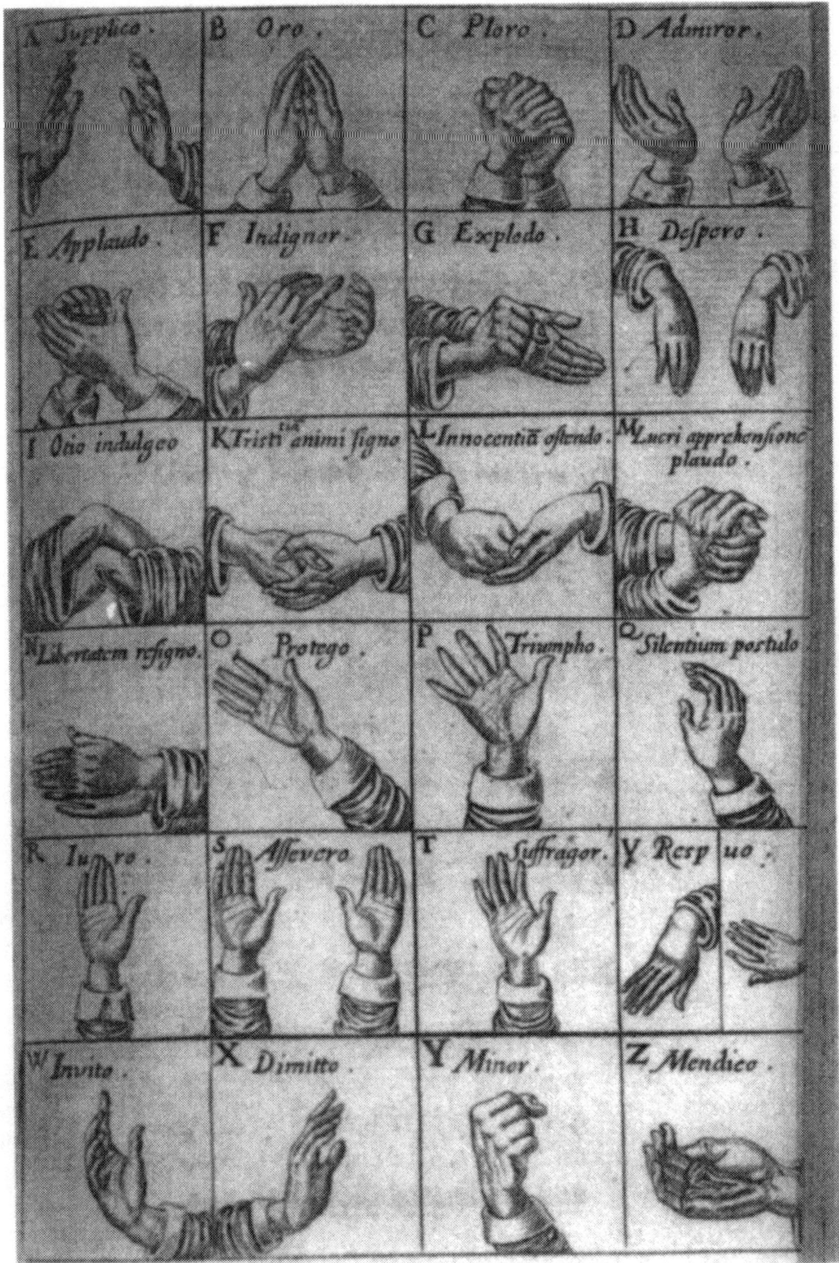

Fig. 2. "Alphabet of naturall expressions." John Bulwer, *Chirologia: Or, the Naturall Language of the Hand*, 1644, page 151. Courtesy of the Philip Mills Arnold Semeiology Collection, Special Collections, Washington University in St. Louis.

disputation of his hands align Kynaston with the court circle, Kynaston's portrait also shares the marked chin, full cheeks, curved eyebrows, and expansive forehead prominent in the engravings of Charles II's mistress Gwyn. Desire, even at the "heterosexual" court of Charles II, was epicene; it marked the place of preferment and not a property of person (gender, for example).

Bulwer's treatises, *Chironomia* and *Chirologia*, can help us analyze the specific gestures of Kynaston's hands. In Lely's portrait, Kynaston's right hand corresponds to Bulwer's gesture "I invite," used, as Bulwer noted, to bid others "*to come near and approach unto us*" (51) [Fig. 2, gesture "W" in the bottom row]. The prominence of the right hand in the portrait first draws our eye as spectators; we are invited to draw near to Kynaston. But almost in the same moment, we notice the turn of Kynaston's eyes to the right. He half raises his left hand in a gesture of hesitation, perhaps based on Bulwer's gesture "I dismiss" [Fig. 2, gesture "X" in the bottom row]. More important is the raised index finger of the left hand, which, like the turn of the eye, suggests a momentary wavering on Kynaston's part, a degree of indecision. As Bulwer noted, "The top or grape of the left index gently apprehended puts the hand into a rhetorical shape for *disputation*" (200). Kynaston looks back and forth between two parties—between the spectator standing before the portrait and the implied spectator to Kynaston's right. This is in keeping with the style of portraiture during the period, constituting a narrative by including the dynamics of spectatorship within the frame of the portrait itself. This exchange of glances directed by the work itself is what Mary Ann Caws has called "The Eye in the Text," a corridor for looking built into the structure of the work, so that the work is incomplete without our look and yet unable to be completed because the look finally does not resolve itself at a fixed point, as it does in perspective proper. Caws has proposed that this technique of pointing elsewhere, to a place of intertextuality outside the frame, is characteristic of mannerism, "the reciprocal interplay between the object pointed out or designated or even created, and the finger pointing, and then the eye regarding finger and object, all this in mutual reflection."[36] The finger pointing does not point out a literal object in the scene, but like the movement of Kynaston's eyes or the gesture of the puppet Dionysius, it points at pointing.

In pointing to a place offstage or outside the text, mannerism forces the issue of spectatorship in a particularly compelling way. It makes urgent the question of whether the object or person pointed out can complete the narrative and, in doing so, stand as origin for the place of spectatorship itself. Art historian J. Douglas Stewart has argued that Lely's portraits combined "pictorial and real space"—that is, combined the space framed by the painting with the space of the spectator—through an incomplete narrative; the presence of a particular spectator was necessary to complete the story.[37] In the Lely engraving, Kynaston rejects us, the actual spectator, in favor of another whom we cannot see. The absence of this spectator provokes our response as actual spectators of the portrait: To align our look with the place of proper spectatorship, we must know the identity of this third party. To describe Kynaston's portrait as mannerist suggests that it does not fix its subject as an object of (our) knowledge. For Bulwer, however, writing in 1644, gestures should not refer themselves to other gestures in an intertextual circle, but should manifest the self openly and sincerely. Bulwer cautioned the orator: "Shun affectation; for all affectation is odious; and then others are most moved with our actions when they perceive all things to flow, as it were, out of the liquid current of nature" (244). But this pointing of the engraving to the "proper" (unseen) spectator, who possesses the image (the boy actor) and organizes its gaze, defers our spectatorship. The gaze of the engraving interpellates us into a triangularity of looks, so that we become other to, and perhaps seen ourselves by, this ideal spectator. The ambivalence of this situation is relieved by being able to read the clues of the narrative and complete it. It is here that the courtly texture/textuality of Kynaston's gestures, languishing eyes, chin, and forehead acquire reference, identifying the place of proper spectatorship as the court. But in completing the narrative, we acquiesce to the place of proper spectatorship, to the given of the referent; the place in which we stand is not our own. By contrast, it was in the interests of the public sphere to assert that the critical faculty created the place from which one looked as exclusively one's own, so that one's place as spectator, or the value of one's look, was not simply determined by one's proximity to sovereignty.

And yet, while our ability to see ourselves as identical to the place of proper spectatorship has been deferred by Kynaston's greater proximity to that place, we have not been completely displaced by these signs of privilege. Kynaston's rejection of the actual spectator in favor of the implied spectator is perhaps only temporary. As the raised index fingers indicate, it is a disputation; it is not final. Lely's portrait is poised at the very moment of transition of ownership of the visual field; Lely must at least flirt with the new dynamics of spectatorship. Kynaston may not be accessible to our look, but neither is he fully performing his submission to patronage. This is a moment of profound possibility, when any paradigm of spectatorship fails to contain the spectacle. Against this failure, Kynaston, as the performative subject of Lely's portrait, becomes present.

Should the boy actor who plays with the duality of this gaze be located within a discourse of vision specific to pederastic desire or within that other discourse underlying the articulation of immutable, but complementary, gender positions? Does the spectacle summon the eye, demanding submission, or does the eye summon the spectacle, creating knowledge? If the gestures of disputation and deferral in Lely's portrait encourage us to see the visual field as a power unmoored from any place of ownership, in circulation and therefore open to negotiation, it may nevertheless be salutary for us to let the portrait raise its questions in terms of a courtly erotics that our own visual epistemology of gender has rendered invisible. Despite, and precisely because of, their circulation downward through the marketplace in mezzotint copies, Lely's portraits were not yet given over to the new way of seeing that we take for granted. The commodification of Lely's court portraits points toward the assimilation by the court of the developing public sphere.

To discuss Kynaston's performances solely in terms of gendered acts, or even in the Platonic terms of androgyny, fails to grapple with the hermaphroditical energy with which some courtiers were occupying and excessively redeploying the very visible margin to which they had been assigned by the increasingly central but visually absent public sphere. Through representations like these, the Cavalier revival and some men's resistance to their equalization within the political nation was being formulated as an occupation—and an increasingly excessive occupation during the Frenchified, virtuosic court of Charles II—of precisely those spectacular places that had been marginalized as effeminate: the places of breeding and of privilege, of spectacle and conspicuous consumption through which the aristocracy had once legitimated its power.

Kynaston's portrait offers no completed narrative. The "answer" to the problem of the portrait is an offstage space that is not realized on stage—a space that is emphatically not that of introspection or confession. With the hegemony of an internalized look possessing authority as the origin and content of representation, this place of sovereign power gives way to that other offstage space, interiority. Kynaston "himself," and no longer the place he occupies and in which he is seen by the other man, becomes the subject of the story. When, by the late seventeenth century, it had become possible to reread Kynaston's association with the Cavalier circle, and by extension the link between sovereignty and theatricality, as indications of gender trouble and sexual suspiciousness, so then the boy actor's deferral of spectatorship could be reread as an ambiguity in his own erotic self-presentation. The textual and textural play of his pointing elsewhere was collapsed inward, so that Kynaston became visible as a self whose internal sexual economy was identical to the ambivalence of his external gestures.

During the period preceding the Glorious Revolution, several satires by enemies of George Villiers, second Duke of Buckingham, denigrated him through allegations of pederastic association with Kynaston. "On the Duke of Bucks" (1678), apparently penned by John Dryden, alleged, "And Kenastons arse knows its own Buggerer."[38] Two years later, "The Litany of the Duke of Buckingham" (1680) included the following satirical prayer for relief from Buckingham:

> From transposing nature upon our *bon gars*,
> On Kynaston acting both Venus and Mars,
> From owning twenty other men's farce,
> *Libera nos.*[39]

Buckingham is accused of taking both positions with Kynaston, an appropriation of the political rhetoric linking sovereignty and sodomy, here used against the country party.[40] (The availability of accusations of sodomy and scandalous inferences about pederasty to *both* sides of the political field should not surprise us. Court and Country, Tory and Whig: Both sides were constituted through appeals to a public sphere of privatized men. The political legitimacy of both would require a demonization of residual pederasty.) In 1935, Montague Summers decided that Kynaston "was notoriously homosexual," but in a footnote added that he "actually was of a bisexual temperament."[41] But the accuracy of either claim, and whether Buckingham even knew Kynaston, are not at issue here.[42] What is important is that the authors of these satires assumed that their audiences would associate a former boy actor with the politically obsolete system of pederasty; that the slur was directed against the country party rather than the court shows how pederasty was losing its specific meaning and being associated more generally with the political differences of "the last age" from the emerging public sphere. Unmoored from its original place in the court, sodomy became a more generalizable charge capable of floating freely across the landscape of political representations. Whereas the boy actor had been aligned with the "sweetness" of Cavalier ideology, by the last quarter of the seventeenth century his effeminacy signaled a failure of the gaze, a lack of self-knowledge, that had become the psychic property of the habitual sodomite.

NOTES

1. Michel de Certeau, *The Practice of Everyday Life*, trans. Steven Rendell (Berkeley: University of California Press, 1984) xix, 36, 117.

2. Leonard Tennenhouse, "Simulating History: A Cockfight for Our Times," *The Drama Review* 34.4 (Winter 1990): 144.

3. Jürgen Habermas, *The Structural Transformation of the Public Sphere: An Inquiry into a Category of Bourgeois Society*, trans. Thomas Burger and Frederick Lawrence (Cambridge: MIT, 1989) 7.

4. Habermas, *The Structural Transformation*, 28.

5. For a detailed discussion, see Linda Woodbridge, *Women and the English Renaissance: Literature and Nature of Womankind, 1540–1620* (Urbana and Chicago: University of Illinois Press, 1984) 159–67, 278–81, 291.

6. Baldesar Castiglione, *The Book of the Courtier*, trans. Charles S. Singleton (Garden City, N.Y.: Doubleday, 1959).

7. John Milton, *Samson Agonistes*, *The Norton Anthology of English Literature. Major Authors Edition. Revised*, gen. ed. M. H. Abrams (New York: W.W. Norton, 1968) 701–44.

8. In *Inigo Jones: The Theater of the Stuart Court*, eds. Stephen Orgel and Roy Strong (London: Sotheby Parke Bernet; Berkeley: University of California Press, 1973) 2: 728–85.

9. See also Lauren Silberman, "Mythographic Transformations of Ovid's Hermaphrodite," *The Sixteenth-Century Journal: A Journal for Renaissance and Reformation Students and Scholars* 19 (1988): 650.

10. For the distinction between subjection and subjectivity, see Francis Barker, *The Tremulous Private Body: Essays on Subjection* (London: Methuen, 1984) 31–32.

11. For other analyses that note the age-asymmetry of male-male erotic practices in the early modern period, see Lisa Jardine, *Still Harping on Daughters: Women and Drama in the Age of Shakespeare* (Totowa, N.J.: Barnes and Noble, 1983) 24; Randolph Trumbach, "The Birth of the Queen: Sodomy and the Emergence of Gender Equality in Modern Culture," *Hidden from History: Reclaiming the Gay and Lesbian Past*, eds. Martin Duberman, Martha Vicinus, and George Chauncey Jr. (New York: Meridian-Penguin, 1989) 130; and James M. Saslow, "Homosexuality in the Renaissance: Behavior, Identity, and Artistic Expression" (*Hidden from History*) 93–94. See also Trumbach, "Sodomy Transformed: Aristocratic Libertinage, Public Reputation and the Gender Revolution of the

18th Century," *Love Letters Between a Certain Late Nobleman and the Famous Mr. Wilson, Discovering the True History of the Rise and Surprising Grandeur of that Celebrated Beau* (1723), ed. Michael S. Kimmel (New York: Harrington Park, 1990) for the transition from a "libertine" model of male-male sexual relations to modern, "egalitarian" male homosexuality.

12. John Wilmot, *Lord Rochester*, ed. Paddy Lyons (London: J. M. Dent-Everyman, 1996) 56.

13. Tennenhouse, "Simulating History," 148.

14. John Downes, *Roscius Anglicanus* [1708], ed. Montague Summers (London: Fortune, 1929) 21.

15. [William Oldys?] Thomas Betterton, *The History of the English Stage, From the Restauration to the Present Time* (London, 1741) 17.

16. Katharine Eisaman Maus, "'Playhouse Flesh and Blood': Sexual Ideology and the Restoration Actress," *ELH* 46:4 (1979) 597, 612. Also, Thomas Laqueur in *Making Sex: Body and Gender from the Greeks to Freud* (Cambridge: Harvard University Press, 1990), and Stephen Greenblatt in "Fiction and Friction" (*Shakespearean Negotiations: The Circulation of Social Energy in Renaissance England*, Berkeley: University of California Press, 1988) have traced the historical discontinuity from the Galenic model of male and female sexual resemblance, in which male and female genitalia were considered reversed, and reversible, copies of each other, to one of absolute male and female anatomical difference. Nancy Armstrong suggested in *Desire and Domestic Fiction: A Political History of the Novel* (New York: Oxford University Press, 1987) that the new model of gender polarity collapsed differences of class among women:

> . . . producing a woman whose value resided chiefly in her femaleness rather than in traditional signs of status, a woman who possessed psychological depth rather than a physically attractive surface, one who, in other words, excelled in the qualities that differentiated her from the male. (20)

17. Colley Cibber, *An Apology for the Life of Mr. Colley Cibber, Written by Himself* (1740), ed. B.R.S. Fone (Ann Arbor: University of Michigan Press, 1968) 71.

18. Elizabeth Howe, *The First English Actresses: Women and Drama 1660–1700* (Cambridge: Cambridge University Press, 1992) 25.

19. Samuel Pepys, *The Diary of Samuel Pepys*, eds. Robert Latham and William Matthews, 11 vols. (Berkeley: University of California Press, 1983) 8: 196.

20. Pepys, *The Diary*, 7: 162.

21. See Woodbridge's classic study of the widespread Jacobean coupling of the male effeminate and the female virago, *Women and the English Renaissance*.

22. John Harold Wilson, *All the King's Ladies: Actresses of the Restoration* (Chicago: University of Chicago Press, 1958) 74.

23. All references to *Epicoene* by Ben Jonson are from *Epicoene: Or, The Silent Woman*, ed. L. A. Beaurline (Lincoln: University of Nebraska Press, 1966).

24. Jardine, *Still Harping*, 31.

25. Quoted in Peter Stallybrass, "Transvestism and the 'Body Beneath': Speculating on the Boy Actor," *Erotic Politics: Desire on the Renaissance Stage*, ed. Susan Zimmerman (London and New York: Routledge, 1992) 67.

26. *An Apology for the Life of Mr. Colley Cibber Written by Himself*, 1740, ed. Robert W. Lowe, 2 vols. (London: J. C. Nimmo, 1889). The extant image is a mezzotint by R. B. Parkes after R. Cooper's copy of Lely's lost original, measuring 4-3/8 by 3-1/4 inches and published in Robert W. Lowe's 1889 edition of Cibber's *Apology* (following 1: 122). The engraving under discussion is certainly the portrait of a boy actor. It is distinguishable from

other Lely portraits of boys in the rhetorical specificity of the gestures; the subject's hands are arranged not to satisfy a painterly interest in contrast and balance, as they are in Lely's pastoral portraits of boys, but to constitute conventional oratorical gestures that can be "read." The attribution to Lely, the prominent portrait painter in London during the Interregnum and Restoration and court painter from October 1661, seems correct. The subject's features and hair resemble that of Lely's famous "Portrait of a Boy." In particular, as I argue below, the subject is represented with the same "sleepy" eyes typical of Lely's portraits of the court circle, including those of Eleanor Gwyn.

27. Lely's "Portrait of a Boy" and self-portrait are reprinted by Oliver Millar, *Sir Peter Lely 1618–80* (London: National Portrait Gallery, 1978) nos. 28 and 70, pages 51 and frontispiece, respectively.

28. Dressing gowns, "Indian gowns," shifts, and classical armor were used by Lely to give his portraits a more timeless feel (Millar 18). Pepys recorded hiring an Indian gown when he sat for the famous portrait by John Hayls, now in the National Portrait Gallery (30 March 1666; 7:85). Pepys's and Kynaston's gowns are virtually identical.

29. Lisa Jardine has argued that "the dependent role of the boy player doubles for the dependency which is woman's lot, creating a sensuality which is independent of the sex of the desired figure . . ." (24). Kristina Straub, in *Sexual Suspects: Eighteenth-Century Players and Sexual Ideology* (Princeton: Princeton University Press, 1992), has noted that actors were constructed as other through their lower-class status; by the mid-eighteenth century, their otherness was increasingly described as effeminacy or sexual suspect-ness (25).

30. [Charles Gildon] *The Life of Mr. Thomas Betterton, the Late Eminent Tragedian* (London, 1710) 41.

31. Robert Burton, *The Anatomy of Melencholy, What it is, With all the kinds, causes, symptoms, prognosticks, & severall cures of it* 7th. ed. (London: 1660) 469ff.

32. John Bulwer, *Chirologia: Or, the Naturall Language of the Hand* (London: 1644) Rpt. As *Chirologia: Or, The Natural Language of the Hand; and Chironomia: Or, The Art of Manual Rhetoric*, ed. James W. Cleary (Carbondale: Southern Illinois University Press, 1974) 63.

33. Quoted in Richard Wendorf, *The Elements of Life: Biography and Portrait-Painting in Stuart and Georgian England* (Oxford: Clarendon Press, 1990) 92.

34. Millar, *Sir Peter Lely*, 26.

35. Compare Pepys's criticism that Lely's "Beauties" were "good, but not like" (21 August 1668; 9: 284).

36. Mary Ann Caws, *The Eye in the Text: Essays in Perception, Mannerist to Modern* (Princeton: Princeton University Press, 1981) 36, 50.

37. J. Douglas Stewart, "Pin-ups or Virtues? The Concept of the 'Beauties' in Late Stuart Portraiture," *English Portraits of the Seventeenth and Eighteenth Centuries: Papers Read at a Clark Library Seminar, April 14, 1973*, eds. Stewart and Herman W. Lubert (Los Angeles: William Andrews Clark Memorial Library, University of California, 1974) 10–11.

38. Quoted in Philip H. Highfill Jr., Kalman A. Burnim, and Edward A. Langhans, *A Biographical Dictionary of Actors, Actresses, Musicians, Dancers, Managers, and Other Stage Personnel in London, 1660–1800* (Carbondale: Southern Illinois University Press, 1973) 83. In *Poems on Affairs of State: Augustan Satirical Verse, 1660–1714* (New Haven and London: Yale University Press, 1965), Elias F. Mengel, Jr., gives a slightly different version of the line: "And Keniston's A- knows the B-r" (194 n.20).

39. Quoted in Mengel, *Poems on Affairs of State*, 194.

40. He is also criticized for "owning" the farce *The Rehearsal* (1670), which he co-authored with several other men. This suggests why Dryden should be bitter toward Buckingham: One of the main intentions of *The Rehearsal* was to parody Dryden in the character of Bayes.

41. Montague Summers, *The Playhouse of Pepys* (New York: Macmillan, 1935) 295, 331 n.78.

42. Terrence Sidney Johnson has suggested in an unpublished dissertation that Kynaston was a member of a group of actors "associated with certain types of sodomitic roles . . . " and "before his retirement he played several roles in which the character's desire for other men plays a significant part, including Frederick in Dryden's *Assignation*, Scipio in Lee's *Sophonisba*, Maximus in Rochester's *Valentinian*, and Marcellus in Lee's *Gloriana*" (41–42). "Representations of Male Homosexuality on the English Restoration Stage." Diss. University of California-Los Angeles, 1992.

Godly Manliness: Defoe's Good Men in Bad Times

Stephen Gregg

Why write an account of the 1665 plague in 1722? The occasion of Defoe's *A Journal of the Plague Year*, its catalyst, has been variously accounted for. Specifically in its depiction of a confused and disordered city, *A Journal* has been seen as a commentary upon the South-Sea Bubble of 1720.[1] The outbreak of plague in Marseilles in 1720 had reanimated fears that the plague would spread across Europe to engulf England. While *A Journal* can be seen to address those particular anxieties with its ostensibly factual historicism of the account, buried within the text is an admonitory and judgmental tone, which implies that Defoe's *A Journal of the Plague Year* is also a critique of moral conduct in times of calamity. Of particular interest to Defoe was how a man might act in order to rise above the chaos of the plague. In this sense, by creating exemplars of what I will term "godly manliness," Defoe's men shine out against the bad times, not only of the plague, but also of the perceived debauchery of the Restoration.

The discourses of "reformation" are instrumental in outlining godly manliness as it appears in *A Journal of the Plague Year*. Defoe himself had close ties with the culture of reform in the late seventeenth and early eighteenth centuries when the term "reformation" held a variety of connotative associations.[2] First, it connoted the type of religious self-reflection that would lead one to personal reformation; second, it carried with it the accusation that the Restoration court had abandoned the ideals of the great Protestant Reformation; and third, the term "reformation" inevitably brought to mind the efforts of the Orange court and the Societies for Reformation of Manners to foster a change in public virtue. It is within these connotative associations that I wish to place *A Journal of the Plague Year*. In this chapter I will argue that the culture of moral reformation in the 1690s—aimed especially at male behaviour—is projected against the backdrop of the plague and the Restoration period, which offered Defoe a paradigmatic moment, where, as Foucault has commented, the "image of the plague stands for all forms of confusion and disorder."[3] Against this backdrop of disorder—the "bad times" of the 1665 plague—*A Journal of the Plague Year* maps out ideals of masculinity through the disciplinary efforts of the moral reformers, efforts that inevitably involve acts of separation, categorisation, and exclusion. In Defoe's *A Journal*, godly manliness is promoted as an ideal of male behaviour subjected to a legal and moral disciplinary rhetoric articulated through the subjection of the masculine subject to the highest of authorities, God. Through the identification and exclusion of irrational and impious men, the qualities of the godly man, an unswerving religious faith, an active, almost martial, courage, and a rational world view, emerge as a new standard of masculine self-deportment.

An unswerving religious belief that one's reward is to be found, not in this life, but in the next, is a quality upheld in the godly man. It appears as a stoiclike courage in the face of perils and setbacks. Thus Hughes, in a sermon before the Societies, exhorts the zealous intervention in public vice by crying "*your reward is safe in heaven*: let the certain prospect of a future glorious recompence [*sic*] animate your attempts to reform a vicious age."[4] Such a faith in the next life is also recommended to a doubting young man in Defoe's *Due Preparations for the Plague*: "Nothing can Animate and Encourage the Mind, like a firm Resignation to the Will of God, and a comfortable Hope that it shall be well with us beyond Life: this is certainly the best preparation for the Distemper."[5] Likewise, such a secure religious foundation will be seen in the figure of Robert, the boat-man, in *A Journal of the Plague Year*.

Taking an active role in a male's spiritual reformation has a parallel with the differing levels of godliness displayed in Bunyan's *The Pilgrim's Progress* (1678).[6] Bunyan's masculine allegory Christian sets out alone from The City of Destruction in the face of ridicule from neighbours and family in search of the Celestial City. Throughout *The Pilgrim's Progress*, Christian is linked to a manhood whose foundation is an active courage. In the face of persecution and the pleasures of the world at Vanity-Fair, Evangelist exhorts Christian and Faithful to "quit your selves like men" (72). Even though warning against the vanity of proclaiming oneself a hero in battle, Christian still underlines the importance of the association of active courage and masculinity: "But for such footmen as thee and I are, let us never desire to meet with an enemy, nor vaunt as if we could do better, when we hear of others that have been foiled, nor be tickled at the thoughts of our own manhood" (107). In part two, which narrates the pilgrimage of his wife and children, Christian is the pattern for their journey, and when they come to the scene of his battle with Apollyon, Great-Heart, their male guide declares, "verily *Christian* did here play the Man, and showed himself as stout, as could, had he been here, even *Hercules* himself" (199). Notably, this paradigmatic male hero is the only classical reference in the two parts of *The Pilgrim's Progress*.

Such an active courage became idealized in the texts of the Societies for Reformation of Manners. The author of *An Account of the Societies for Reformation of Manners* declares that "you are all confessedly, by your baptismal Engagement, listed Soldiers for God's service, against the Devil's Kingdom."[7]

Matthew Henry echoes this fervent exclamation in his sermon to the Societies: "The undertaking is *bold* and *great*, and in which the Spirit of a truly *Christian Hero* appears as much as in anything."[8] The male, Christian hero is categorised by the expulsion of a passivity characterised as effeminate. Godliness and manliness go hand-in-hand in these texts because any failing in the nation's virtue is automatically associated with a failing in the nation's masculinity. Edward Stillingfleet's sermon, "Reformation of Manners the true way of Honouring God," makes this clear: "The Sins of a Nation do naturally tend to the Weakness and Dishonour of it. . . . Who can deny that Luxury and Debauchery, and all sorts of Intemperance, not only sink the Reputation of a People, but effeminates and softens them."[9] Here, effeminacy clearly poses a threat to the security and stability of the nation, which must be combated by the godly men of England.

Godly manliness also rests upon a rationality which excludes religious delusions and superstition. Again, Stillingfleet offers us a glimpse of the perceived dangers when imagination overcomes rationality. He exhorts his readers to keep a "true and setled [*sic*] Notion of God to reform our Disorders . . . and keep us from being led aside by the violent and impetuous Heats of *Imagination*" and adds, "*Reason and Understanding* is a steady and uniform Principle, and being well fixed from a due and thorough Consideration of the Nature and *will of God*, keep the Mind even and constant."[10] Religious faith in the providences of God is here linked to the workings of human reason and rationality, which were, of course, traditional gendered attributes of the male. In Dryden's fable "The Cock and the Fox" (1700), it is the world of female imagination that overthrows reason: "When monarch reason sleeps" (326), dreams are mistaken for truth, and "The nurse's legends are for truths received" (335).[11] Further, in *Paradise Lost* (1667), there is the continual suspicion that Adam's reason was undermined by Eve, voiced most succinctly by the archangel Michael:

> From Man's effeminate slackness it begins.
> Said the angel, who should better hold his place
> By wisdom, and superior gifts received.[12]

The overthrow of reason breaks the "naturalized" bond between men and masculine behavior, thus effeminizing the male. Likewise, fancy and religious superstition in *A Journal of the Plague Year* also become linked with the female sex and produce a similar destabilization of manliness.

What importance, then, does the Restoration setting of *A Journal of the Plague Year* have for the early eighteenth-century reader's understanding of manliness? Defoe's own interest in the period is evident as many of his characters inhabit the latter half of the seventeenth century. Moll Flanders's tale is dated 1683, implying a life spanning at least the Interregnum and the Restoration; *Roxana* (1724) is ostensibly set during the reign of Charles II; Captain Singleton has his years of piracy in the 1690s, a period in which Colonel Jack spends part of his youth also; Robinson Crusoe is born in 1632, is shipwrecked on his Caribbean island in 1659, and is rescued in 1687; and H. F., the narrator of *A Journal of the Plague Year*, obviously lives via the events of 1665.

My brief listing of the chronology of Defoe's fiction is, of course, naive. Approaching Defoe's fiction from a limited understanding of realism invalidates any expectations of chronological consistency. For example, Roxana is born in 1673, yet the title page refers to the person known as "Roxana" (a grown woman) as living during the reign of Charles II who died in 1685. Such inconsistencies should not be measured solely against the expectations of realism. Instead, it is more productive to examine Defoe's use of chronology against an understanding of time as emblematic. "Emblematic time" is Paul Alkon's phrase for describing a way of reading time for its symbolic significance, not its temporal realism. "To Defoe," he writes, "the past was of interest primarily for exemplary purposes. Any such exploration of the past for help in solving present problems transforms history into a variety of deliberate rhetoric."[13]

Of course, Defoe is not alone in reading the past for emblematic significance; Christian typology was a longstanding system of reading historical figures and events as post-figurations of the Bible. Indeed, the most basic form of typology was to read the Old Testament events and figures as pre-figurations of those in the New Testament. Paul Korshin stresses the importance of this "complex mode of literary figuralism"[14] in the transformation of this purely theological system of exegisis to its use in imaginative literature where both writers and readers share, what Alkon calls a "typological habit of mind."[15] Between the events of the Bible and those of the early eighteenth century, figures and events of recent history could be read and written as both postfigurations of the Bible as well as prefigurations of the present. Defoe's narratives echo this typological reading of history, containing what can be described as an idiosyncratic, double-time scheme. By reading Defoe's narratives typologically, especially *A Journal of the Plague Year*, it becomes apparent that his characters and their actions recall certain figures and events of the Bible, yet they also reverberate from their setting in the recent past of the late seventeenth century forward to Defoe's own time. This provides a narrative framework, which allows Defoe's characters to act as mediating figures connecting the "truths" of the Bible with the postreformative culture of Defoe's own historical moment. As such, the ideals of masculinity evident in *A Journal of the Plague Year* are contained within this narative reverberation. Primarily, these ideals echo those of godly manliness constructed by the culture of reform in the 1690s.

Stressing the importance of the culture of reform, D.W.R. Bahlmann comments that "a tremendous enthusiasm for a reformation of morals broke forth in the years after 1689. . . . The phrase 'reformation of manners' appeared everywhere."[16] In an apparent aside, *A Journal of the Plague Year*'s narrator, H. F. alludes to several connotations of "reformation":

> The Court removed early, (*viz.*) in the Month of *June*, and went to *Oxford*, where it pleased God to preserve them; . . . for which I cannot say, that I ever saw they shew'd any great Token of Thankfulness, and hardly any thing of Reformation, tho' they did not want being

told that their crying Vices might, without Breach of Charity, be said to have gone far, in bringing that terrible Judgment upon the whole Nation.[17]

H. F.'s remarks implicitly link various late seventeenth-century perceptions of the term beyond the scope of personal reformation, and establish "reformation" as a condition for secure nationhood: first, the notion of the plague as a visitation of God's judgment upon the English nation (a notion that relies, implicitly, upon the typological view of England as the next Israel); second, the common perception of the dissoluteness of the court of Charles II; and third, that the burdens of "Reformation" included not only a reformation of manners pervasive from the 1690s, but also of the great Protestant Reformation of the sixteenth century.

Examining H. F.'s comment upon the court of Charles II, we see that his ire is not raised merely because they have abandoned the capital, but because they have shown no signs of religious self-reflection. In his opinion, the court have not reflected upon their "crying vices"; neither have they recognised that it is God who should be thanked for their preservation. This recognition would serve as a clear sign of repentance for sins past, a repentance that should bring about the reformation of the court. Instead, as Defoe laments in a *Review* of 1708, with the Restoration the nation suffered a kind of blindness: "We could see no Evil in universal Debauchery, no Mischief in a *P . . . pus* Government, a lewd Court, a drunken Country, a debauched M . . . ch, or an immoral Nation."[18] For Defoe, the Restoration did not necessarily cause a reformation of courtly excess and abuse; instead, it legitimized a profane and ungodly code of conduct.

Part of the reformative initiatives of the 1690s was to reform the nation's moral standing and reactivate the private and public connotations of the term "reformation" by appealing to a sense that England had abandoned the ideals of the great Protestant Reformation. Tony Claydon outlines what he terms a "courtly reformation" where the Williamite stress upon moral virtue was initially one of the strategies for legitimating William's rule. The Orange court developed a "biblically based discourse . . . which presented William as a providential ruler who had a divine commission to protect the protestant church in England, and to return the nation to its pristine faith, piety, and virtue." Claydon identifies, particularly in the sermons of the leading Williamite propagandist, Gilbert Burnet, "a mid-Tudor mental universe." The court, then, resurrected the ideals of the sixteenth-century Protestant Reformation, of which an important strand "was a peculiar understanding of the importance of moral reform."[19]

In his sermon at St. James's on twenty-three December 1688, Gilbert Burnet puts the events of that year in the context of the continuing war between the true church (Protestantism) and the false church (Catholicism), and claims William's role as a sign of God's providential concern for those who willingly help in His cause. Burnet explicitly constructs a typological link with William as a Davidic ruler leading the nation to salvation. Lamenting the debauchery and atheism of the preceding reigns (those of Charles II and James II), Burnet declares, "we have not forgot the Criminal Excesses of the year Sixty, and how that great Revolution that seemed to promise all that a Nation that had been so long tossed with wars and dangers of Government, could wish for, was so unsuccessful."[20] Burnet calls for a moral reformation after the debaucheries of the Restoration court had mocked the ideals of the Reformation. In his sermon at William and Mary's coronation, Burnet again outlines the need for a godly prince to lead the nation in a moral reform: "the encouraging and promoting of a vigorous Piety, and sublime Vertue, and the maintaining and propagating of True Religion, by ways and means suitable to it, is the chief design of their Rule."[21] Through such rhetoric, Burnet echoed the strategies of this courtly reformation, presenting William as a monarch who would clear the court of the sin and debauchery of recent reigns; who would turn the nation back toward God by instituting an intense period of fast-days; who would support the reformation of the nation's manners through the law; and who would vigorously defend the Protestant cause throughout Europe.[22]

Defoe was aware of the full implications of these discourses of reformation. In the context of Scots' accusations that the Act of Union would mean a union with a dissolute nation, Defoe refers to the work of reformation under the Orange court and the Societies for Reformation of Manners:

> *England*, BAD AS SHE IS, is yet a reforming Nation . . . the Work of Reformation has made more Progress in *England*, from the Court even to the Street . . . Let any Man look back to the Days of King Charles II when Rampant Vice over-run that Court, when all Sort of Lewdness spread the Face of Authority: Let them view the Example of the late Royal Pair of King *William* and Queen *Mary*, how Vice learned to blush, and being banish'd from the Court by the Royal Example, Virtue and good Manners became the Mode there.[23]

Although following the traditional gendering of the nation as female, the call "Let any Man look" distinctly interpellates a male subject. The project for reforming the nation's morals had at its heart an assumption that it was the nation's men whose morals were under scrutiny, and the effort at reforming male manners offers a revealing paradigm of changing attitude toward men's public recreational and sexual activities. Both the propaganda of the Williamite court and the texts of the Societies for Reformation of Manners utilised religious discourse to discipline and construct a godly manliness. Specifically, the efforts of the Societies were aimed at the nation's men, "responding," notes G. J. Barker-Benfield, "most immediately and continuously to the proliferating, modernizing, 'irreligious,' masculine culture in post-Reformation Britain, centred on alehouse and tavern."[24] After all, the Williamite propaganda was written and organised by men for a male court; sermonising was by an all-male clergy; the Societies for Reformation of Manners was an all-male organization.[25] This is not to say, of course, that in the attempts to reform the nation's morals, women did not come under observation. Rather, the androcentric culture of the late seventeenth and early eighteenth centuries viewed women's vices, most notably prostitution, primarily in terms of how they affected men. The vice of prostitution, although, of course, sinful for the individual woman, represented a far greater threat for the nation's men: Indulging in prostitution rendered men sickly, enervated, effeminate, and also endangered patrilineal descent, and thereby undermining the nation's protection and self-esteem.[26]

The clearest representation of an irreligious, dissolute, Restoration masculinity in *A Journal of the Plague Year* occurs, inevitably, in a tavern: "there was a dreadful Set of Fellows that used [this] House, and who in the middle of all this Horror met there every Night, behaved with all the Revelling and roaring extravagances, as is usual for such People to do at other Times" (*Journal*, 64). The revellers taunt passersby lamenting the dead and a lonely gentleman silently grieving inside the tavern by "some very profane, and even blasphemous Expressions" (*Journal*, 64). H. F. reproves the revellers with an account of his own preservation, which depicts the plague as a visitation of God's judgement:

> in this terrible Judgment of God, many better than I was swept away . . . that I was mercifully preserved by that great God, whose Name they had Blasphemed and taken in vain, by cursing and swearing in a dreadful Manner; and that I believed I was preserv'd in particular, among other Ends, of his Goodness, that I might reprove them for their audacious Boldness, in behaving in such a Manner, and in such an awful Time as this was. (*Journal*, 65)

More particularly, H. F. implies that his preservation is a sign of God's especial care, and a call to a pious duty to reform the revellers. God rewards the pious and punishes the wicked: A belief affirmed when the revellers all die from the plague within the succeeding days. *A Journal of the Plague Year*, through H. F., polices the margins between acceptable male behaviours and the unacceptable. Foucault's account of the institutional practices that came about to control the outbreak of plague offer a paradigm for the workings of Defoe's strategy for the depiction of masculinity in *A Journal*: "Rather than the massive, binary division between one set of people and another," Foucault writes, the plague "called for multiple separations, individualizing distributions, an organization in depth of surveillance and control."[27] Rather than a rejection of an amorphous mass of the ungodly, separating them from the godly, H. F. carefully specifies the qualities of ungodly men against a combination of qualities embodied in godly men.

Swearing, cursing and blasphemy, all behaviors of the ungodly man, were prime targets in the movements for reformation of manners. Queen Mary's letter to the Justices of the Peace of Middlesex in 1691 urged the enforcing of the laws against Sabbath-breaking, drunkenness, lewdness, and "Prophane swearing and Cursing." William III's proclamation in 1697 represents the danger posed to well-ordered government by swearing.[28] The danger the blasphemers pose in *A Journal of the Plague Year*, then, is not merely to themselves, but also to the nation. The constant rhetoric of the propaganda of the Williamite court, but most especially in the sermons of the Societies for Reformation of Manners, was that these sins are national sins. The keynote of these sermons being "National Sins" bring down "National Judgments":

> O *England! England!* To what Misery have thy Sins brought thee! But the Cause of

> Reformation is God's Cause. His Providence hath seemed to me to favour the poor Endeavours of it, which are represented in these Papers, and therefore I hope they will, with his Blessing, so prosper and prevail, that such a National Reformation may be effected as may prevent His heavy Judgments falling upon us.[29]

This is exactly the note H. F. strikes in *A Journal of the Plague Year*, strenuously affirming that "I looked upon this dismal Time to be a particular Season of Divine Vengeance" (*Journal*, 68); and declaring "that this was a Day of Visitation; a Day of God's Anger; and those Words came into my Thought. *Jer.* v. 9. *Shall I not visit for these things, saith the Lord, and shall not my Soul be avenged of such a Nation as this?*"(*Journal*, 68). H. F. stresses that God's judgment is not only upon these individual blasphemers, but upon the nation: "he had, as it were, his Sword drawn in his Hand, on purpose to take vengeance, not on them only, but on the whole Nation" (*Journal*, 69).

Citing verse nine of *Jeremiah*, H. F. alludes to the idolatry of the people of Israel and the resulting falsehood and deceit in their nation. This mobilises the powerful typology, in the seventeenth and eighteenth centuries, which portrayed England as a post-figuration of Israel. Such a typology was taken up by Josiah Woodward in his Fast-day Sermon of 1695. Speaking of Moses's pleas to God on behalf of the Jews, he singles out the story of their deliverance by the hand of God (Moses leading the Israelites from Egyptian bondage across the Red Sea), and remarks, "in this respect also some Plea may be made for *England*. It is a land which God has by a *Series of Wonders* freed from the *Slavery and Corruptions* of *Popery*."[30]

However, the underside of the metaphor of England as new Israel was the history of the Israelites' corruption and the resultant destruction and diaspora of the Jewish nation. In *An Account of the Societies*, the author laments the destruction and scattering of the Jewish people: "No Nation seems ever to have been so terrible and lasting Monument of God's Displeasure for National Sin."[31] The texts of the Societies for Reformation of Manners use the association of England with Israel, stressing the notion that the parallel offers a contemporary warning. Woodward once again affords us a glimpse of this anxiety: "when I consider what a Favourite *People* the *Jews* once were, and by what a dreadful destruction they were cut off at last. I am sure *Favourite England* has reason to look about her."[32] The metaphor became not only a positive identification, but a bleak warning to avoid the same fate.

Indeed, H. F. goes on to make this connection explicit at the end of *A Journal of the Plague Year*. The figure of Israel offers a dire pre-figuration of England's backsliding after the plague has passed:

> for the Generality of the People it might too justly be said of them, as was said of the Children of *Israel*, after their being delivered from the Host of *Pharoah*, when they passed the *Red-Sea*, and look'd back, and saw the *Egyptians* overwhelmed in the Water, *viz*. That *they sang his Praise, but they soon forgot his Works*. (*Journal*, 248)

Significantly, referencing *Psalm* 106, 12–13, Defoe also chooses the moment of

Israel's deliverance to point out England's tottering moral status. The typology, so often mobilised by the texts of the Societies in the 1690s, is used by Defoe to project back into the plague year of 1665 a moral interpretation of Williamite propaganda. The reign of Charles II is pitted against the moral reformation of the 1690s; the blasphemers, revelers, and the unrepentant constitute a corrupt, Restoration-era masculinity against which H. F. pits an ideal of godly manliness informed by the culture of reform later in the century.

Godly manliness was further enunciated through the discourse of nationhood and Protestant rhetoric. Jeremiah Gill, in his sermon to the Societies in 1700, draws upon a direct parallel between the incipient corruption of manners in England and the corruption in Biblical Jerusalem, then embellishes it with the language of plague and contagion. Describing the Degeneracy of Jerusalem, he exclaims, "this threatening Contagion had Unhappily insinuated into the Whole Body . . . Prophets, Priests, Princes, People; *Nobility, Gentry, Commonalty; Ecclesiasticks, Liacks* [*sic*]; All Corrupt."[33] He continues, "here we read *England's Character* and *Case* too much *drawn to the Life*!" (*Sermon*, 4). Gill then imagines God castigating the Jews of Jerusalem:

> O *Jerusalem*! You that are *Professedly* my People; *Mine*, both by *Natural Right* and *Covenant-Obligation*. You've hitherto been guarded by a Securing *Hedge*, or *Wall*. . . . Have been the Peculiar *Care* and *Charge* of my Providence. But You've forgot Your God and Special Engagements . . . Your Sins (which are of the deepest) have broken down that *Fence* that was about you, and have Open'd a Wide *Gap* to desolating Judgments. (*Sermon*, 6–7)

A gap in Jerusalem's imaginary topography seems to be an inlet to invasion and corruption of the nation-body. To Gill, God's words seem:

> Congruous and Pertinent to our Case, and rather the more so, because a Disposing Providence has Order'd our Lot in a *Garrison-Town*, where our *Walls* are accounted, *as Means*, a considerable Part of our Defence. A *Breach* in *these*, and the furious Approach of an Implacable Enemy, wou'd fully persuade Us, that 'twas a Time of Common Danger. (*Sermon*, 8)

The use of the fortress-nation metaphor posits those of corrupt or unreformed manners outside the virtuous nation, symbolically excluding them from the England that Gill wants to construct. Ideally, the ejection of those with undesirable manners enables an imaginary, virtuous England to coincide with the topographical England and a virtuous nation-body. He tells us how the breach in the nation's virtue, the nation's body, can be stopped up:

> *Couragiously* and *Resolvedly*—He that steps into such a *Breach*, and endeavours to *make it up*, had need to be a Person of Courage and Resolution. He must be a MAN, One of a *Masculine*, brave Spirit. An inglorious *Effeminacy*; a creeping *Pusillanimity* prevents the Undertaking or Effecting any thing that's *Great*. (*Sermon*, 31)

The saturation of gender associations testifies to the anxiety that underlies this passage; a fear that perhaps the breach has let in a contagion that has diseased the men of England. The piling up of traditional masculine attributes such as courage, resolution, bravery,—no "creeping" cowardice here—apparently strengthen the associations in opposition to "inglorious *Effeminacy*." Such an active courage reiterates the Societies' conception of the Christian soldier and parallels the fortitude earlier valorised in *The Pilgrim's Progress*. At the heart of Gill's declaration is a desperate tautology: "He must be a MAN." The description only apparently leads us up to his disclosure that it is a "MAN" who is the only effective agent, when, in fact, the disclosure has already been mapped out in traditional gender assumptions. The tautology, in fact, testifies to an underlying anxiety that those gender attributes normally given to the male sexed body are in danger of becoming unattached, and echoes Stillingfleet's and Milton's anxieties that the naturalised bond that fuses the male to masculinity may be broken by ungodly behaviour. Gill's conception of the ideal English masculinity has striking parallels with Thomas Sprat's depiction of another calamity that befell the Restoration capital, the great fire of 1666. In his *History of the Royal Society* (1667), Sprat offers an idealised construction of the artisan class:

> Nor was their courage less, in sustaining the *second calamity*, which destroyed their *houses*, and *estates*. Thus the greatest losers indur'd with such undaunted firmness of mind, that their example may incline us to believe, that not only the most *Natural*, but the best *Moral* Philosophy too, may be learn'd from the shop of the *Mechaniks*. . . . no *unmanly bewailings* were heard in the few *streets*, that were preserv'd: they beheld the Ashes of their *Houses* and their *Gates*, and *Temples*, without the least expression of Pusillanimity.[34]

Once again, the idealisation of an almost-stoic manliness occurs through the rejection of feminised behaviour: "*unmanly bewailing*" and "Pusillanimity." Yet, in addition to upholding the qualities of active courage and a steady mind, which underpin the concept of godly manliness, Sprat aligns these qualities with the artisan class. "If *Philosophers* had done this, it had well become their profession of Wisdom: if *Gentlemen*," Sprat continues, "the nobleness of their *breeding*, and *blood* would have required it."[35] Qualities that inhere in the biological and hereditary status of aristocracy become, instead, attached to the artisan class.

Commenting upon the representations of plagues, Armstrong and Tennenhouse perceive a valorisation of the artisan class by the time of the 1665 plague, in opposition to the depiction of the plague in texts such as Boccaccio's *Decameron* and Thomas Dekker's *Rod for Run-Awais* (1625), where the plague provides opportunities for the aristocratic class to mirror its own interests and concerns. They note, "whereas despairing men and wanton women had filled the plague-riddled streets of Elizabethan and Jacobean cities, a noble and manly figure arises from the ashes of Restoration London and transfigures it. The city no longer languishes in a state of lawlessness, abandoned by the elite cast of people."[36] Yet, crucially for Defoe and *The Journal*, London was abandoned by its elite: The court of Charles II's abandoning of the capital implies the abandoning of the nation's moral well-being, and the turning of their backs upon the ideals of the Reformation. Writing from a post-Williamite perspective, Defoe represents the court culture of Charles II as undermining the nation's morals and bringing down God's judgment, while he upholds a godly manliness in H. F., who embodies the values of the culture of reform prevalent in the 1690s. If the capital is under a well-ordered rule by a "noble and manly figure," it is, for Defoe, embodied in the godly manliness of the merchant and artisan classes of urban London, precisely the makeup of the members of the Societies of Reformation of Manners. In their analysis of the class makeup of the Societies, T. C. Curtis and W. A. Speck comment that the majority were from a variety of trades and crafts including porters, schoolmasters, goldsmiths, carpenters, bakers, grocers, and butchers; "very few," they note, "were gentlemen."[37] Matthew Henry's "Christian Hero"—the groundtroops and zealous workers of the societies—came not from the upper echelons of life, but from the urban artisan class. Like Sprat's depiction of the movement of aristocratic qualities to the artisans, the qualities of faith and stoic courage situate the urban artisan class, not the nobility, as exemplars of English manliness.

Defoe's own concern to strip the aristocracy of its hereditary nobility is nowhere more clear than in *The True-Born Englishman* (1700–1701):

> What is't to us, what Ancestors we had?
> If Good, what Better? or what worse, if Bad? (1205–06)
>
> . . . .
>
> For Fame of Families is all a Cheat,
> *'Tis Personal Virtue only makes us great.* (1215–16)[38]

If the aristocracy no longer held a monopoly upon personal virtue, then, for Defoe, the urban middle classes could transform themselves with the availability of these qualities. Of course, such a valorisation of the middle class has its most notable expression in *Robinson Crusoe* (1719). Crusoe's father delivers an encomium upon the "middle Station," declaring:

> that the middle Station had the fewest Disasters, and was not expos'd to so many Vicissitudes as the higher or lower Part of Mankind; nay, they were not subjected to so many Distempers and Uneasinesses either of Body or Mind, as those who, by vicious Living, Luxury and Extravagancies on one Hand, or by hard Labour, Want of Necessaries, and mean or insufficient Diet on the other Hand, bring Distempers upon themselves by the natural Consequences of their Way of Living.[39]

The association of the "middle Station" with a healthy body and a healthy mind constructs a moral hierarchy where the higher classes become a repository for extravagant consumption and vice. The very poor, on the other hand, forced into a life of hard labour, are unable to break out of a circle of mean dietary health, and are therefore responsible in a different way for their own lack of spiritual and bodily well-being.

Throughout *A Journal of the Plague Year*, there are careful qualifications concerning ideals of class and manliness. The exemplary figures, though varying in their precise position in the urban hierarchy, are all valorised against the figures of the court, the superstitious, the revellers, and the irreligious poor who all share an unreflective and ungodly view of God's workings during the city's calamity. The exemplary figures who do emerge are H. F. himself, a saddler; Robert, the boatman; and the two brothers, John and Thomas, one an ex-soldier, and the other an ex-seaman. Finally, H. F. records his praise for the body of clergy and physicians that made up the upper part of what Crusoe's father terms the "middle Station," and "the Civil Officers, such as Constables, Headboroughs, Lord Mayor's, and Sheriff's-men, as also Parish-Officers, whose Business it was to take Charge of the Poor, did their Duties in general with as much Courage as any, and perhaps with more" (*Journal*, 238). This is in stark contrast to the court of Charles, who "concern'd themselves so little, and that little they did was of so small Import, that I do not see it of much Moment to mention any Part of it here" (*Journal*, 234). H. F.'s explicit aim, therefore, is to represent the concerns and interests of the urban populace, especially the males, and to demonstrate their godly attributes as basic criteria for a reformed ideal of true, English manhood.

Yet his praise of the urban classes does not extend to all as H. F. characterises a section of the very poor in disparaging terms. Recognising that the plague hit the poor the hardest, he finds this at odds with their behaviour, "yet, were the Poor the most Venturous [*sic*] and Fearless of it [the plague], and went about their Employment, with a sort of brutal Courage; I must call it so, for it was founded neither on Religion or Prudence" (*Journal*, 89–90). When the plague begins to abate, this irrational courage is echoed in his description of the mob-like "People," whose "precipitant Courage" (*Journal*, 225) and "rash and foolish Conduct" (*Journal*, 227) in suddenly venturing abroad leads to further infection. The necessary faith in the providences of God, the calmness of mind and spirit in times of disorder and confusion, exemplified in the texts of the Societies and in *Due Preparations for the Plague*, are missing in the hasty and unreflective conduct of the very poor. H. F. divides the populace who stayed in London on the basis of this religious reflection, for courageous godly conduct should be "not so much a valuing our selves upon our Boldness in staying, as if all Men were Cowards that fly from the Hand of God, or that those who stay, do not sometimes owe their Courage to their Ignorance, and despising the Hand of their Maker, which is a criminal kind of Desperation, and not a true Courage" (*Journal*, 238). Interpellating a male subject position, H. F. presents to the reader an ideal masculinity whose courage rests firmly in a godly world view.

Significantly, this type of religious reflection is measured by rationality. Such a formulation is found in Stillingfleet, who declares that "the *Clouds and Vapors* [*sic*] of *Imagination*" divert the mind from the true course of reason. "Nothing," he goes on, is "so ungovernable as a *restless Imagination*; and when it is oppressed with a *Religious* Melancholy, then every thing seems dark and confused; we neither know God nor our selves as we ought to do."[40] Irrational conduct becomes the yardstick by which to measure behaviour in H. F.'s descriptions of the signs, comets, ghosts, voices and flaming swords that appeared to the superstitious:

So Hypchondriac Fancy's represent
Ships, Armies, Battles, in the Firmament;
Till steady Eyes the Exhalations solve,
And all to its first Matter, Cloud, resolve. (*Journal*, 22)

Reason—"*steady Eyes*"—banishes the hypochondriac's delusions.[41] Reason becomes distinctly masculinized in this formulation when H. F. explicitly associates hypochondria with women. Disparaging the fanciful reading of comets as forewarnings, he notes that "the old Women, and the Phlegmatic Hypochondriac Part of the other Sex, who I could almost call *old Women* too," were most affected with these sights (*Journal*, 19). Irrationality and hypochondria break apart the naturalised bond between male and masculinity, and give rise to potentially destructive effeminacy. Rationality, then, as we have also seen in Stillingfleet's sermonising, is the basis of true religion and, further, the basis for godly manliness.

Against the rash, unthinking conduct of the very poor, the superstitious, and the blasphemers of the tavern, Defoe sets Robert, the Thames water-man. Robert explains to H. F. that he does not go near his infected wife and children:

> But said I, *Why do you not come at them? How can you abandon your own Flesh, and Blood? Oh, Sir!* says he, *the Lord forbid; I do not abandon them; I work for them as much as I am able; and blessed be the Lord, I keep them from Want*; and with that I observ'd, he lifted up his Eyes to Heaven, with a Countenance that presently told me, I had happened on a Man that was no Hypocrite, but a serious, religious good Man. (*Journal*, 106–07)

The image of abandonment is particularly resonant with the perceived actions of the Court of Charles II; both in H. F.'s observation of their escaping the city, and also by the reformers of the 1690s in their depiction of the Restoration court abandoning the principles and morality of the English Reformation. Robert, in contrast, preserves himself while not abandoning his family ("*I keep them from want*"). Ultimately, Robert, and not the King, becomes the figure of ideal masculine identity whose godly manliness enables him to fulfill his familial obligations. For Defoe, the social cohesion necessary for England to survive the "bad times" is best exemplified by the godly manliness of this type of poor working man.

Robert also recognises and resigns himself to the workings of God. Saying of his wife, "*I hope she will recover*," he adds, "*I fear the Child will die; but* it is the Lord!"; he breaks off, weeping, which moves H. F. to observe, "*Well, honest Friend, . . . thou hast a sure Comforter, if thou hast brought thy self to be resign'd to the will of God, he is dealing with us all in Judgment*" (*Journal*, 108). H. F. reiterates the advice given in *Due Preparations for the Plague* for calmness of mind in times of calamity, by resting one's life in the hands of God. Robert, supporting H. F.'s opinion declares, "*it is infinite Mercy, if any of us are spar'd; and who am I to repine!*" (*Journal*, 108). H. F. ruefully reflects upon "how much better this Poor Man's Foundation was, on which he staid in the Danger, than mine . . . mine was meer Presumption, his a true Dependance [*sic*], and a *Courage resting on God*" (*Journal*, 108, emphasis mine). In opposition to the unthinking courage of the irreligious, Robert exemplifies the type of stoicism praised by Gill and Sprat. Even while he weeps, Robert displays a manly courage that has its foundation in a resignation to God's providences.

If Robert is given the exemplary qualities of godly manliness, then *A Journal of the Plague Year* pits these qualities against the cataclysmic disorder of the times. This imperative to offer a didactic account that is both a warning and a pattern echoes the rhetorical tactics in the sermons and texts of Williamite propaganda and the Societies for Reformation of Manners; specifically, the past was used primarily for emblematic purposes to critique the ideals and corruption of contemporary society and, in particular, contemporary masculinity. H. F.'s story of the two brothers and a kinsmen offers masculine figures who are explicitly given exemplary status: "the story of those three Men . . . I shall give as distinctly as I can, believing the History will be a very good Pattern for any poor Man to follow" (*Journal*, 58). John is an old soldier from the wars with Holland and Spain in the 1650s and is now a biscuit baker; his brother, Thomas, is a wounded seaman, now a sailmaker; the third is a carpenter. Their condition is constructed so as to exclude the possibility of their being destitute and echoing the unthinking, irreligious action of the very poor. Coming from the stratum of the working poor and having been in the service of their nation, they are constructed as exemplary urban men, possessing and exhibiting the ideals of godly manliness.

As with Robert, Defoe represents the interests and concerns of the urban workers through John and Thomas, as Wainwright points out, "the objects of the narrative thus become here, as elsewhere in Defoe's work, its subjects."[42] The first reported dialogue between the two brothers explores the nature of their rights in obtaining charity if they leave London. Having nowhere outside London to go, their rights as subjects are severely circumscribed; it is illegal to move from place to place under the laws of vagrancy, thus, the two brothers have no legal right to escape the plague. Yet the ex-soldier, John, questions this legal subjection by arguing their rights upon an alternative basis. He first uses a Biblical allusion, which, while not having any revelatory application, rhetorically suggests a religious and divine precedent for them: "*I am of the same Mind with the Lepers of Samaria, if we stay here we are sure to die*" (*Journal*, 124). Thomas reminds him that it is not lawful under the vagrancy laws to move about, to which John forcefully asks, "*Is not flying to save our Lives, a Lawful Occasion?*" (*Journal*, 124). John mobilises Natural Law, the right of self-prèservation, against what he sees as unreasonable laws; the Law of Nature also being known as the Law of Reason.[43] Underpinning this is his appeal to a sense of nationhood: "*The whole Kingdom is my Native Country as well as this Town. . . . I was born in* England, *and have a Right to live in it if I can*" (*Journal*, 124).

John is the voice of that active, courageous representation of ideal masculine attributes praised by Jeremiah Gill. As Defoe, and Bunyan before him, recognised, piety alone does not reach the heights of an ideal godly manliness; one must pray, yes, but one must pray and fight. In the context of a tradesman in despair, Defoe remarks, "A MAN that will lie still, should never hope to rise; he that will lie in a Ditch and pray, may depend upon it he shall lie in the Ditch and die."[44] In a striking parallel with Bunyan's hero, Christian, whose pilgrimage takes him away from his city, The City of Destruction, the three travellers set out from the desolation of Restoration London. That stoic courage exemplified by Robert has given way to a martial sense of Christian courage, and it comes as no surprise that when the three travellers meet up with another group of refugees, John is silently acknowledged as their leader. In times of calamity and vice, the rhetoric of reform picks out a man who will step into the breach of the nation's virtue. Entering into this service, the author of *An Account of the Societies for Reformation of Manners* declares, is "as Holy *David* of old, *Who will rise up for me against the Evil doers? Who will stand up for me against the Workers of Iniquity?*"[45]

While not strictly analogous to David's call against evil-doers, John and his fellow travelers encounter versions of uncharitable behaviour in the local villagers of Epping. In his dialogue with the constable, the figure of legal authority, John argues that "we have a Right to seek our own safety as well as you, and you may see we are flying for our Lives, and 'tis very unchristian and unjust to stop us" (*Journal*, 137). When this fails to move the villagers, John implicitly threatens violence (he has already fashioned fake weapons for the others of their band): "We have offer'd no Violence to you yet, why do you seem to oblige us to it? I am an old Soldier, and cannot starve" (*Journal*, 137). The offer of violence is rhetorically aligned with impugning the villagers' Christian charity. For John, manly force and godliness go hand in hand. John's martial values and his ability to talk and argue "rationally" (*Journal*, 144) are at an extreme from the values of such ungodly men as the revellers in the tavern and the feminised superstitious.

Everett Zimmerman has recognised that "what the story seems to inculcate is the personal effort that, in addition to reliance on God, is necessary for Salvation," yet adds that "H. F.'s passive trust in God is presumptuous."[46] I have already indicated that this unquestioning faith in awaiting the will of God is not so much presumption, but one of the ideal qualities of the godly man. H. F. does, however, question the moral and religious basis for his staying when faced with Robert, thinking that his decision, not based upon ties of duty to family, is "meer Presumption" (*Journal*, 108). Earlier, H. F.'s brother had advocated "that the best Preparation for the Plague was to run away from it" (*Journal*, 9). Yet it is hard to believe H. F.'s self-castigation for staying. Finding that all his attempts to get away were frustrated by an accident, H. F. believes that these are "Intimations from Heaven" (*Journal*, 10). H. F. reasons that to attempt to flee London would be to act "contrary to these Intimations, which I believed Divine, it was a kind of flying from God" (*Journal*, 11). He turns to the Bible for help, and opening the Bible at random for divination—the practice of *Sortes Biblicae* that Crusoe employs on his island when suffering from a fever—alights on the 91st Psalm. H. F. reads of his protection from the plague in these verses: "*I will say of the Lord, He is my refuge, and my fortress, my God, in him will I trust. Surely he shall deliver thee from the snare of the fowler, and from the noisome pestilence*" (*Journal*, 13).

If H. F. finds his resolve in these lines, then we see another justification for H. F. to remain in the city: "*Only with thine Eyes shalt thou behold and see the reward of the wicked. Because thou hast made the Lord which is my refuge, even the most High, thy habitation*" (*Journal*, 13). In his resignation to the will and providences of God, H. F. is also given an engagement to observe the morals of the time, to see the judgments of God at a time of calamity. As V. L. Wainwright observes, "the moral imperative underlies and sanctions the compulsion to stay, observe, record and narrate."[47] On a more secular level, H. F. is appointed as an Examiner of Houses, whereby he may enact a disciplinary gaze over the chaos and disorder of the city (*Journal*, 159). However, the ambivalence of the 91st Psalm which comforted H. F.—is it a command or merely a statement?— reappears in H. F.'s apparently ingenuous denial that he is "preaching a Sermon instead of writing a History, making my self a Teacher instead of giving my Observations of things" (*Journal*, 247). In his idealisations and moral judgments of central men in *A Journal of the Plague Year*, Defoe's narrator finds it impossible to divide observation from teaching and even sermonising. To the ostensible readers after the time of the narrator's writing, he declares that "I desire this Account may pass with them, rather for a Direction to themselves to act by, than a History of my actings" (*Journal*, 8).

H. F. not only reports and analyses the plague year, he passes judgment upon those men who fail to exemplify godly manliness, and marks out for special attention those men who stand out in their affirmation of godly manliness above the chaos of the plague. H. F.'s project, then, is not dissimilar to the project of the moral reformers: to mark out those suitable for carrying out the effort of reform, and to judge and discipline through religious rhetoric and the law those men deemed unfit for England. Yet, as we have seen, H. F. himself embodies many of the qualities of godly manliness Defoe so admires. His call to attempt to reform the revellers in tavern echoes the active involvement of the urban citizens of the Societies, and as a saddler, he is a member of the urban artisan class that made up the army of reform. His scepticism toward apparitions and the superstitions of the mob, and his rational arguments to stay, exemplify the rationality of the godly man. Further, his acceptance of the will of God, his unswerving faith, parallels the qualities found in the ideals of the Societies' men. H. F. not only records and judges masculine behaviour, he is also a template for the godly man. Indeed, he encompasses both roles at the very end of *A Journal of the Plague Year*. After lamenting "the Unthankfulness and Return of all manner of Wickedness among us, which I was so much an Eye-Witness of my self" (*Journal*, 248), he proclaims:

> *A dreadful Plague in* London *was,*
> *In the Year Sixty Five.*
> *Which swept an Hundred Thousand Souls*
> *Away: yet I alive!* (*Journal*, 248)

H. F. the saddler, Robert the boatman, and John the ex-soldier now biscuit baker, are constructed in opposition to a domain of unacceptable masculine and feminized behaviour. Their exemplary status of godly manliness is articulated via discourses of English Protestant nationhood, and also through the valorisation of the urban artisan class contrasted against the irreligious Restoration court. Defoe's use of emblematic chronology enables him to pit against the "bad times" of the plague a series of exemplary figures who stand out against the confusion and disorder of London. Against the backdrop of the calamity-stricken capital, itself emblematic of the perceived dissoluteness of the Restoration court, arises the figure of the urban male artisan. Through his godly manliness, expressed through the rejection of irrationality, superstition, and cowardice—all implicitly feminized—he is a figure projected back from the culture of reform in the late seventeenth and early eighteenth centuries. In choosing to use the plague of 1665 as the backdrop for the concerns of manliness, "Reformation" becomes the crucial rhetorical underpinning of Defoe's *A Journal of the Plague Year*; it is the catalyst for imagining an ideal masculinity that ultimately finds its foundation in the "godly" fortitude and example of the urban, working class.

NOTES

1. Pat Rogers, *Eighteenth-Century Encounters. Studies in Literature and Society in the Age of Walpole* (Brighton: The Harvester Press Ltd., 1985) 151–67.

2. His classmate at a Dissenting academy was John Shower, whose sermons to the Societies for Reformation of Manners were published, and who preached at Salter's Hall, the center of the Dissenting arm of the Societies' sermons and one of Defoe's local chapels. Further, Defoe had almost certainly been a member of one of the London Societies in the late 1690s and early 1700s, and was certainly a member of the Edinburgh Society in 1707. Paula Backsheider, *Defoe: His Life* (Baltimore: The Johns Hopkins University Press, 1989) 71–72; for Shower, see 40, 85–86; for membership, see 235–40.

3. Michel Foucault, *Discipline and Punish: The Birth of the Prison*, trans. Alan Sheridan (Harmondsworth: Penguin, 1977) 199.

4. O. Hughes, *A Sermon to the Societies for Reformation of Manners; Preach'd at Salter's-Hall, July 1, 1728* (London, 1728) 40.

5. Daniel Defoe, *Due Preparations for the Plague as well for Soul as Body* (London, 1722) 142. The largest part of the text is taken up with the narrative of a family from the 1665 plague, and the religious behaviour of two brothers.

6. John Bunyan, *The Pilgrim's Progress*, ed. N. H. Keeble (Oxford: Oxford University Press, 1984). Subsequent page references are given after quotations in the text.

7. [Yates], *An Account of the Societies for Reformation of Manners in London and Westminster, and other Parts of the Kingdom. With a Persuasive to Persons of all Ranks, to be Zealous and Diligent in Promoting the Execution of the Laws against Prophaness and Debauchery, for the Effecting of a National Reformation* (London, 1699) 148.

8. Matthew Henry, *A Sermon Preach'd to the Societies for Reformation of Manners, at Salter's-Hall. On Monday, June 30, 1712* (London, 1712) 4.

9. Edward Stillingfleet. *Reformation of Manners the true way of Honouring God. With the necessity of putting the Laws in Execution against Vice and Profaneness* [*sic*]. *In a Sermon Preach'd at White-Hall* (London, 1700[?]) 15.

10. Stillingfleet, *Reformation of Manners*, 9–10.

11. John Dryden, "The Cock and the Fox," *The Poetical Works of John Dryden*, ed. W. D. Christie (London: Macmillan and Company, 1873) 571.

12. John Milton, *Paradise Lost*, ed. Alistair Fowler (London and New York: Longman, 1971) 9: 634–36.

13. Paul K. Alkon, *Defoe and Fictional Time* (Athens: University of Georgia Press, 1979) 59, 37.

14. Paul J. Korshin, *Typologies in England, 1650–1820* (Princeton: Princeton University Press, 1982) 17. For his typological reading of *A Journal of the Plague Year*, see 221–23.

15. Alkon, *Defoe and Fictional Time*, 40.

16. Dudley W. R. Bahlmann, *The Moral Revolution of 1688* (New Haven and London: Yale University Press, 1957) 14.

17. Daniel Defoe, *A Journal of the Plague Year*, ed. Louis Landa (Oxford: Oxford University Press, 1969. 1990) 15–16. Subsequent page references are given after quotations in the text.

18. Daniel Defoe, *Review* (13 March 1708) 4: 678.

19. Tony Claydon, *William III and the Godly Revolution* (Cambridge: Cambridge University Press) 3, 33, 44.

20. Gilbert Burnet, *A Sermon Preached in the Chappel* [sic] *of St. James's, Before His Highness the Prince of Orange the 23rd of December, 1688* (London, 1689) 1–5, 22–24.

21. Burnet, *A Sermon preached at the Coronation of William III and Mary II. King and Queen of England,— France, and Ireland, Defenders of the Faith; in the Abby-Church* [*sic*] *of Westminster, April 11. 1689* (London, 1689) 19.

22. Claydon, *William III*, 90.

23. Defoe, *Review* (26 December 1706) 3: 613.

24. G. J. Barker-Benfield, *The Culture of Sensibility: Sex and Society in Eighteenth-Century Britain* (Chicago: Chicago University Press, 1992) 57.

25. Josiah Woodward, in *An Account of the Rise and Progress of the Religious Societies in the City of London, &c, And of the Endeavours for Reformation of Manners which have been made therein* (London, 1698), describes the Societies as a "*Christian-Brotherhood*" (his italics) 61. See also T. C. Curtis and W. A. Speck, "The Societies for the Reformation of Manners: A Case Study in the Theory and Practice of Moral Reform," *Literature and History* 3 (1976): 47. They do note that one woman was a member, and that the male members were mostly from the merchant and artisan class. They base their figures from a manuscript from 1694.

26. Woodward, *An Account of the Rise and Progress*, vi–vii. This masculinist position is echoed in the court of William III, and involved a similar disavowal of the female body, and certain representations of strong femininity. The decision to have William rule, instead of Mary who was in the direct line of (Protestant) succession, was an indicator of the new court's masculinist intentions—William declaring he would not be his "wife's gentleman usher." See Lois G. Schwoerer, "Women and the Glorious Revolution," *Albion* 18:2 (1986): 211–13. Gilbert Burnet credits himself for persuading Mary in this choice. Further, Shakespeare's *King Lear*, with its weak father and strong daughters, was banned; whereas *Dido and Aeneas*, a classical narrative that celebrated a hero who accomplishes a grand national duty in spite of an interfering and sexualised woman, was first staged by Purcell in 1689. See Ruth Perry, "Mary Astell and the Feminist Critique of Possessive Individualism," *Eighteenth-Century Studies* 23 (1990): 449.

27. Foucault, *Discipline and Punish*, 198.

28. Queen Mary's letter and William III's proclamation are reproduced at the head of [Yates], *An Account of the Societies for Reformation of Manners*. See also Defoe, *Review*, no. 61, 23 August 1709, vol. 6, 242–43, for animadversions upon swearing and drunkenness.

29. [Yates], *An Account of the Societies*, 163.

30. Woodward, *A Sermon Preached before The Right Honourable the Lord-Mayor and Aldermen of the City of London, At St. Mary le Bow. On Wednesday the 19th of June, 1695. A Day Appointed for a Solemn Fast* (London, 1695) 17.

31. [Yates], *An Account of the Societies*, 103.

32. Woodward, *A Sermon*, 20.

33. Jeremiah Gill, *A Sermon preach'd before the Society for the Reformation of Manners, in Kingston upon Hull: Sept. the 25th, 1700* (London, 1701) 3. Subsequent page references are give after quotations in the text. The notion of the covenant obligation in Puritan thought also invokes Hebraic notions of the covenant which stressed the possibilities of an integrated society. See Harold Fisch, *Jerusalem and Albion: The Hebraic Factor in Seventeenth-Century Literature* (London: Routledge and Kegan Paul, 1964) 109–11.

34. Thomas Sprat, *History of the Royal Society*, ed. Jackson I. Cope and Harold Whitmore Jones (St. Louis: Washington University Studies, 1958) 121.

35. Sprat, *History*, 121.

36. Nancy Armstrong and Leonard Tennenhouse, *The Imaginary Puritan: Literature, Intellectual Labour, and the Origins of Personal Life* (Berkeley: University of California, 1992) 96.

37. T. C. Curtis and W. A. Speck, "The Societies for the Reformation of Manners," 47–48.

38. Defoe, *The True-Born Englishman*, in *Poems On Affairs of State*, 6: 308–09. For the transvaluation of aristocratic values, see Michael McKeon, *The Origins of the English Novel, 1600–1740* (Baltimore: The Johns Hopkins University Press, 1987) 131–75.

39. Daniel Defoe, *The Life and Strange Surprizing Adventures of Robinson Crusoe*, ed. J. Donald Crowley (Oxford: Oxford University Press, 1972) 4–5.

40. Stillingfleet, *Reformation of Manners*, 9.

41. The association between hypochondria, the imagination, and religious melancholia is outlined in Robert Burton's *The Anatomy of Melancholy* (1621), 3 vols. (London: Dent, 1932). See, especially, part 3, section 4.

42. V. L. Wainwright, "Lending to the Lord: Defoe's Rhetorical Design in *A Journal of the Plague Year*," *British Journal of Eighteenth-Century Studies* 13 (1990): 67.

43. For Natural Law, see Maximillian Novak, *Defoe and the Nature of Man* (Oxford: Oxford University Press, 1963), chapter one.

44. Daniel Defoe, *The Complete English Tradesman: Directing him in several Parts and Progressions of Trade*, 2 vols. (London, 1732) 2. 183.

45. [Yates], *An Account of the Societies*, 148–49.

46. Everett Zimmerman, "H. F.'s Meditations: *A Journal of the Plague Year*," *PMLA* 87 (1972): 422.

47. Wainwright, "Lending to the Lord," 61.

Clarissa's "Man of Violence" and *Grandison's* "Truly Good Man": Masculine Homogeneity in Richardson

Susan Korba

In a recent study of Samuel Richardson's novels, Tassie Gwilliam observes that the novelist's works "offer an extraordinarily rich—and immense—textual field for the investigation of both gender and sexuality."[1] In fact, much of the material to be found in Richardson's novels prefigures work that is currently being done on gender, particularly in the study of what feminist theorist Alice Echols has called "patriarchally-conditioned masculinity."[2] And while it is, by now, a critical commonplace that gender is a cultural construction rather than a biological reality, "a social category imposed on a sexed body,"[3] it may be argued that a focus on men as explicitly gendered individuals is a relatively recent development, despite the fact that, as Scott Coltrane points out, research on men is "as old as scholarship itself."[4] Jane Flax explains that, while women have always been defined as "a 'question' or the 'sex' or the 'other'," men have traditionally been seen as "the universal (or at least without gender)."[5] With the advent of feminist scholarship, masculinity has come to be seen "not as a normative referent but as a problematic gender construct."[6] Accordingly, one of the aims of current critical studies of men and masculinity, whether theoretical or empirical, is "to *name* men and masculinity; to make those categories visible and to recognize their power; and to *deconstruct* them, to undermine, subvert, and dismantle them."[7] This seems to be exactly what Samuel Richardson was attempting to do as early as 1748, the year in which he published *Clarissa*, and the term "masculinity" had its first recorded usage in England.[8]

In the creation of *Clarissa*'s Robert Lovelace, one of literature's most infamous rakes and rapists, Richardson explores the damaging imperatives underlying the acquisition and maintenance of a particular type of masculine identity, revealing masculinity to be very much a "problematic gender construct." Having stated his intention of warning young women against "that dangerous but too commonly received notion that a reformed rake makes the best husband,"[9] Richardson subsequently demonstrates how the masculinist ideology to which Lovelace subscribes, and the particular masculine identity he struggles to maintain, result in Clarissa's rape, suffering, and death, as well as his own state of emotional and mental torment, and subsequent violent end. Yet, ironically, Richardson's most powerful, albeit unwitting, critique of masculinity is to be found, not in *Clarissa*, but in *The History of Sir Charles Grandison* (1753), which, as Tassie Gwilliam points out, is "the novel that was written to supply the portrait of the 'good man'—to match Richardson's virtuous women and to redeem masculinity from the rakes he had represented."[10]

The masculine behaviour displayed by *Clarissa*'s Lovelace elicited responses of both approbation and distress from Richardson's public; consequently, in his creation of the character of Grandison, Richardson complied with the exhortations of readers such as Thomas Edwards, who implored him to create a "manly Clarissa,"[11] and Lady Bradshaigh, who urged him to "set about reforming your own sex" and to "Exhibit the man we ought to prefer."[12] Thus, in *The History of Sir Charles Grandison,* Richardson explicitly attempts to redefine manhood and reconstruct masculinity anew through his male exemplar—"Sir Charles Grandison, the Example of a Man acting uniformly well thru' a variety of trying Scenes, because all his Actions are regulated by one steady Principle: A man of Religion and Virtue; of Liveliness and Spirit; accomplished and agreeable; happy in himself, and a Blessing to others."[13] However, despite his desire to provide a corrective to Lovelace with a chaste yet manful man who illustrates "what a degree of excellence may be attained and preserved amidst all the infection of fashionable vice and folly" (3: 466), Richardson reinscribes within the character of Grandison the very lethal brand of masculinity he so pointedly deconstructs in *Clarissa*. Richardson wrote to Lady Bradshaigh: "I think the characters, the sentiments, are all different from any of those in my two former pieces, though the subjects are still love and nonsense, men and women."[14] But the imperatives and principles informing Sir Charles's masculine identity are essentially the same as those which Richardson impugns in the character of Lovelace. Thus, Richardson's attempt to set up a dichotomy between two versions of manhood ultimately collapses in on itself.

In Lovelace, Richardson embodied a particular conception of eighteenth-century manhood that he was anxious to dismantle, that of the libertine and rake. In *The Culture of Sensibility*, G. J. Barker-Benfield explains that the rake's actions "were literally a display of a certain style of masculinity,"[15] exemplified by the figure of John Wilmot, Second Earl of Rochester. Barker-Benfield further observes that there are "ample" correspondences between Rochester and Richardson's Lovelace, and argues that "Rochester symbolizes a new kind of man. In his wit and dandyism, young Rochester was 'the pattern of the modern fine gentleman,' the leader of a new, postwar generation. . . . [that] 'affected' a manly style of 'apparent hardness'."[16] Rakes and libertines were desirous of being seen as "men of the World," and displayed their masculinity through conduct that included sexual licentiousness, the pursuit of pleasure, misogyny, and duelling. Richardson's most scathing description of this particular model of masculinity is expressed in a letter from Clarissa's cousin, Colonel Morden, who warns her of the dangers of an alliance with a rake, as he delineates and condemns the traits that constitute the rakish identity:

> A libertine, my dear cousin, a *plotting*, an *intriguing* libertine, must be generally *remorseless*—*unjust* he must always be. The noble rule of doing to others what he would have done to himself, is the first rule he breaks; and every day he breaks it; the oftener, the greater his triumph. He has great contempt for your sex. He believes no woman chaste, because he is a profligate. Every woman who *favours him*, *confirms him* in his wicked incredulity . . . To be a libertine, *at setting out*, all compunction, all humanity, must be overcome. To *continue* to be a libertine, is to continue to be everything vile and inhuman. (2: 259–60)

Clearly, Richardson believed this style of masculine behaviour to be dangerous and pernicious, and was committed to revealing "to all the barbarity which lies below the genteel veneer of rakery."[17]

Richardson first attempted to implement his design in *Pamela* (1740), wherein he hoped to show "the Character of a Libertine in its truly contemptible Light" (G1: 3). He made Mr. B. a "rakish squire,"[18] who resorts to deceit, kidnapping, and violence in an effort to deflower Pamela, his mother's serving-girl. Despite Mr. B.'s endeavours, he is ultimately "too completely and youthfully masculine" to convey the kind of male threat Richardson would incarnate in Lovelace.[19] Richardson confers upon Lovelace the complexity that his first rakish protagonist lacked; although possessed of "a lively, witty mind stocked with much learning, a disposition to do good, and an immitigable charm of manner,"[20] Lovelace is consumed by his need for power and control, given to violent fantasies involving the degradation and subjugation of women, and intractable in the arrogant conviction of his masculine prerogative.

In investigating the masculine identity of the rake so much more thoroughly in *Clarissa* than in *Pamela*, Richardson is careful to expose the viciousness and self-delusion involved in the construction and maintenance of this brand of male subjectivity. As a self-professed libertine and leader of a rake brotherhood, Lovelace commits himself to a particular set of misogynistic beliefs and behaviours codified in the maxims of "the Rake's Creed." For Lovelace and his brother rakes, adherence to these maxims supersedes considerations of decency, virtue, and honour, qualities that Richardson later would enshrine in his masculine exemplar, Sir Charles Grandison. Jack Belford, Lovelace's fellow-rake and best friend, ruefully acknowledges that "Neither are gratitude and honour motives to be mentioned . . . to men such as we are . . . For *our honour* and *honour* in the *general acceptation* of the word are two things" (2: 158). Lovelace's own sense of honour is based on the fact that he has "*never lied to man, and hardly ever said truth to woman.* The first is *what all free-livers cannot say*: the second, *what every one can*" (4: 445). He believes himself justified because "*no wickedness is comparable to the wickedness of a woman*," and "every woman is a rake in her heart" (2: 55–56). He writes to Belford:

> Libertines . . . seldom meet with the stand of virtue in the women whom they attempt. And by the frailty of those they have triumphed over, they judge of all the rest. "*Importunity* and *opportunity* no woman is proof against, especially from a persevering lover who knows how to suit temptations to inclinations": this, thou knowest, is a prime article of the rake's creed. (2:35)

Since it is apparent that, according to Lovelace's code, a persevering lover may employ deceit, kidnapping, constraint, and violence, it is not surprising that the stand of virtue Lovelace encounters is not proof against his tests. He proposes that it is up to women "by their *actions* to prove the contrary, if they can" (2:55); yet his avowed policy of deceiving women reveals the vicious contradiction inherent in his belief system. Moreover, his desire to prove whether Clarissa will or not, "*if once subdued*, be *always subdued*?" (2: 41), another of the libertine maxims, demonstrates how restricted a view of human value and potential the rake's creed offers: All women are to be reduced to the lowest common denominator, and "exalted ladies" such as Clarissa are to be "abased" (2: 30). Ultimately, both his own worth and that of any woman with whom he has a relationship is to be determined solely by sexual [mis]conduct, as deemed by this type of masculinity.

Immoderate sexual behaviour is, of course, a defining feature of the rake. Lovelace refers to himself as "so universal a lover" (1: 150), boasting that "I am perjured ... by priority of obligation, if I am faithful to any woman in the world!" (1: 149). His reputed sexual prowess is the primary means through which he affirms his masculinity, and is a frequent subject of his letters to Belford. In his discussion of eighteenth-century sexual mores, Roy Porter asserts that "sexual liberty and libertinism were often boasted about. Philandering was construed as free and liberal behaviour. It was manly."[21] Apparently, rape could be considered one of these "free and liberal" behaviours; Lovelace states complacently to Belford that "Nor are women ever angry at bottom for being disobeyed through excess of love. They like an uncontrollable passion. They like to have every favour ravished from them ... Don't I know the sex?" (2: 209). He later asserts that "a rape, thou knowest, to us rakes, is far from being an undesirable thing" (3: 214). Certainly, although the rape of Clarissa is the central focus of the novel, she is by no means the only woman who has been victimized by Lovelace in this way. Lovelace reminds his friend: "Thou knowest that I have more than one, twice, or thrice, put to the fiery trial young women of name and character; and never yet met with one who held out a month; nor indeed so long as could puzzle my invention. I have concluded against the whole sex upon it" (2: 40). Miss Betterton suffered a fate similar to that of Clarissa; Joseph Leman, Lovelace's underling, recounts how "Your Honner got her away, it seems, by a false letter. . . . Miss Batirton was not harde of for a month or so. And when ... her frends found her oute and would have prossekutid your Honner, you Honner was gone abroad; and so she was broute to bed . . . and lanquitched, and soon died" (2:148). Lovelace is also largely responsible for the corruption of Sally Martin, who, "had she not met with a Lovelace ... had avoided a Sinclair" (4: 540), and Polly Horton, who likewise "fell a sacrifice to the successful intriguer" (4: 546). Each girl becomes his mistress and is eventually reduced to playing bawd for him. Yet Lovelace is able to excuse his actions, as he expostulates to Belford: "A rake's a rake, Jack! And what rake is withheld by principle from the perpetration of any evil his heart is set upon and in which he thinks he can succeed?" (3: 280).

Anna Howe deprecatingly characterises Lovelace as "the head of a gang of wretches . . . who join together to betray innocent creatures, and to support one another afterwards by violence" (2: 279), and Clarissa labels his pride in the seduction of "the innocent" as "unmanly" (4: 354). However, Lovelace sees himself and his cohorts as audacious, intrepid, and paradigmatically masculine. He maintains that all men would do as he does, given the opportunity and the nerve, as he assures Belford and himself many times: "Were every rake, nay, were every man, to sit down, as I do, and write all that enters his head or into his heart, and to accuse himself with equal freedom and truth, what an army of miscreants should I have to keep me in countenance!" (2: 492). Unfortunately, it is not only Lovelace who believes this style of masculinity to be attractive and compelling. When asked about Lovelace's behaviour toward women, one of Lovelace's comrades asserts that he merely "did as every young fellow would do" (1: 250); and Anna suggests that "This very Hickman, I make no doubt, would be as saucy as your Lovelace, if he dared. He has not half the arrogant bravery of the other, and can better hide his horns; that's all. But whenever he has the power, depend upon it, he will *butt* at one as valiantly as the other" (1: 340).

Throughout *Clarissa*, Lovelace shows himself determined to act the rake's part, no matter the cost. He asserts that "*Hard-heartedness*, as it is called, is an *essential* of the *libertine's character*. Familiarized to the distresses he occasions, he is seldom betrayed by tenderness into a complaisant weakness unworthy of himself" (2: 315). Thus, Lovelace is scornful of Belford's distress over his dying uncle, and determinedly sceptical of Clarissa's very real concern for her virtue. Clarissa remarks upon the price exacted by Lovelace's masculinity:

> What *sensibilities* . . . must thou have suppressed! What a dreadful, what a judicial hardness of heart must thine be; who canst be capable of such emotions as sometimes thou hast shown; and of such sentiments as sometimes have flowed from thy lips; yet canst have so far overcome them all, as to be able to act as thou hast acted, and that from settled purpose and premeditation; and this, as it is *said*, throughout the whole of thy life. (3: 152)

Richardson illustrates the growing struggle Lovelace experiences between his very real feelings for Clarissa and his desperate adherence to his code. On a number of occasions, Lovelace is "exceedingly affected" by his encounters with Clarissa (2: 316), admitting that "my heart often misgives me" (2: 399). But any weakening of resolve or admission of more tender feelings is quickly suppressed, and he feels "ashamed to be surprised into such a fit of unmanly weakness—*so ashamed*, that I was resolved to subdue it at the instant, and to guard against the like for the future" (2: 316). As the situation with Clarissa wears on, he feels more and more that "my invention is my curse, my pride my punishment," and wonders

"Drawn five or six ways at once, can *she* possibly be so unhappy as *I*?" (2: 460). Lovelace increasingly comes to feel trapped by the dictates of his masculine identity, yet he cannot bring himself to renounce it: "And yet . . . am I not a *rake*, as it is called? And whoever knew a rake stick at anything?" (2: 97). His ability to demonstrate his "rakish" efficacy to others is the foundation of his entire identity. If Clarissa should escape him, he broods that he would be rendered "unworthy . . . to be the prince and leader of such a confraternity as ours!—how unable to look up among men! or to show my face among women!" (2: 18). He repeatedly makes reference to the figure he will cut in "rakish annals" (2: 417; 3: 144). At Belford's suggestion that he abandon his plan to overcome Clarissa, Lovelace exclaims: "Were I to take thy stupid advice . . . what a figure should I make in rakish annals! The lady in my power . . . her family expecting the worst *hath* passed; herself seeming to expect that the worst *will* be attempted . . . What! wouldst thou not have me act in character?" (2: 250). Although he attempts to assure himself that "I am no machine" (2: 400), ultimately he is forced to admit that, in modelling himself on a masculine code that negates his very humanity, he is "a machine at last, and no free agent" (3: 146).

Richardson found it distressing that, despite his efforts, this "style of manhood" continued to prove attractive and compelling.[22] In a letter to Lady Bradshaigh, he expresses his dismay that there had been "such kindness shewn to . . . Lovelace" by some of his readers.[23] Richardson himself prefigured this response in a scene in *Clarissa*, in which Lovelace, appearing at a ball after Clarissa's rape, behaves "as if nothing had happened," and Anna reports "how pleased half the giddy fools of our sex were with him, notwithstanding his notorious wicked character" (4: 23). Lovelace observes cynically that "half the female world [is] ready to run away with a rake, because he is a rake; and for no other reason; nay, every other reason against their choice of such a one" (2: 472). Feminist critic Anna Clark, observing that the typical eighteenth-century hero was often a rake, explains that "much libertine literature celebrated the heroic rapist and excused men's abandonment to their 'uncontrollable' passions."[24] Accordingly, Richardson wrote contemptuously of those "many modern fictitious pieces, in which authors have given success (and *happiness*, as it is called) to their heroes of vicious, if not of profligate, characters" (G3: 456). In *The History of Sir Charles Grandison*, Richardson's intention of creating a male character who is the antithesis of such "heroes" and of his own Lovelace is made very explicit, both in his editorial remarks and in the novel itself. In his conclusion to the novel, Richardson states that "Sir CHARLES GRANDISON is . . . in the general tenor of his principles and conduct . . . proposed for an Example" (3: 466). How to represent such a character was no easy task; Richardson was reluctant "To draw a character that the better half of the world, both as to number and worthiness, I mean the women, would not like," particularly "after such a reception . . . as Mr. Hickman has met with."[25] Gerard A. Barker suggests that Richardson's solution was "to lend his hero Lovelace's manly qualities without his vices"; Sir Charles thus represents "an effort to bring together the most attractive features of the bold, virile rake and the diffident good man . . . to develop a hero who is humane yet manly, modest yet worldly, gentle yet forceful."[26]

The History of Sir Charles Grandison presents a new and, according to Richardson, superior standard of masculinity. Unlike Lovelace, who, in slavishly adhering to the principles of the rake's creed, eventually feels himself to be nothing more than a machine, Grandison "is used to do only what he *ought*," (2: 157), and he proclaims, "I live not to the world: I live to myself; to the monitor within me" (1:206). Grandison asserts his masculinity in opposition to earlier models; his masculine attributes are demonstrated through the renunciation of violence, sexual wantonness, and the seduction of women. One of the differences Richardson most emphasises between his exemplar and other contemporary "heroic" representations of masculinity is that Sir Charles "is govern'd by another set of principles, than those of false honour" (1: 209). He makes it clear that Grandison is indisputably brave, *because of* his refusal to engage in violence. In considering "the Laws of Honour," those that require a man to "give . . . the satisfaction of a Gentleman" by engaging in a duel, Grandison queries: "Of whose making . . . are the Laws of Honour you mention? I own no Laws, but the Laws of God and my Country" (1: 242). He admits to Mr. Reeves that, while he is "naturally passionate" and "never could bear a design'd insult," he "will not meet any man . . . as a duellist" (1: 206). However, if offered a threat, he asserts, "I never avoid a threatener" (1: 242). Richardson gives him a number of opportunities to display his courage, including his rescue of Harriet from the clutches of Sir Hargrave Pollexfen, and his subsequent meeting with that irate and violent peer. Sir Hargrave, bent on getting "satisfaction" from Sir Charles, tells him, "If you are a *man*, Sir Charles Grandison, take your choice of one of those pistols." Sir Charles responds, "As I AM a *man*, Sir Hargrave, I will *not*" (1: 250). Sir Charles manages to cow Sir Hargrave through sheer force of his "manly" rhetoric; Sir Hargrave, manoeuvred out of his determination to duel with Grandison, is completely overcome, declaring: "Curse me, if I can bear my own littleness!" (1: 254). Further, Sir Charles converts his enemies into admirers through his behaviour; Pollexfen's own cronies are in awe of his masculine example. Mr. Merceda claims that he would "rather have Sir Charles Grandison for [his] friend than the greatest prince on earth," and Mr. Bagenhall declares that he would "rather be Sir Charles Grandison in this past hour, than the Great Mogul all [his] life" (1: 252).

Richardson also reconceptualizes the notion of masculine virility in *Grandison*. Sir Charles is a male virgin, a masculine type that Lovelace mocks in *Clarissa*. In discussing Hickman, whom he characterises as "a very innocent fellow—a *male-virgin*, I warrant!"—Lovelace asserts that "the ladies generally prefer a rake to a sober man" and "like not novices . . . They are pleased with a love of the sex that is founded in the *knowledge of it*" (3: 81). Richardson suggests that, in fact, quite the opposite is true by showing Grandison to be every bit as sexually compelling as Lovelace. Grandison's virility is never questioned, despite his known chastity, and he is the object of desire of many women. In one instance, "no fewer than Five Ladies, out of one circle, declared, that they would stand out by consent, and let you pick and choose a wife from among them" (2:43). Both Harriet and Clementina are deeply in love with him, and the passionate Lady Olivia offers herself to him on a number of occasions. Grandison not only rejects her unwanted advances, but also chides her for her own immodesty. Olivia is forced to acknowledge that Grandison is a man "of sentiments the most delicate, of life and manners the most unblamable"; while her own amorous proposals were "*too plainly* intimated to him; proposals that owed their existence to inconsiderate Love . . . mingled . . . with passions of the darkest hue" (2:645). Grandison's refusal to give in to sexual temptation is seen to be one of his manly strengths, rather than the opposite; whereas, by exerting sexual agency and avowing her desire for him, Olivia has rendered herself shameful to both herself and her sex. Harriet ruefully notes that Sir Charles "has been used . . . to check the passions of us forward girls" (2: 157); his self-denial is a reproach to those who would behave unchastely.

Not only does Grandison successfully resist sexual temptation, he openly advocates male chastity. In a letter to his young friend Jeronymo della Porretta, he makes his contempt very clear for the sort of sexual conduct engaged in by dissolute men; in attempting to convince Jeronymo to avoid "guilty attachments," he asks: "How can that crime be thought pardonable in a man, which renders a woman infamous?" (2: 140). Many of his opinions on the issue seem to directly address the sort of behaviour Lovelace revels in in *Clarissa*. Whereas Lovelace asserts confidently that "Virtue . . . is less to be dispensed with in the woman than in the man" (2: 39), Grandison asks scornfully: "What can that man say for himself, or for his proud pretension, who employs all his arts to seduce, betray, and ruin the creature whom he should guide and protect?" (2: 140). Grandison reminds Jeronymo that he is "a MAN, a rational and immortal agent"; consequently, he must "act up to the dignity of [his] nature. Can sensual pleasure be the great end of an immortal spirit in this life?" (2: 140–41). Clearly, for Grandison, it cannot. For him, there are "innocent delights enough to fill with joy every vacant hour" (2: 141), and the sexual relationship is meant to be strictly a conjugal one.

Obviously, Lovelace's and Grandison's notions of appropriate masculine behaviour could not be more different. Yet, upon closer examination, it is equally apparent that Lovelace and Sir Charles share a number of rather obvious similarities, as various critics have noted. Morris Golden argues that "Grandison no less than Lovelace is a projection of Richardson's dominance fantasies,"[27] while David Robinson believes that Lovelace can be seen as Sir Charles's "evil twin," noting that "both men share the same fault: an excess of pride, a desire for power, a need to occupy the superior position in a relationship."[28] Moreover, both Richardson's rake and his model of male virtue are deeply misogynistic. Although Lovelace's misogyny is much more overt and vicious than that of Grandison, Grandison's is just as pernicious. Whereas Lovelace spends a great deal of his energy convincing himself of woman's basic depravity, Sir Charles clearly needs to believe in woman's inherent weakness, both of mind and of person. He is smugly convinced that "Women's minds have generally a lighter turn than those of men. They should be innocently indulged" (2: 8). While his outward benevolence, courtesy, and chivalry mark most of Grandison's dealings with women, the underlying contempt with which he views them is not that difficult to perceive. In claiming to "know a little of the sex," Grandison's sentiments are not far off from those expressed by Lovelace: "a man of common penetration may see to the bottom of a woman's heart . . . You are not . . . such Mysteries, as some of us think you" (2: 280). He characterises women as "Charming copiers!" (2: 97), who emulate "the behaviour of your common grandmother," Eve, in their coyness and affectation (2: 97), and suggests that "Waller was not absolutely wrong . . . when he said, 'that women were born to be controuled'" (2: 94). While Grandison does not describe women's inferiority through graphic metaphors such as the ones Lovelace employs—the caged birds, the vermin some men pursue—his comments illustrate his patronising and dismissive attitude. Women must "Guard . . . against . . . imbecilities of tender minds" (3: 242); "Ladies, where Love and their own happiness interfere, are the most incompetent judges of all others for themselves" (1: 415). Even his more playful comments are equally offensive. In discussing the forthcoming marriage of Lord G. to his sister Charlotte, Grandison suggests that Lord G. may give up some of his amusements "when he has a more considerable trifle to amuse himself with"—meaning, of course, Charlotte (2: 85). As Harriet notes, "he has not an high opinion of our sex in general" (2: 272).

Ultimately, Richardson's attempt to create two antithetical conceptions of masculinity, one embodied in "the vilest of libertines" (2: 162), and the other in the "Man of TRUE HONOUR" (1: 4), is unsuccessful. Since both Lovelace's and Grandison's masculinity has been "patriarchally-conditioned," their masculine identities are, at the very foundation, the same. Although his deconstruction of rakish masculinity reveals that the principles which structure such an identity are specious and destructive, Richardson does not question the assumptions and precepts upon which masculinity *itself* is based. These derive from a patriarchal model that prescribes specific qualities and behaviours for the achievement of manliness, referred to in the *OED* as "the appropriate excellences of the male sex." Thus, a man, in order to *be* a man, must be "manly, virile, vigorous, powerful." As Grandison further explains:

> Weaker powers are given generally for weaker purposes, in the economy of Providence. . . . I, for my part, would only contend, that we men should have power and right given us to protect and serve your Sex; that we should purchase and build for them; travel and toil for them; run through, at the call of Providence, or of our King and Country, dangers and difficulties; and, at last, lay all our trophies, all our acquirements, at your feet. . . . (3: 248)

Grandison approves wholeheartedly of the differentiation for which he argues, for "Were it not so, their offices would be confounded, and the women would not perhaps so readily submit to those domestic ones in which it is their province to shine, and the men would be allotted the distaff, or the needle; and you yourselves, Ladies, would be the first to despise such" (3: 248). Not only, then, does the possession of "manly" qualities and behaviours demonstrate that a man is "masculine," but, more importantly, they make it clear that he is not "feminine"—being *a man* means *not being like a woman*.[29] Consequently, in the acquisition of masculine gender identity, a man learns "to devalue all women in his society, as the living embodiments of those traits in himself he has learned to despise,"[30] which explains the common strain of misogyny underlying both Lovelace's and Grandison's beliefs about gender. Thus, at the heart of contemporary and historical conceptions of manhood lies a notion of antifemininity. This was to become an increasingly significant factor in the developing concept of masculinity in the eighteenth century. As Michael McKeon points out, although masculinity was an unstable category in the eighteenth century, "a new standard of gender difference was achieved in part through the separation out of the limiting negative case for masculinity," whereby formerly acceptable "male types"—linked to effeminacy—were excluded from what came to be considered "normative masculine roles."[31] The concept of masculinity, both historically and developmentally, is therefore achieved "in the renunciation of the feminine, not in the direct affirmation of the masculine, which leaves masculine gender identity tenuous and fragile."[32] The repression of the feminine, which remains present in the unconscious, is a constant threat to "the stability of gender identification, denying its unity, subverting its need for security."[33] In order to combat the anxiety associated with this fragility, a man must engage in a constant struggle to prove his masculinity against the perceived threat of the feminine. This struggle characterises both Lovelace's and Grandison's masculine performances throughout the two novels.

Barker-Benfield argues that the continuing appeal of the masculinity epitomised by the rake can, in part, be explained "by the apparent inadequacy of men of feeling. . . . To advance men's sensibility was to bring them closer to women. To make men more sensitive, more delicate, was, in the eighteenth century's own terms, to run the risk of making them too 'effeminate' or 'feminine.'"[34] This was, of course, one of the risks Richardson faced in creating Grandison and his new model of manhood. As such, Richardson repeatedly reinforces Grandison's admirable masculinity: "So much goodness, so much sensibility, so much compassion . . . never met together, in a heart so manly" (2: 134). Grandison himself makes it clear that he despises effeminacy; in his discussion on the differences "in the *constitution*, in the *temperament*, of the two Sexes, that gives to the one advantages which it denies to the other," he refers scathingly to one of the "more odious" of characters, that of the effeminate man: "There are, indeed, *men*, whose minds, if I may be allowed the expression, seem to be cast in a Female mould; whence the fops, foplings, and pretty fellows" (3: 247). For Grandison, the qualities that define masculinity and femininity are very explicit: "delicacy, softness, grace" belong to the persons of women; "strength, firmness . . . a capacity to bear labour and fatigue; and courage, to protect the other," to men (3: 247). To illustrate his point, Grandison invokes the image of the protector, the role in which Harriet first encounters him: "Were it not . . . for male protectors, to what insults, to what outrages, would not your Sex be subject?" (3: 248). For Grandison, gender identity is clearly contingent upon the successful performance of appropriate gendered behaviour; he thus places himself firmly in a masculine category antithetical to that of men who belong to the despised "Female mould." Moreover, the distinction he makes involves a moral valuation: His description of "fops, foplings, and pretty fellows" as men who merely "buz about your Sex at public places" (3: 247) implies their inherent worthlessness, whereas, men who possess a "real" masculinity actually preserve the social order, safeguarding women's virtue and peace of mind, even their very lives.

A similar disdain for/fear of effeminacy characterises Lovelace's efforts at self-construction. Lovelace is at great pains to make his contempt for Mr. Hickman known throughout his correspondence with Belford. In his eyes, Hickman, described as "whining" and "submissive" (2: 104), is a figure of questionable masculinity. Lovelace accordingly refers to him as a "prancer" (2: 418), and characterises his behaviour as "mincing" (2: 366) and "prim" (2: 421). In his wild scheme to abduct and rape Anna Howe and her mother, Lovelace dismissively lumps Hickman with the women he intends to punish (2: 420); and he later mocks Hickman's response to Clarissa's distress:

> But this honest fellow, it seems, with *tears in his eyes*, and with *humble prostration*, besought the vixen to *permit* him to set out . . . *in order to give himself the glory of protecting such an oppressed innocent, in the face of the whole world.* Nay, he *reddened*, it seems; and *trembled* too! as he read the fair complainant's letter. How *valiant* is all this! Women love *brave* men; and no wonder that his *tears*, his *trembling*, and his *prostration*, gave him high reputation with the *meek* Miss Howe. (3:173)

Lovelace then draws a comparison between himself and Hickman, asking Belford: "But dost think, Jack, that I in the like case (and equally affected with the distress) should have acted thus? Dost think that I should not first have rescued the lady, and then, if needful, have asked excuse for it, the lady in my hand?" (3: 173). In a particularly tense and telling scene between himself and Clarissa, Lovelace is rendered momentarily powerless as Clarissa, comporting herself "like a haughty and imperious sovereign," makes clear her intention to leave Mrs. Sinclair's home. Having been reduced to stammering and trembling—decidedly unmasculine responses—Lovelace finds himself in the humiliating position of "the spiritless Hickman" (2: 381). In order to regain his sense of himself as potent and powerful, Lovelace must resort to verbal and physical violence, smashing a teacup and "seizing her hand," while intimating further violence if Clarissa does not capitulate.

In this instance, Lovelace's masculine display is for his own and Clarissa's benefit. But it is the public affirmation of masculinity that really matters; as Michael S. Kimmel explains, masculinity is "a *homosocial* enactment" that is "demonstrated for other men's approval."[35] A man's masculinity is affirmed when it is witnessed. Although Lovelace and Grandison perform the masculine "excellences" in different ways, perform them they must, if they are to be considered men at all. Lovelace's masculine displays are more carefully orchestrated than those of Grandison. A case in point is the dinner party Lovelace arranges at Mrs. Sinclair's, to which he invites Belford, Mowbray, and Belton in order to show Clarissa off to them. He admits that "So generous a spirit as mine is cannot enjoy its happiness without communication. If I raise not your envy and admiration both at once, but half-joy will be the joy of having such a charming fly entangled in my web" (2: 214). Lovelace asks Belford, "Think you that I do not long to have your opinion of my fair prize?"(2: 223). Indeed, the entire trial of Clarissa—all of her responses, all of his stratagems, the "liberties" taken, the fantasised scenarios—is conducted in front of an audience, in the person of Belford. Lovelace's letters to Belford detail his masculine ingenuity, his pride in his contrivances, and his extravagant claims about his greatness—they are an elaborate record of masculine self-construction. Significantly, the briefest, least detailed letter written by Lovelace is that which describes the rape: "And now, Belford, I can go no farther. The affair is over. Clarissa lives" (3: 196). The rape, carried out with the assistance of opiates and the supervision of Mrs. Sinclair and her minions, represents a failure of Lovelace's masculinity, not a triumph. His refusal to depict it as he has depicted every other aspect of his relationship with Clarissa reveals the empty reality of Lovelace's public posturings.

Public affirmation is no less crucial to Grandison's sense of masculine identity. Each of Sir Charles's acts of benevolence and masculine virtue are carefully recorded, often by himself, and distributed to the members of his admiring circle. Everyone learns of his match-making between a worthy, yet impoverished gentlewoman and his morally careless uncle, which happily brings about that lady's material comfort and his uncle's reformation; they are given the minutiae of his negotiations with Lady Beauchamp, which secure his deserving best friend Edward's rightful allowance; and they are made privy to his redistribution of an inheritance that he does not feel rightfully entitled to, an action that has the beneficiaries "invoking blessings upon me" (1: 456). Grandison's encounter with Pollexfen is particularly significant in establishing his virtuous manliness. Not only does he overcome Sir Hargrave in front of his own friends through his refusal to duel, humiliating him far more effectively than if he had actually run him through; he requests a copy of the whole affair after it has been recorded by Pollexfen's scribe. This he forwards to Harriet and her friends. His manly example is thus established against that of the rakish and violent Pollexfen, evoking everyone's reverence. Harriet asks her grandmother: "What . . . is the boasted character of most of those who are called HEROES, to the un-ostentatious merit of such a TRULY GOOD MAN?" (3: 462). Grandison's prolific accounts of his own exemplariness are anything but "un-ostentatious," and they secure for him that general admiration and acclamation that confirm his sense of masculine identity—the same response Lovelace seeks through his extravagant letters to Belford.

Far from being the polar opposites he envisioned, Richardson's two models of masculinity share a number of disturbing commonalities, but it is in the examination of his protagonists' exertion of power, that primary masculine "excellence," that Richardson's design to construct alternate masculinities can be seen to rebound on itself. Gerard A. Barker, in considering Sir Charles's "affinities to Lovelace," concludes, finally, that "what primarily distinguishes . . . Richardson's hero and villain is their morality: their means are similar, only their ends differ."[36] However, while their means are quite different, their ends are, in fact, the same. Lovelace's need for power causes him to destroy Clarissa, and, ultimately, himself. Like Lovelace, Grandison is consumed by the need for power, and he, too, destroys the woman he claims to love above all others. The difference between them, then, is not that they exert different kinds of masculine power, or that one's exertion of power is less destructive than the other's—quite the contrary. The difference is that Grandison's will to power manifests under the guise of virtue; as the acknowledged standard of manhood, he is given virtual carte-blanche to reduce whom he chooses to his puppets. As the exemplar of ideal masculinity, no one can take issue with his attitudes or his actions, as they can with those of Lovelace. In *Clarissa*, Lovelace does his worst, and he is punished for it. Grandison's worst, however, is disguised as exemplariness, which Richardson endorses.

Power is fundamental to both Lovelace's and Grandison's conception of masculinity. It is a term that encompasses concepts of control, authority, and even force, and can be understood as "a complex negotiating process," wherein those who can provide or withhold that which is necessary or valorised, "thereby rewarding or punishing (or promising or threatening to do so), can impose their will on others."[37] Power, in this sense, is seen to be power over something or someone else. Power sets a man apart from that which he is not—weak, dependent, feminine. It is in a man's capacity to exercise power and control that the successful performance of masculinity is ultimately achieved. Lovelace's obsession with power is very overt; he is desperate to be perceived as strong, brave, capable, and in control. He represents himself as "such a one . . . who have been used to carry all before me, upon my own terms" (1: 144), and he boasts to Belford: "Many and many a pretty rogue had I spared, whom I did not spare, had my power been acknowledged, and my mercy in time implored" (1: 170).

It is apparent that Lovelace is engaged in an unceasing battle with the world to prove his manhood and to have it acknowledged. His constant attempts to exert power and control reassure him of his masculinity, the fragility and incoherence of which becomes increasingly apparent as the novel progresses. Patricia Spacks writes that "Lovelace's need for effective power is . . . compelling, and . . . elaborately realized. . . . In his relations with other men he finds it necessary to be the leader, the 'emperor' of a troop of rakes . . . The only role Lovelace can imagine with a woman is one of equally absolute dominion."[38] Yet, he is ineffective, as Carol Houlihan Flynn observes: "Lovelace repeatedly demands and never receives public recognition of his greatness. He reigns over his fantasy world, but in the drawing room he is only the rakish Bobby Lovelace."[39]

Lovelace's relationship with Clarissa represents the ultimate test to his masculine identity. His attempts to ingratiate himself with Clarissa before her abduction are largely unsuccessful, and he confesses: "All my fear arises from the little hold I have in the heart of this charming frost-piece . . . and *I*, the hitherto successful

Lovelace, the addresser—how can it be?" (1: 148). Clarissa's "haughty treatment" (2: 314) of him threatens his very identity; he is held in contempt by a woman, a creature who, by definition, is powerless and weak. Instead of becoming "her emperor," he complains that she makes him look like "an abject slave" (2: 32), and treats him "like her vassal" (2: 381), and he feels that, because of Clarissa, he has been made to "bear insults, which *unman* me to bear" (1: 149). However, once he has Clarissa safely ensconced in Sinclair's brothel, he feels himself in control and is able to reassure himself with the dual refrains "is she not IN MY POWER?" (1: 514), and "Marriage will always be in my power" (1: 516). Yet it becomes increasingly clear to Lovelace that no matter what he does, what schemes and stratagems he employs, he cannot subjugate Clarissa's will. He admits to Belford that, "In my power or out of my power, all one to this lady" (2: 15). And ironically, he begins to find that "every time I attend her . . . she is less in *my* power; I more in *hers*" (1: 515). Moreover, he is taunted by the prostitutes whom he has involved in his elaborate plan: "They . . . ridicule me . . . *It was not always so with me*, poor old man! Sally told me; saucily flinging her handkerchief in my face" (2: 471). He vows: "I will not long, my fair one, be despised by *thee*, and laughed at by *them*!" (2: 316). The perceived threat to his masculinity, to his very identity, is too much for him to bear. Terrified at the prospect of emasculation, Lovelace becomes desperate, resorting to the most basic and violent power he can exert over Clarissa: rape. It is in this ultimate act of violence that Lovelace attempts to cement his masculine identity, and fails. In an anguished letter to Belford, he writes: "By my soul, Belford, this dear girl gives the lie to all our rakish maxims— *Once subdued, always subdued!*—'tis an egregious falsehood!—But, oh Jack, she never *was* subdued. What have I obtained but an increase of shame and confusion!" (3: 261). Clarissa, though physically violated, achieves a triumph of sorts over her rapist: "Though a slave, a prisoner, in circumstance, I am no slave in my will! Nothing will I promise thee. Withheld, compelled—nothing will I promise thee!" (3: 260).

Lovelace brings to bear upon Clarissa all of the means at his disposal to make her submit to his will—to have her acknowledge the power of his masculine identity: He flatters her, tricks her, terrorises her, violates her, and finally brings about her death. Thus, Richardson demonstrates the destructive potential inherent in the form of masculinity that Lovelace represents. The example of Lovelace, he hopes, will "afford many useful Lessons to the gay Part of Mankind against that Misuse of Wit and youth, of Rank and Fortune, and of every outward Accomplishment, which turns them into a Curse to the miserable Possessor, as well as to all around him" (G1: 4).

"Wit and youth . . . Rank and Fortune, and . . . every outward Accomplishment" are also the happy lot of Sir Charles in whom these qualities are wedded to virtue, chastity, and a rigid sense of personal integrity and righteousness. It is this fact that legitimates Sir Charles's exertion of masculine power, demonstrated most clearly, though by no means exclusively, in his relationship with Harriet Byron. On the surface, Harriet's and Sir Charles's relationship seems to be very different from that of Clarissa and Lovelace. Sir Charles rescues Harriet from Sir Hargrave Pollexfen, a Lovelaceian rake; and although she naturally falls in love with Sir Charles, he is forced to keep her at a modest distance throughout much of the novel because of a prior romantic entanglement. However, once that affair has been honourably resolved, Sir Charles declares his love for Harriet, they are married, and, we presume, live happily ever after.

And why shouldn't we? After all, Harriet has married the most wonderful man who has ever lived, which she compulsively acknowledges throughout the novel. She claims that "It is virtue, it is goodness, it is generosity, it is true politeness, that I am captivated by; all centred in this one *good man*" (1: 389). Near the novel's close, she delivers the following panegyric:

> Sir Charles Grandison's Love is a Love to be gloried in. Magnanimity and tenderness are united in his noble heart. Littleness of any kind has no place in it: All that know him are studious to commend themselves to his favourable opinion; solicitous about what he will think of them: and, suppressing common foibles before him, find their hearts expand. . . . (3: 457)

This description merely reiterates the view of Grandison that everyone in the novel comes to have, particularly after he has proven his inimitable superiority at everyone else's expense, what Harriet refers to as "the art he has of making everybody proud of acknowledging an inferiority to him" (1: 211). As the exemplar of a new masculine code, one based on a virtuous virility and an honour that abhors violence, he is the standard against which all other men can now be measured; Sir Hargrave Pollexfen calls him "the man of men" (3: 75), and Charlotte Grandison asserts that he is, in fact, "more than a man" (3: 68). Grandison's exemplary manliness is certainly a key factor in the power he is able to exert over all with whom he comes in contact. As Lipman-Blumen points out, "the perceived omnipotence of those currently in power is . . . mythical and seriously immobilizing to the less powerful. It is the mythic proportions, however that tend to keep the less powerful intimidated."[40] But what Harriet's speech also articulates is the power dynamic between herself and Sir Charles; indeed, between him and any other person in the novel with whom he develops a relationship. It is not the virtuous example set by Grandison that embodies his power; rather, it is the example of what happens to those who do not meet his expectations and standards which, to use Lipman-Blumen's words, "keep the less powerful intimidated"—and in the world of Sir Charles Grandison, the category of "less powerful" includes everyone, save himself. Grandison, who makes it known "that he lived to himself, and to his own heart" (1: 182), does not extend this same right to others. Although Harriet suggests that Grandison "but accommodates himself to the persons he has to deal with" as a method of achieving his ends (2: 272), it becomes clear that those who defy Sir Charles, whether it be to act against his advice or to adopt a perspective different from his own, are threatened with the withdrawal of not only his approval, but of his love. Whereas Lovelace is quite open in his declaration that

"I always considered opposition and resistance as a challenge to do my worst" (2: 15), Grandison recasts all opposition to his wishes as a failure of virtue; thus, his "worst" is to punish the offender by repudiation. In responding to the news of his sisters' supposed defiance of their father's authority, Grandison states that "their want of consideration shall receive no countenance from me. I shall let them know, that my love, my esteem, if it be of consequence with them, is not founded on relation, but merit . . ." (3: 52). It is important to note that it is Grandison who determines what constitutes merit, and his love and esteem are distributed accordingly. Charlotte later remarks: "Very happy . . . to have such a character that every-body must be in fault who differs from him, or offends him" (2: 87). This is graphically illustrated in Grandison's early relationship with Jeronymo della Porretta and his attempts to wean him away from dissolute companions and loose women. On being, in Grandison's words, "expostulated with," Jeronymo has the temerity to resent "the friendly freedom. He was passionate. . . . He even defied his friend" (2: 120). Sir Charles decides that he "could not be over-solicitous to keep up a friendship with a young man who . . . would not allow of remonstrances, in cases that concerned his morals" (2: 142). Similarly, Grandison informs his cousin Everard that, had he seduced a certain young girl through promises of marriage, "I must have made it a condition of our continual friendship, that you had married her" (2: 573). Not surprisingly, Harriet internalises the examples she both reads of and witnesses first-hand, noting "is not his conduct such, as would make a considerate person, who has any connexion with him, tremble?" (2: 609).

What Grandison cannot effect through manipulation or badgering, he will accomplish through rejection, a serious punishment when it comes from a man who embodies every virtue and desirable manly attribute. Harriet admits, "It is impossible . . . but Sir Charles Grandison must carry every point he sets his heart upon" (2: 317). This, of course, is as necessary to his sense of masculine identity as sexual triumph is to Lovelace's. Harriet certainly experiences Grandison's coercive, relentless influence. He pressures Harriet unmercifully in order to get her to concede to an "early day." Certainly this could be attributed to the fervency of his love for her, until we remember that he pressured his sister Charlotte in exactly the same way. Grandison wishes to have all of his affairs in order before he returns to Italy; it would be convenient for him if Charlotte were to marry Lord G. prior to his departure. Despite the fact that Charlotte "vehemently opposed so early a day" (2: 314), he dismisses her reluctance with impatience: "You have sacrificed enough to female punctilio, Charlotte. . . . Leave the day to me. Let it be Tuesday next" (2: 316). Charlotte responds: "Good heaven! I can't bear you" (2: 316). Although Charlotte makes it clear that she "hate[s] his peremptoriness" (2: 315), she is forced to bow to her brother's will: "It was agreed for Charlotte, whose assent was given in these words—'Do as you will—or, rather, as my brother will.—What signifies opposing him?' that the nuptials shall be solemnized" (2: 335-36). On Charlotte's wedding day, Harriet contemplates the fact that though marriage is supposed to be a joyful solemnity:

on the woman's side it can be only so, when she is given to the man she loves above all men in the world. . . . What a victim must that woman look upon herself to be, who is compelled, or even *over-persuaded*, to give her hand to a man who has no share in her heart? Ought not a parent or guardian, in such circumstance . . . to be chargeable with all the unhappy consequences that may follow from such a cruel compulsion? (2: 347)

She hastily retracts the imputation of cruelty to Grandison, managing to convince herself that his "over-persuasion" is really for the best: "But this is not the case with Miss Grandison . . . She hates not Lord G. . . . she may be happy, if she will . . . her brother was kind in persuading her to shorten her days of coquetting and teazing, and allow him to give her to Lord G. before he went abroad" (2: 347). Clearly, Grandison's convenience supersedes his sister's right to be "given to the man she loves above all the men in the world."

Grandison's treatment of Harriet is no less coercive, and no less successful. Although he reassures her that her "*chearful* compliance with my wishes is the great desireable," and "Whatever shall be your pleasure must determine me" (3: 156), his response to her decision to set six weeks until their marriage is less than supportive: "'Six weeks! For Heaven's sake, madam'—He looked, he spoke, impatience" (3: 134). Virgin modesty be damned! Grandison's own celebrated "delicacy" does not prevent him from securing what he wants, when he wants it. Moreover, Grandison's repeated hints to Harriet that any reluctance she might have can only be based on punctilio (3: 57) replicates his intolerant response to his sister's aversion to an early day; he fears that her "known delicacy," as he tells her, "would descend into punctiliousness" (3:78). The implication, of course, is that such a failing on Harriet's part would be a grave disappointment to him, and Harriet, to whom Grandison's opinion means more than anything, is herself "afraid of being thought affected" in the matter (3: 99). After all, "to unwomanly faults, to want of morals, and even to want of delicacy, no man is more quicksighted" than Sir Charles (2: 45). The situation merely echoes Harriet's earlier anxieties regarding Grandison's approbation: "I dread . . . every-thing that may be construed into officiousness or particularity, by so nice a discerner. Does he not say, that no man is more quick sighted than himself, to those faults in women which are owing to want of delicacy?" (2: 63).

Harriet spends much of her time trying to "deserve" Sir Charles's love (despite the fact that she is his second choice). She endures his constant praise of Clementina, the pious young Italian woman he almost married. Harriet lives with the intolerable suspense of not knowing if he will actually marry Clementina or not. Even after her engagement to Grandison, the threat that Clementina will change her mind constantly torments Harriet. And, worst of all, Grandison admits that Clementina's welfare is as much behind his proposal of marriage to Harriet as are his feelings for her. During his actual proposal, he tells her that "I am urged by all [Clementina's] family, for the sake of setting her an example, to address myself to a Lady of my own country. This *impels* me, as I may say, to *accelerate* the humble tender of my vows to you, madam" (3: 57). Moreover, Clementina's renunciation of Sir Charles is discussed and admired constantly; Harriet is never allowed to forget the superior example of her predecessor. Sir Charles's praise of Harriet is invariably mixed with tender praise for his first love: "I observed in her [Harriet's] mind and behaviour that true dignity, delicacy, and noble frankness, which I ever thought characteristic in the sex, but never met with, in equal degree, but in *one* Lady" (3: 53); "Sweet Excellence! Did I ever hope to meet in woman with such an enlargement of heart!—Clementina only, of all the women I ever knew, can be set in comparison with you . . . " (3: 151). And, when Harriet is finally his wife, Grandison, that paragon of delicacy, introduces her on one occasion as "the sister-excellence of Lady Clementina" (3: 310).

Harriet is further distressed when she discovers that Sir Charles has refused Mr. Deane's offer of a financial settlement upon the marriage; her pride is wounded, and she admits, "My poverty . . . has added to my pride" (3: 38). To Charlotte, she writes: "Yet think you, my dear, that I am not mortified? How can I look round upon my congratulating friends . . . with that modest confidence which the sense of laying an obligation on a favoured object . . . gives to diffident merit?" (3: 39). And, despite feeling guilty, she cannot help but entertain the thought that "in declining so greatly their offers," Sir Charles is offering "a bribe to make me sit down satisfied with half, nay, *not* half, a heart" (3: 39). It is the deeper implication of Grandison's action, however, that is most significant. Grandison is described as "A man . . . who takes pleasure in conferring obligations, yet never lays himself under the necessity of receiving returns" (2: 645). In rejecting Mr. Deane's offer, Grandison indicates that he "will not permit [Harriet] to owe uncommon obligations to any but himself" (3: 38). We are reminded of Lovelace's views on conferring obligations:

> But is it not a confounded thing that I cannot fasten an obligation upon this proud beauty? I have two motives in endeavouring to prevail upon her to accept of money and raiment from me: one, the real pleasure I should have in the accommodating of the haughty maid . . . the other, in order to abate her severity and humble her a little. (2: 67)

Although Grandison's action is, as always, attributed to his generosity, it is difficult to deny Lovelace's cynical observation that "Nothing sooner brings down a proud spirit than a sense of lying under pecuniary obligations" (2: 67). Eventually, the stress of her situation wears Harriet down. In the course of meeting and becoming involved with Sir Charles, Harriet, by her own admission, "a saucy creature" (1: 22), whom Uncle Selby used to call "My sweet Sparkler," which she explains "was the name he used to call me, before Sir Charles Grandison taught me a lesson that made me thoughtful" (3: 70), is transformed into a woman possessed of an "overburdened heart" and beset by "anxieties" (3: 29). She is plagued by "The sense I have of my own littleness" (3: 41), and on a number of occasions declares, with real pain: "I am such a nothing!" (1: 295). This is most disturbingly evident in several remarks she makes about herself since she has known Sir Charles:

> I was supposed once to be so good a creature . . . Ah, my partial friends! you studied your

Harriet in the dark; but here comes the sun darting into all the crooked and obscure corners of my heart; and I shrink from his dazling eye; and, compared to Him (and *Clementina*, let me add) appear to myself such a Nothing. (3: 132)

Harriet exhibits a great deal of trepidation over what she sees as Grandison's superior prudence and largeness of spirit in comparison to her inferiority. "But is not his conduct such, as would make a considerate person, who has any connexions with him, tremble? Since if there be a fault between them, it must be all that person's" (2: 609). As a further consequence of her distress, Harriet experiences a fairly serious physical decline. Mr. Deane, on seeing her for the first time after her rescue and very early in her relationship with Sir Charles says, "She is as lovely as ever; but I think, not quite so lively, and somewhat paler . . . she has more meekness and humility in her countenance, than, methinks, I would wish her to have" (2: 30). Later, when Sir Charles appears to be going through with his marriage to Clementina, Harriet becomes increasingly debilitated: "She visibly falls away; and her fine complexion fades. Mr. Deane . . . was so much startled at the alteration in her lovely countenance, that he broke from her, and shed tears to Lucy" (2: 516). However, nowhere is Harriet's torment more apparent than in her disturbing dream:

But such contradictory vagaries never did I know in my slumbers . . . For example—I was married to the best of men: I was not married: I was rejected with scorn, as a presumptuous creature. I sought to hid myself in holes and corners. . . . I again dreamed I was married: Sir Charles again was the man. He did not love me. My grandmamma and aunt, on their knees, and with tears, besought him to love their child; and pleaded to him my Love of him of long standing, begun in gratitude; and that he was the only man I ever loved. O how I wept in my dream! My face and bosom were wet with my real tears. (3: 148)

In later parts of the dream, Sir Charles is killed, first by Clementina's brother, the General, and then by Greville, one of Harriet's more persistent suitors. Admittedly, the latter parts of the dream originate in some of Harriet's legitimate fears about Grandison's safety, but it also speaks to a very real anger she feels, a desire to punish him in turn for what she has suffered, and continues to suffer. Certainly, there are points in the relationship when Harriet's anger at the intolerable position she has been put in erupts. Having been stood up by her suitor one morning, Harriet breaks out with: "But let me try to excuse him. . . . May he not have overslept himself?—Some agreeable dream of the Bologna family—I am offended at him—did he learn this tranquillity in Italy?" (3: 46). She notes later, "I know my heart: It is all his own: and I am *loth* to disoblige him—But he was far, far more attendant on Lady Clementina's motions" (3: 122). She is bitter about the course events have taken:

But he has no doubts, no suspenses, from us, to keep Love awake: His path is plain and smooth before him. He has demanded his day. . . . Am I not perverse? . . . I believe I am. Yet . . . truly as I honour and revere Lady Clementina, my mind is not always great enough

. . . to carry itself above apprehension and petulance, noble as is the man. (3: 122)

Yet, finally, both Harriet's anger and Harriet herself are completely, probably irrevocably, subsumed by Grandison. Gaining Grandison's approval becomes everything, and seems to be the only way through which Harriet can escape the sense of her intolerable "nothingness": "It was making me great . . . to have it in my power, as I may say, to convince Sir Charles Grandison, that my compassion, my love my admiration of [Clementina] the noblest of women, was a sincere admiration and love" (3: 330). Harriet, no less than Clarissa, has been subjected to a rigorous test of virtue. Whereas Clarissa passes Lovelace's test by refusing to succumb to his manipulations, dying in the process, Harriet passes Grandison's by schooling herself to make his will her own, also dying in the process. Grandison remarks approvingly of his wife, "my Harriet has found, for the first time, a will. It is her own, we know, by its obligingness" (3: 289). At one point she is so grateful for proof of his love that she "threw myself at his feet; embraced his knees; and has speech been lent me, would have offered him the fervent vows of a heart overflowing with Love and Gratitude" (3: 275). Interestingly, this duplicates one of Lovelace's fantasies about Clarissa, wherein she is finally humbled and prostrate before him, speaking her gratitude and humility with her eyes, but otherwise silent (2: 251–52). Lovelace's power is here only fantasised; Grandison's is actual.

In comparing *Clarissa* and *The History of Sir Charles Grandison*, Jocelyn Harris concludes that, "having shown in *Clarissa* a woman destroyed by the tyrannical misuse of authority, Richardson now offers the more practical solution of turning patriarchal power to good ends,"[41] a sentiment echoed by Margaret Doody, who sees the world of *Grandison* as "a place in which male sexual and aggressive power is to be used solely for good."[42] Yet, Harriet's self-esteem and, finally, her *self*, virtually disappear as a result of her relationship with Grandison. The Harriet we meet at the beginning of the novel is nowhere to be found in the compliant, even servile wife of Sir Charles. Ultimately, Harriet is humbled by Grandison in a way that Clarissa, for all the indignities and violence she suffers at the hands of Lovelace, never was humbled. Thus, in creating a masculine ideal to oppose his model of masculine baseness, Richardson does not actually posit an alternative to hegemonic forms of "patriarchally-conditioned masculinity." In Grandison, he merely gives us another, supposedly better form of the same thing. Ironically, his model of masculine virtue manages to accomplish what Lovelace could not: It is Harriet, not Clarissa, of whom it can be said "*Once subdued, always subdued!*"

The History of Sir Charles Grandison is a significant work in the canon of novelistic fiction and profoundly influenced subsequent literary representations of masculinity in the works of later eighteenth-century authors, including those of Burney, Godwin, and Austen.[43] Yet, while Grandison's model was intended to serve as a new exemplar of masculinity, implicit in its construction was the message, as Terry Eagleton points out, that "male hegemony was to be sweetened but not undermined."[44] Accordingly, while the authors of novels such as *Evelina*

(1778), *A Simple Story* (1791), and *Emma* (1816), offered modifications and even implicit critiques of Richardson's standards for ideal masculinity, they did not question the imperatives informing the model itself. Burney's Lord Orville, Inchbald's Dorriforth, and Austen's Mr. Knightley are, like Sir Charles Grandison, constructed from the same masculine material as Richardson's Lovelace. Thus, Evelina is ultimately infantilised by Orville's overwhelming superiority and comes to feel that she "could scarce breathe under the weight of gratitude that oppressed" her;[45] Jane Spencer remarks that "the best key to understanding [Dorriforth] is his insistence on controlling any wilfulness in his subordinates, especially in women";[46] and the willful and oft-mistaken Emma is finally overpowered by the paternalistic Mr. Knightley, and learns to do "Just what she ought, of course."[47] Like Lovelace and Sir Charles Grandison, the male protagonists who followed in the wake of Richardson's attempt to reconstruct masculinity are characterized by the need to ultimately subdue their female counterparts. Moreover, if, as Sue Warrick Doerdelein contends, we need to acknowledge what Richardson's novels add "to the complex network of power/knowledge relationships" that shaped a "then inarticulate 'femininity' into words and gestures,"[48] we must also credit him with not only representing, but reshaping notions of masculinity—what it means to be a man—at a time when gendered identities were becoming defined in ways they never had before.

NOTES

1. Tassie Gwilliam, *Samuel Richardson's Fiction of Gender* (Stanford: Stanford University Press, 1993) 1.

2. Alice Echols, "The Taming of the Id: Feminist Sexual Politics, 1968–83," *Pleasure and Danger: Exploring Female Sexuality* (Boston: Routledge & Kegan Paul, 1984) 53. Echols's use of this term begs the question of whether there can be a masculinity that is not patriarchally-conditioned, a question underlying this analysis of Richardson's masculine representations.

3. Joan W. Scott, "Gender: A Useful Category of Historical Analysis," *American Historical Review* 91 (1986): 1056.

4. Scott Coltrane, "Theorizing Masculinities in Contemporary Social Science," *Theorizing Masculinities*, eds. Harry Brod and Michael Kaufman (Thousand Oaks: Sage Publications, 1994) 41. In their introduction to *Manful Assertions: Masculinities in Britain Since 1800* (London and New York: Routledge, 1991), Michael Roper and John Tosh observe that traditional scholarship has been "highly resistant to problematizing the masculinity of its male subjects" (2).

5. Jane Flax, "Postmodernism and Gender Relations in Feminist Theory," *Signs* 12 (1987): 629.

6. Michael S. Kimmel, preface, *Theorizing Masculinities*, 11.

7. Jeff Hearn and David Collinson, "Theorizing Unities and Differences Between Men and Between Masculinities," *Theorizing Masculinities*, 98.

8. Anthony Fletcher, *Gender, Sex, and Subordination in England 1500-1880* (New Haven and London: Yale University Press, 1995) 322–33.

9. Samuel Richardson, *Clarissa, Or the History of a Young Lady*, 4 vols. (New York: Everyman's Library, 1906) 1: xv. Subsequent references will be to this edition and will be noted in the text by volume and page.

10. Gwilliam, *Samuel Richardson's Fiction*, 111.

11. Samuel Richardson, *Correspondences*, ed. Anna L. Barbauld, 6 vols. (London: Richard Phillips, 1804) 3: 140.

12. *Correspondences*, 6: 75.

13. Samuel Richardson, *The History of Sir Charles Grandison*, 3 vols., ed. Jocelyn Harris (London: Oxford University Press, 1972) 1:4. Subsequent references will be to this edition and will be noted in the text by volume and page.

14. *Correspondences*, 6:22.

15. G. J. Barker-Benfield, *The Culture of Sensibility: Sex and Society in Eighteenth-Century Britain* (Chicago: The University of Chicago Press, 1992) 40.

16. Barker-Benfield, *The Culture of Sensibility*, 38.

17. Ian Watt, *The Rise of the Novel: Studies in Defoe, Richardson, and Fielding* (Harmondsworth: Penguin Books, Ltd., 1985) 258.

18. Margaret Anne Doody, *A Natural Passion: A Study of the Novels of Samuel Richardson* (Oxford: Clarendon Press, 1974) 47.

19. Doody, *A Natural Passion*, 48.

20. Jean Hagstrum, *Sex and Sensibility: Ideal and Erotic Love from Milton to Mozart* (Chicago: University of Chicago Press, 1980) 209.

21. Roy Porter, "Mixed Feelings: The Enlightenment and Sexuality in Eighteenth-Century Britain," *Sexuality in Eighteenth-Century Britain*, ed. Paul Gabriel Bouce (Manchester: Manchester University Press, 1982) 12.

22. In one of his editorial additions to the third edition of *Clarissa*, Richardson lamented the fact that "many of the sex (we mention it with regret) . . . has been readier to censure [Clarissa] for over-niceness . . . than him for artifices . . . not less cruel and ungrateful, than ungenerous and unmanly" (2:33).

23. *Correspondences*, 4: 312.

24. Anna Clark, *Women's Silence, Men's Violence: Sexual Assault in England 1770-1845* (London: Pandora Press, 1987) 24.

25. *Correspondences*, 4: 312.

26. Gerald A. Barker, *Grandison's Heirs: The Paragon's Progress in the Late Eighteenth-Century English Novel* (London: Associated University Presses, 1985) 15.

27. Morris Golden, *Richardson's Characters* (Ann Arbor: University of Michigan Press, 1963) 17.

28. David Robinson, "Unraveling the 'Cord Which Ties Good Men to Good Men': Male Friendship in Richardson's Novels," *Samuel Richardson: Tercentenary Essays*, eds. Margaret Doody and Peter Sabor (Cambridge: Cambridge University Press, 1989) 127.

29. Michael S. Kimmel discusses this point in "Masculinity as Homophobia: Fear Shame, and Silence in the Construction of Gender Identity" (*Theorizing Masculinities*) 126.

30. Kimmel, "Masculinity as Homophobia," 128.

31. Michael McKeon, "Historicizing Patriarchy: The Emergence of Gender Differences in England, 1660–1760," *Eighteenth-Century Studies* 28 (1995): 312–14. McKeon argues that, in fact, "the modern category of the masculine" emerged from the "interstices of . . . two gender types, the feminine and the effeminate" (310).

32. Kimmel, "Masculinity as Homophobia," 127.

33. Scott, "Gender," 1063.

34. Barker-Benfield, *The Culture of Sensibility*, 340–41.

35. Kimmel, "Masculinity as Homophobia," 128–29.

36. Gerard A. Barker, "The Complacent Paragon: Exemplary Characterization in Richardson," *SEL* 9 (1969): 518–19.

37. Jean Lipman-Blumen, "The Existential Bases of Power Relationships: The Gender Role Case," *Power/Gender: Social Relations in Theory and Practice*, eds. H. Lorraine Radtke and Henderikus J. Stam (London: Sage Publications, 1994) 128.

38. Patricia Meyer Spacks, "Early Fiction and the Frightened Male," *Novel* 8 (1974): 144.

39. Carol Houlihan Flynn, *Samuel Richardson: A Man of Letters* (Princeton: Princeton University Press, 1982) 233.

40. Lipman-Blumen, "Existential Bases," 114.

41. Jocelyn Harris, *Samuel Richardson* (Cambridge: Cambridge University Press, 1987) 144.

42. Margaret Anne Doody, "Saying 'No,' Saying 'Yes': The Novels of Samuel Richardson," *Tennessee Studies in Literature* 29 (1985): 98.

43. Barker, *Grandison's Heirs*, 9–10.

44. Terry Eagleton, *The Rape of Clarissa: Writing, Sexuality and Class Struggle in Samuel Richardson* (Oxford: Basil Blackwell, 1982) 95.

45. Frances Burney, *Evelina, Or the History of a Young Lady's Entrance Into the World* (London: Oxford University Press, 1968) 367.

46. Jane Spencer, introduction, *A Simple Story*, by Elizabeth Inchbald (London: Oxford University Press, 1988) xix.

47. Jane Austen, *Emma* in *The Novels of Jane Austen*, 3d. edition, ed. R. W. Chapman (London: Oxford University Press, 1933) 430.

48. Sue Warrick Doerdelein, "Clarissa in the Hands of Critics," *Eighteenth-Century Studies* 16 (1982–83): 403.

Selected Bibliography

Alkon, Paul. *Defoe and Fictional Time*. Athens: University of Georgia Press, 1979.

Amussen, Susan. *An Ordered Society: Gender and Class in Early Modern England*. Oxford: Basil Blackwell, 1988.

Armstrong, Nancy. *Desire and Domestic Fiction: A Political History of the Novel*. New York and Oxford: Oxford University Press, 1987.

August, Eugene. *Men's Studies: A Selected and Annotated Interdisciplinary Bibliography*. Littleton: Libraries Unlimited, 1985.

Barker-Benfield, G. J. *The Culture of Sensibility: Sex and Society in Eighteenth-Century Britain*. Chicago: University of Chicago Press, 1992.

Barrell, John. "'The Dangerous Goddess': Masculinity, Prestige, and the Aesthetic in Early Eighteenth-Century Britain." *Cultural Critique* 12 (1989): 101–31.

Bartky, Sandra. *Femininity and Domination: Essays on the Phenomenology of Oppression*. London and New York: Routledge, 1990.

Bernheimer, Charles. "Penile References in Phallic Theory." *Differences: A Journal of Feminist Cultural Studies* 4.1 (1992): 116–32.

Boone, Joseph A., and Michael Cadden, eds. *Engendering Man: The Question of Male Feminist Criticism*. London and New York: Routledge, 1990.

Breitenberg, Mark. *Anxious Masculinity in Early Modern England*. Cambridge: Cambridge University Press, 1996.

Brittan, Arthur. *Masculinity and Power*. New York: Basil Blackwell, 1989.

Brod, Harry, and Michael Kaufman, eds. *Theorizing Masculinities*. Thousand Oaks, CA.: Sage Publications, 1994.

Brooks, Harold. "Principal Conflicts in the Restoration Comedy of Manners: The Battle of Sex, and Truewits v. Witwoulds and Lackwits." *Durham University Journal* 80 (1988): 201–12.

Budd, Michael Anton. *The Sculpture Machine: Physical Culture and Body Politics in the Age of Empire*. New York: New York University Press, 1997.

Bushnell, Rebecca. *Tragedies of Tyrants: Political Thought and Theater in the English Renaissance*. Ithaca: Cornell University Press, 1990.

Butler, Judith. *Bodies That Matter: On the Discursive Limits of "Sex."* London and New York: Routledge, 1993.

Carnes, Mark C. *Secret Ritual and Manhood in Victorian America*. New Haven and London: Yale University Press, 1989.

Chernaik, Warren. *Sexual Freedom in Restoration Literature*. Cambridge: Cambridge University Press, 1995.

Cohen, Michele. *Fashioning Masculinity: National Identity and Language in the Eighteenth Century*. London and New York: Routledge, 1996.

Coltharp, Duane. "'Pleasing Rape': The Politics of Libertinism in *The Conquest of Granada*." *Restoration: Studies in English Literary Culture, 1660–1700* 21.1 (1997): 15–31.

Connell, R. W. *Masculinities*. Berkeley: University of California Press, 1995.

Craft, Christopher. *Another Kind of Love: Male Homosexual Desire in English Discourse, 1850–1920*. Berkeley: University of California Press, 1994.

Dellamora, Richard. *Masculine Desire: The Sexual Politics of Victorian Aestheticism*. Chapel Hill: University of North Carolina Press, 1990.

DiGangi, Mario. "Asses and Wits: The Homoerotics of Mastery in Satiric Comedy." *English Literary Renaissance* 25.2 (1995): 179–208.

Doody, Margaret Ann. *A Natural Passion: A Study of the Novels of Samuel Richardson*. Oxford: Clarendon Press, 1974.

Doty, William. *Myths of Masculinity*. New York: Crossroads, 1993.

Dubbert, Joe. *A Man's Place: Masculinity in Transition*. Englewood Cliff, N.J.: Prentice-Hall, 1979.

Dubrow, Heather. *Echoes of Desire: English Petrarchism and its Counterdiscourses*. Ithaca: Cornell University Press, 1995.

Eagleton, Terry. *The Ideology of the Aesthetic*. Oxford: Basil Blackwell, 1990.

Easthope, Anthony. *What a Man's Gotta Do: The Masculine Myth in Popular Culture*. London: Paladin, 1986.

Enterline, Lynn. *The Tears of Narcissus: Melancholia and Masculinity in Early Modern Writing*. Stanford: Stanford University Press, 1995.

Eyler, Ellen C. *Early English Gardens and Garden Books*. Ithaca: Cornell University Press, 1963.

Ferguson, Margaret, Maureen Quilligan, and Nancy J. Vickers, eds. *The Renaissance: Discourses of Sexual Difference in Early Modern Europe*. Chicago: University of Chicago Press, 1986.

Finkelpearl, Philip. *Court and Country Politics in the Plays of Beaumont and Fletcher*. Princeton: Princeton University Press, 1990.

Fletcher, Anthony. *Gender, Sex and Subordination in England, 1500–1880*. New Haven and London: Yale University Press, 1995.

Flynn, Carol Houlihan. *Samuel Richardson: A Man of Letters*. Princeton: Princeton University Press, 1982.

Gilmore, David. *Manhood in the Making: Cultural Concepts of Masculinity*. New Haven and London: Yale University Press, 1990.

Goldberg, Jonathan. *Sodometries: Renaissance Texts, Modern Sexualities*. Stanford: Stanford University Press, 1992.

Greenblatt, Stephen. *Shakespearean Negotiations: The Circulation of Social Energy in Renaissance England*. Berkeley: University of California Press, 1988.

Gwilliam, Tassie. *Samuel Richardson's Fictions of Gender*. Stanford: Stanford University Press, 1993.

Hagstrum, Jean. *Sex and Sensibility: Ideal and Erotic Love from Milton to Mozart*. Chicago: University of Chicago Press, 1980.

Hearn, Jeff. *The Gender of Oppression: Men, Masculinity, and the Critique of Marxism*. London: Wheatsheaf, 1987.

Howard, Jean. "Crossdressing, the Theater, and Gender Struggle in Early Modern England." *Shakespeare Quarterly* 39:4 (1988): 418–40.

Illich, Ivan. *Gender*. New York: Random House, 1982.

Jardine, Alice, and Paul Smith, eds. *Men in Feminism*. New York: Methuen, 1987.

Jordan, Constance. *Renaissance Feminism: Literary Texts and Political Methods*. Ithaca: Cornell University Press, 1990.

Kahn, Coppelia. *Man's Estate: Masculine Identity in Shakespeare*. Berkeley: California University Press, 1981.

Kann, Mark E. *On the Men Question: Gender and Civic Virtue in America*. Philadelphia: Temple University Press, 1991.

Kaufman, Michael, ed. *Beyond Patriarchy: Essays by Men on Pleasure, Power, and Change*. New York: Oxford University Press, 1987.

Kelly, Veronica, and Dorothea E. Von Mucke, eds. *Body and Text in the Eighteenth Century*. Stanford: Stanford University Press, 1994.

Kimmel, Michael S., ed. *Changing Men: New Directions in Research on Men and Masculinity*. Newbury Park Calif.: Sage, 1987.

———. "From Lord and Master to Cuckold and Fop: Masculinity in Seventeenth-Century England." *University of Dayton Review* 18.2 (1986–87): 93–109.

———, ed. *The Politics of Manhood: Profeminist Men Respond to the Mythopoetic Men's Movement (And the Mythopoetic Leaders Answer)*. Philadelphia: Temple University Press, 1995.

Laqueur, Thomas. *Making Sex: Body and Gender from the Greeks to Freud*. Cambridge: Harvard University Press, 1990.

Legouis, Pierre. *Andrew Marvell: Poet, Puritan, Patriot*. Oxford: Oxford University Press, 1968.

Levine, Laura. *Men in Women's Clothing: Anti-Theatricality and Effeminization, 1579–1642*. Cambridge: Cambridge University Press, 1994.

Loughlin, Marie H. *Hymeneutics: Interpreting Virginity on the Early Modern Stage*. Lewisburg: Bucknell University Press, 1997.

Low, Anthony. *The Reinvention of Love: Poetry, Politics and Culture from Sidney to Milton*. Cambridge: Cambridge University Press, 1993.

Mahdi, Louise Carus, Steven Foster, and Meredith Little, eds. *Betwixt and Between: Patterns of Masculine and Feminine Initiation*. Chicago: Open Court, 1987.

Mangan, J. A., and James Walvin, eds. *Manliness and Morality: Middle-class Masculinity in Britain and America 1800–1940*. New York: St. Martin's Press, 1987.

Masten, Jeffrey. *Textual Intercourse: Collaboration, Authorship, and Sexualities in Renaissance Drama*. Cambridge: Cambridge University Press, 1997.

McGeary, Thomas. "Warbling Eunuchs: Opera, Gender, and Sexuality on the London Stage, 1705–1742." *Restoration and 18th Century Theater Research* 7 (1992): 1–22.

McKeon, Michael. "Historicizing Patriarchy: The Emergence of Gender Difference in England, 1660–1760." *Eighteenth-Century Studies* 28 (1995): 295–322.

McLuskie, Kathleen. "The Act, the Role, and the Actor: Boy Actresses on the Elizabethan Stage." *New Theater Quarterly* 3:10 (1987): 120–30.

Minnich, Elizabeth Karmarck. *Transforming Knowledge*. Philadelphia: Temple University Press, 1990.

Monick, Eugene. *Phallos: Sacred Images of the Masculine*. Toronto: Inner City Books, 1987.

Moore, Robert, and Douglas Gillette. *King, Warrior, Magician, Lover: Rediscovering the Archetypes of the Mature Masculine*. San Francisco: Harper Collins, 1990.

Moss, George. *The Image of Man: The Creation of Modern Masculinity*. Oxford: Oxford University Press, 1996.

Nussbaum, Felicity. *The Autobiographical Subject: Gender and Ideology in Eighteenth-Century England*. Baltimore and London: The Johns Hopkins University Press, 1989.

———. *The Brink of All We Hate: English Satires on Women, 1660–1750*. Lexington: University Press of Kentucky, 1984.

Osherson, Samuel. *Finding Our Fathers: The Unfinished Business of Manhood*. New York: Macmillan, 1986.

Pearson, Jacqueline. *The Prostituted Muse*. New York: St. Martin's Press, 1988.

Radtke, Lorraine, and Henderikus J. Stam, eds. *Power/Gender: Social Relations in Theory and Practice*. London: Sage Publications, 1994.

Rochlin, Gregory. *The Masculine Dilemma: A Psychology of Masculinity*. Boston: Little, Brown and Company, 1980.

Rogers, Pat. *Eighteenth-Century Encounters: Studies in Literature and Society in the Age of Walpole*. Brighton: The Harvester Press Ltd. 1985.

Roper, Michael, and John Tosh, eds. *Manful Assertions: Masculinities in Britain Since 1800*. London and New York: Routledge, 1991.

Rutherford, Jonathan. *Forever England: Reflections on Race, Masculinity and Empire*. London: Lawrence and Wishart, 1997.

Sedgwick, Eve. *Between Men: English Literature and Male Homosocial Desire*. New York: Columbia University Press, 1985.

Segal, Lynne. *Slow Motion: Changing Masculinities, Changing Men*. New Brunswick: Rutgers University Press, 1990.

Senelick, Laurence. "'Mollies or Men of Mode': Sodomy and the Eighteenth-Century London Stage." *Journal of the History of Sexuality* 1 (1990): 36–67.

Shapiro, Susan. "'Yon Plumed Dandebrat': Male 'Effeminacy' in English Satire and Criticism." *Review of English Studies* 39 (1988): 400–12.

Sharpe, Kevin. *Criticism and Compliment: The Politics of Literature in the England of Charles I*. Cambridge: Cambridge University Press, 1987.

Shattuck, Roger. *Forbidden Knowledge: From Prometheus to Pornography*. New York: Harcourt Brace, 1996.

Shepard, Paul. *Man in the Landscape: A Historic View of the Esthetics of Nature*. New York: Knopf, 1967.

Silverman, Kaja. *Male Subjectivity at the Margins*. London and New York: Routledge, 1992.

Smith, Bruce R. *Homosexual Desire in Shakespeare's England: A Cultural Poetics*. Chicago: University of Chicago Press, 1991.

Staves, Susan. "A Few Kind Words for the Fop." *Studies in English Literature* 22 (1982): 413–28.

Stone, Lawrence. *The Family, Sex and Marriage in England 1500–1800*. New York: Harper Torchbooks, 1979.

Straub, Kristina. *Sexual Suspects: Eighteenth-Century Players and Sexual Ideology*. Princeton: Princeton University Press, 1992.

Tennenhouse, Leonard. "Simulating History: A Cockfight for Our Times." *The Drama Review* 34.4 (1990): 137–55.

Thomas, Calvin. *Male Matters: Masculinity, Anxiety, and the Male Body on the Line*. Urbana and Chicago: University of Illinois Press, 1996.

Traub, Valarie. *Desire and Anxiety: Circulations of Sexuality in Shakespearean Drama.* London and New York: Routledge, 1997.

Tuana, Nancy. *The Less Noble Sex.* Bloomington: Indiana University Press, 1993.

Turner, James Grantham, ed. *Sexuality and Gender in Early Modern Europe: Institutions, Texts, Images.* Cambridge: Cambridge University Press, 1995.

Underwood, Dale. *Etherege and the Seventeenth-Century Comedy of Manners.* New Haven and London: Yale University Press, 1957.

Wall, Wendy. *The Imprint of Gender: Authorship and Publication in the English Renaissance.* Ithaca: Cornell University Press, 1993.

Watt, Ian. *The Rise of the Novel: Studies in Defoe, Richardson, and Fielding.* Harmondsworth: Penguin Books Ltd. 1985.

Weber, Harold. *The Restoration Rake-Hero: Transformations in Sexual Understanding in Seventeenth-Century England.* Madison: University of Wisconsin Press, 1986.

Weed, David M. "Sexual Positions: Men of Pleasure, Economy, and Dignity in Boswell's *London Journal.*" *Eighteenth-Century Studies* 31 (1997–98): 215–34.

Williams, Andrew P. *The Restoration Fop: Gender Boundaries and Comic Characterization in Later Seventeenth-Century Drama.* New York: Edwin Mellen Press, 1995.

Williams, Carolyn. *Pope, Homer, and Manliness: Some Aspects of Eighteenth-Century Classical Learning.* London and New York: Routledge, 1993.

Index

Contributors

TAYLOR CORSE is an Associate Professor of English at Arizona State University. He is the author of *Dryden's Aeneid: The English Virgil* (1994), and edited, along with Allison Coudert, *Anne Conway: The Principles of the Most Ancient and Modern Philosophy* (1996). Dr. Corse is the author of numerous articles published in *Notes and Queries*, *Milton Quarterly*, and *Restoration: Studies in English Literary Culture, 1660–1700*.

STEPHEN GREGG teaches "Literature: 1660–1790" at the University of Leeds. His essay "Strange Longing and Horror in *Robinson Crusoe*" will appear in the forthcoming volume *Signs of Masculinity* (1999). Mr. Gregg is currently completing his doctoral thesis, "That Het'rogeneous Thing, An Englishman: Masculinities and Nations in the Writing of Daniel Defoe."

LISA HOPKINS is a Senior Lecturer in English at Sheffield Hallam University. She is the author of two books, *John Ford's Political Theater* (1994), and *The Shakespearean Marriage: Merry Wives and Heavenly Husbands* (1997). Currently Dr. Hopkins is working on the *Macmillan Literary Life of Marlowe*, and serves as the Associate Reviews Editor for *Early Modern Literary Studies*.

THOMAS A. KING is co-editor of the forthcoming volume, *Pleasure Praxis: Essays on Contemporary Gay Performance* (1999). Dr. King's previous publications include reviews and essays in *The Politics and Poetics of Camp*, *The Drama Review*, and *The Gay and Lesbian Studies Newsletter*. Currently, Dr. King is completing *The Gendering of Man*, a contribution to the early modern history of masculinity and sexual subjectivity. He teaches early modern cultural studies, performance studies, queer/gender studies, and dramatic literature at Brandeis University.

SUSAN KORBA is a doctoral candidate at Queen's University in Kingston, Ontario, where she received an M.A. in English Literature in 1990. She has recently published an article on Jane Austen's *Emma* in *Studies in the Novel* (29.2.97). Currently, Miss Korba is completing her dissertation on the problematic nature of masculine identity in the novels of Samuel Richardson.

IAN McADAM is an Assistant Professor at the University of Lethbridge. Dr. McAdam's previous publications have appeared in *Studies in Philology* and *English Literary Renaissance*. His article "Masculinity and Magic in Friar Bacon and Friar Bungay" is forthcoming in *Research Opportunities in Renaissance Drama*. Also forthcoming is *The Irony of Identity: Self and Imagination in the Drama of Christopher Marlowe* (1999). Currently, Dr. McAdam is working on another book-length project, *Masculinity and Magic in Renaissance Drama*.

GORAN STANIVUKOVIC is an Assistant Professor of English at University College of Cape Breton. Specializing in Renaissance literature, Dr. Stanivukovic is the editor of a forthcoming critical edition of Emmanuel Ford's *Ornaus and Artesia* (1999), and is currently working on a critical study of the politics of masculinity in English popular, prose romances. His work has also appeared in *Narrative Strategies in English Fictions*, *The Canadian Journal of Rhetorical Studies*, and *Notes and Queries*. Dr. Stanivukovic also has an article forthcoming in *Forum for Modern Language Studies*.

EDWARD J. WHITELOCK is an Assistant Professor of English at Gordon College. Dr. Whitelock's primary research focus is on Romantic poetry, especially the poetry of Wordsworth. A poet himself, Dr. Whitelock is the former editor of *The New Growth Arts Review*. He is currently completing a book-length manuscript of poems, *In Upland*.

ANDREW P. WILLIAMS is an Assistant Professor of Literature and Creative Writing at North Carolina Central University. He is the author of *The Restoration Fop: Gender Boundaries and Comic Characterization in Later Seventeenth-Century Drama* (1995), and has been a frequent reviewer for *Studies in the Humanities*. Dr. Williams's work has appeared in various scholarly journals including *The Midwest Quarterly*, *The Gay and Lesbian Studies Newsletter*, and *Early Modern Literary Studies*. Currently, he is working on *Fops, Fools, and Fumblers*, a book-length study of masculine anti-ideals in the eighteenth century.

CPSIA information can be obtained at www.ICGtesting.com
Printed in the USA
BVOW040153090113

309802BV00010B/317/P

9 780313 307669